How Long
Till My Soul
Gets It Right?

How Long Till My Soul Gets It Right?

100 Doorways on the Journey to Happiness

Robert M. Alter
with Jane Alter

Previously published under the title
The Transformative Power of Crisis

ReganBooks
An Imprint of HarperCollinsPublishers

Honor thy father and thy mother.
—Exodus 20:12

This book is dedicated, with great respect and love,
to the memory of my mother,
Sylvia Celene Alter (1917–1999),
who taught me candor, precision, love, and love of words
and to the memory of my father,
Jack Alter (1912–2000),
who taught me discipline, righteousness, kindness, and manhood.

SPECIAL THANKS

We would like to express our special thanks to Nancy Peske, our stellar editor, for tough and true questions that forced us to deeper answers; for superb creative input when better writing was needed; for editorial assistance that felt like genius to us; and for brilliantly and artfully shaping the manuscript into this book.

CONTENTS

FOREWORD

I want to congratulate you on choosing to read *How Long Till My Soul Gets It Right?* by Robert and Jane Alter. You are in for a wonderful journey of information, experience, wisdom, and reflection, which, if you take it seriously, will change your life.

I am often asked to review books for a possible endorsement, and I pass on most of them after a brief scan. Not because they are not good books, but because they may not be in my field and I do not have the competence to evaluate them, or because they do not interest me and thus I cannot, in good conscience, endorse them. Whatever my decision, I am always honored that anyone would want my opinion.

When I received this book, I was intrigued by the title and began to thumb through it, doing my usual scan. I found myself shifting from scanning to reading, and before I knew it, I was reading every word and eagerly turning the pages. When I finished the last page, my first thought was: This book is a labor of love. Not just a love of self-expression, but a love of the reader and of humankind. This love is expressed in the depth of each piece of wisdom as well as in the richness of the quotes that adorn each page. The authors not only shared their intelligence and wisdom but the wisdom of the ages. I eagerly endorsed the first version and then was given the privilege of writing this foreword to this final version.

What impresses me is the sheer scope and depth of experience and wisdom. The authors have clearly lived life fully and reflected upon it deeply. And they have interacted with many people over the years with wise insight and deep compassion. It is clear to me that they are more than mere clinicians treating clients with psychological knowledge, although they exhibit a seasoned professionalism. They are not technicians of healing but philosophers with a deep understanding of the human condition, born out of their experience in the helping role. Reflecting deeply upon the suffering and struggles of all types of people, they are brilliant in distilling from their experience seminal insights and wisdom for us all.

Whatever your life experience is, you will find yourself addressed in these pages with warmth, kindness, and compassion. It is a comprehensive book, inclusive of almost any human situation, problem, or question. When you find yourself addressed in these pages, you will also find yourself confronted by your defenses, denials, rationalizations—and possibilities. Whether you are in a marriage, suffering from a divorce, struggling with your life's meaning, coping with your addictions, trying to improve your parenting, dealing with your fears, searching for your sexuality, or struggling with your identity—to list but a few subjects—you will be invited to look at your life deeply and realistically, and challenged to take charge of your existence and plumb your potential.

What I found here, in addition to wisdom and compassion, is hard-hitting realism. No punches are pulled with regard to your need for honest self-assessment, discovering the imprisonment of your immaturity, or claiming the possibility of your self-transcendence. This book will assist you in being yourself, loving yourself, loving others as they are rather than as extensions of yourself, and taking charge of your life. Do not look for mere comfort, but join the authors in the hope and joy that can be yours if you face your truth.

I wish you the enrichment, challenge, and vision I experienced as I read these pages.

Blessings and peace,

HARVILLE HENDRIX, PH.D., author of *Getting the Love You Want*, *Keeping the Love You Find*, and coauthor with his wife, Helen Hunt, of *Giving the Love That Heals*

Just as there is fragrance in a flower, there is a transforming divine power in every one of us.

—Gurumayi Chidvilasananda

As we begin to heal ourselves as individuals, we also naturally shift the consciousness of the entire planet.

—Shakti Gawain,
"Listening to Inner Wisdom"

I asked him if he still believed, as he once had written, "that we are at this moment participating in one of the very greatest leaps of the human spirit to a knowledge not only of outside nature but also of our own deep inward mystery."

He thought a minute and answered, "The greatest ever."

—Bill Moyers,
speaking of Joseph Campbell in
The Power of Myth

Wisdom is the principal thing; therefore, get wisdom: and with all thy getting, get understanding.

—Proverbs 4:7

Good therapy helps patients do two things: get launched onto a path leading toward enlightenment and learn some navigational techniques and tools to expedite their journeys.

The journey itself is life; therapy is no more than a major intervention along the way.

—John Fortunato,
Embracing the Exile

Let no one ever come to you without leaving better and happier. Be the living expression of God's kindness: kindness in your face, kindness in your eyes, kindness in your smile, kindness in your warm greeting.

—Mother Teresa

Bear in mind, Child, and never for an instant forget that there are higher planes, infinitely higher planes, of life than this thou art now traveling on. Know that the goal is distant, and upward, and is worthy of all your life's effort to attain to.

—Henry David Thoreau,
Journal, September 12, 1851

And it's alright, Ma, I can make it.

—Bob Dylan,
"It's Alright, Ma (I'm Only Bleeding)"

PREFACE

After a time of darkness comes the turning point. The old is discarded and the new appears. Persevere quietly on the path of inner truth. To return to the light in yourself, depend on the teachings of the sages. All is well.

　　　　　　　　　—"Fu: The Turning Point," *I Ching*

Until the juice ferments a while in the cask, it isn't wine. If you wish your heart to be bright, you must do a little work.

　　　　　　　　　—Jalaluddin Rumi,
　　　　　　　　　　"Be Lost in the Call"

In 1992, the Indigo Girls came out with their great song "Galileo," which is an exhilarating, foot-tapping look at life, truth, and psychological and spiritual growth. "Galileo" is one of those songs that once it gets in your head, it's hard to get out, especially these two lines from the refrain:

How long till my soul gets it right?
Did any human being ever reach the highest light?

I have been a psychotherapist for the past twenty-five years. I have sat in my office for approximately forty-five thousand hours talking with individuals and couples who are trying to get their souls right. They come in to therapy with all the problems, stresses, losses, messes, misfortunes, transitions, crises, and conundrums that life tends to present to us human beings, and, like the rest of us, are bravely trying to deal with it all without completely freaking out. The therapy is done on many levels by my clients—from fixing an immediate life problem to fixing a lifelong emotional problem—but on the deepest level, down in the soul, my clients are involved in a much larger and momentous psychological and spiritual process that is happening to many of us these days. It is that deep process, down in the soul, that really brings them into therapy with me.

This process goes by many names, and takes many forms. At bottom, it is an attempt by human beings to find physical, psychological, and spiritual well-being. It is an awakening to our magnificent potential as human beings. It's about finally getting the human soul right.

No one coming in to therapy has ever actually said to me, "I want to get my soul right." Usually people come in saying they're depressed, or anxious, or unfulfilled, or they don't like their jobs, or their marriages, or themselves. Sometimes they don't know how to deal with their parents, or their children, or a sudden misfortune in their lives. Sometimes they say that everything is actually going quite well in their lives, and then they ask, "So why aren't I happy?"

Then we start talking—for weeks, for months, sometimes for years—and under all the talking about this or that, under the symptom or the problem or the heartache they came in with, under their age, appearance, occupation, gender, marital status, and personal history, there sits before me a person or a couple who, on the deepest level of their being, is trying to clean up and clean out of their being anything in there—like childhood wounds, social and gender conditioning, addiction, immaturity, and negativity—that keeps them from being their best and highest selves, reaching their highest light, and living good, happy lives spreading goodness and joy to all they meet.

This is the process that I see happening in myself, in my marriage, in friends, in clients, and all over the world. Millions of people in our time are exerting tremendous psychological and spiritual effort to get their souls right. It's the best thing happening in our time. And if enough of us get our souls right, in due course of time, perhaps we can get the soul of the world right.

☽ ☽ ☽

What does it mean to get the soul right? It means to be on a journey from our present state of consciousness, in which there is much negativity, to another state of consciousness, a better and higher and happier state that is completely positive. This better, higher, happier state exists in us. It is, in fact, our natural state. It is who we are in our heart. In other words, we already are what we are trying to become, and getting the soul right is really a matter of learning to *be* who we already are.

In our present state of consciousness, for some of us, there are negativities like depression, loneliness, anxiety, fear, anger, aggression, jealousy, cynicism, boredom, and self-hatred. There's an emotional roller coaster we're all bouncing along on, moods that come over us like renegade weather systems, and a mind that's careening around like a maniac in there. There are hurts and resentments from the far past, a set of compulsions, addictions, and other out-of-control behaviors that run our lives and ruin our health, and some downright bad behaviors that hurt other people. Our marriages and families and children are troubled, our sexuality is wanton, and everybody's "stressed."

This does not have to be. There's a way out of this. We have work to do. The work is to get the human soul right.

Getting the soul right is to engage in a long, interesting, intrepid inner journey of looking at all our negative stuff, understanding where it comes from, feeling some of it, talking about most of it, and ultimately getting rid of all of it. It's a journey of complete self-purification. Getting the soul right is having the belief that there is that journey to take, and then taking it.

It's really a spiritual journey, because our soul—our true nature—is Spirit, and Spirit is the indwelling God who lives in our hearts. *Know ye not that ye are the temple of God, and that the Spirit of God dwelleth in you?* The spiritual journey, it turns out, is also a psychological journey, because the effulgent cave of the spiritual heart can be entered only through the narrow, musty passageways of our personal psychology. Psychological understanding takes us into our personal self, with all its past experiences, wounds, thoughts, feelings, and failings; and spiritual understanding takes us completely through and beyond that self to the divine Self that is at the core of our being.

Psychology can bring our pain to consciousness—and must, because nothing can permanently depart from our being unless it passes through consciousness to be burned up in the purifying fire of consciousness. Spirituality takes us beyond the pain to the stunning, scintillating realization that we *are* Consciousness, the pure unmodified Awareness within us, watching and witnessing everything, including ourselves, in a state of perfect stillness and love. This inner Awareness is sometimes called the Self. Psychology takes us through self-examination; spirituality takes us to Self-realization. Combining the two of them, we enter the inner splendor of the heart.

It's a spiritual journey, and a great journey. When we finally understand that the purpose and meaning of human life *is* this great spiritual journey, we become eager to know what needs to be changed in ourselves, and able, with work and time, to change it. Getting the soul right is the journey of permanent, profound positive inner change. Though we may take somewhat different paths, it's the same basic journey, and we all eventually get to the same great place.

We get to the happiness that is the essence of our nature. We get to the light of Consciousness, the lightness of being, the laughter, the power, the inner peace, the intuitive wisdom, and the great love and respect that are the essence of our nature. Having seen the Self within us, we see that same Self in all beings and in all things, so we treat ourselves, all beings, and all things with great love and respect, and we bring to the present culture of the world a new culture based on love and respect.

This is the state of the soul when we get it right. This is who we are, and this is the world we are here to create.

☽ ☽ ☽

For forty-five thousand hours over the past twenty-five years, it has been my labor, my service, and my honor to help individuals and couples get their souls right. This help has taken four basic forms.

THE ALLIANCE

When I am with my clients, I listen very hard to the life problem or character flaw or painful emotional state they are presenting to me, and I relate that problem or flaw or emotional state to the same or a similar one within myself. Then I say to the client the words that spontaneously arise from within me in that moment of identification and empathy. It is because of my own personal experience with most human problems, flaws, and states—I think of myself, actually, as universally dysfunctional—that I can speak with understanding, conviction, and credibility to clients about what they can do when they're experiencing them.

The Attention

I help my clients get their souls right by paying very close attention to everything in their souls that isn't yet right. I watch their postures, gestures, facial expressions, choices of words, and tones of voice. I am looking for the visible speech and behavior patterns that lead down into the invisible emotional wounds and cultural conditioning that create those patterns. I'm looking for all that is unclear, unpowerful, immature, self-abasing, manipulative, coercive, defensive, and deluded about my clients, and, looking deeper, for the troubles and traumas that happened to them that made them that way. The therapist "does not need to reconstruct a traumatic moment; the traumatic moment continues to exist in every breath the patient takes, in every gesture he makes."[1] When I point out to my clients the patterns I'm seeing, they can see them too, and see the whole inner network of wounds and scars that drives those patterns; and then they can work on their wounds and scars, and replace the old patterns with new ways of thinking, feeling, speaking, and acting that have self-respect, clarity, power, truth, and love in them.

The Clear Bead

I help my clients get their souls right when I see that deep inside them their souls are already right. With the eyes of my heart, I see through their patterns and their pain to their heart, to the pure one at their center, the one who is free of pain, full of love, totally good, fully aware, supremely intelligent, confident, tranquil, humble, and happy. Because I see my clients with the eyes of my heart, they start to see themselves with the eyes of their hearts too, as already in the state of consciousness that they're aspiring to, and they start to live their lives in that state, lighthearted, with love and respect for all, including themselves. When you finally learn that you don't have to become anything except what you already truly are, a radical transformation begins in you. "The clear bead at the center changes everything," says Rumi.[2]

THE DOORWAYS

I help my clients get their souls right by trying to elucidate and explain to them how I think the journey to the inner Self works, psychologically, spiritually, and behaviorally. How do I know how this journey works? Sometimes I've heard it from a friend or a mentor or a sage—or I've read it in a book—and I'm just passing it on. Sometimes I've learned it from my own journey through life and into myself. Sometimes, as I listen to clients in my office, a spontaneous insight occurs to me, a momentary glimpse into the workings of things, often in the form of an analogy. And sometimes I'll just hear myself suddenly saying, "The way it works is . . ." without knowing anything about how anything works, and for the next few minutes I try manfully to keep my mind thinking up to the speed of what my mouth is saying, all the while wondering if I'm right and praying that nobody disagrees with me.

The purpose of these elucidations is to open doorways of understanding for people on the journey of self-knowledge. On the long and winding road into ourselves, we need to understand many things: how our past experiences, especially our childhood experiences, affect us in the present; how the mind works and how it can be brought under control to harness its power; what feelings are, where they come from, and what to do with them; what compulsions and addictions are, where they come from, and what to do with them; how relationships, especially partner relationships, help us—in fact, force us—to get our souls right, and how to make those relationships flower and flourish; how to raise children with love and respect, so they flower into strong, self-respecting, wonderful adults; how to do contemplation, meditation, and other practices of psychological and spiritual self-awareness; the importance of discipline, effort, perseverance, patience, and time on this journey; and the great destination of this journey, which is the realization of God within us. In our meetings I try to share with clients a radiant awareness that illumines and brightens their journey into themselves, and elucidates the sublime meaning and purpose of their lives. These elucidations are the 100 Doorways on the Journey to Happiness in this book.

☽ ☽ ☽

Like all journeys, getting the soul right takes a while, but we just get going and keep going because we know there are other human beings who got going and kept going . . . and reached the highest light! Lots of them. They are the wise beings, the sages and seers and mystics and masters, the saints and Self-realized beings, the enlightened and awakened souls who have lived on the earth throughout all time, in all cultures and traditions, and have spoken and written scripture and poetry and philosophy and song, the highest words to teach us how to take the journey to the highest light. Their lives demonstrate and illustrate that the journey of Self-realization can be completed, and their words are essential illuminations along the way. The words of wise beings decorate and illuminate this book in the form of enlightened quotations that begin the book, the eight chapters, and each of the hundred doorways.

When I refer to God with a pronoun in these pages, I use the masculine form "He" because, even though I know, with St. Juliana of Norwich, that God is both genders ("As truly as God is our Father, so truly is God our Mother"), and even though I know that God is the formless, attributeless Being with no gender, still, I grew up calling God He, and it sounds natural to my ear.

All of the narratives about clients in therapy sessions are imagined, though based on my experiences as a therapist in a very generalized way. The identifying characteristics, including name, occupation, age, or other details of life experience used for the purposes of this book, are not accurate with respect to any particular individual or couple. To all clients who have journeyed into their souls in my office in these twenty-five years, please know that I have written this book with great respect and admiration for the work you did here.

☽ ☽ ☽

How Long Till My Soul Gets It Right? is a collection of twenty-five years of trying to help individuals and couples who are trying to find happiness in their lives. Every elucidation, every quotation, every sentence, every word is the result of a nine-year collaboration between me, who is the writer, and my wife, Jane, who is also a therapist, and who, for the past thirty-two years, in matters psychological, spiritual, and marital, has meticulously and lovingly checked both the writer and his writing for clarity and honesty and truth and goodness. This book is the fruit of that collaboration, our marriage, and our lives. We hope it is helpful to you.

HOW LONG
TILL MY SOUL
GETS IT RIGHT

1

PAST TO PRESENT

*We are all the products of thousands of years of failed parenting . . .
because the human species has not yet evolved to the point that it knows
how to raise its young without injury.*

> —Harville Hendrix,
> the audiotape *Safety*

*Mama always said you gotta put the past behind you before you
can move on.*

> —from the movie *Forrest Gump*

*Receive the child in reverence. Educate the child in love.
Let the child go forth in freedom.*

> —Rudolf Steiner

At the same time that we are moving forward in our journey toward our inner Self, we have to move backward to our childhood. We must face what happened in those early years that was so disappointing, hurtful, terrifying, or infuriating that we had to leave behind major parts of our emotional selves in order to deal with it all. All of it that you can remember you have to face, and the parts that you can't quite remember, you have to infer and intuit and face. You can do all that in therapy because you have a guide accompanying you on the trip who has himself been back there, in his own childhood, and knows the neighborhood. He might not know your specific neighborhood—the exact events that happened to you back then—but he knows the general size and significance of these events, and their emotional, behavioral, and spiritual consequences in your adulthood. He knows all the hiding places we crouched in when we were children, and the ones we retreat to now—

because he himself has hidden in most of them, and come out of some of them. "Healing occurs when a person returns to the pain of the past and finds she is not alone this time."[1] In therapy, we return to the pain of the past accompanied by the therapist, who looks at the facts with us, and helps us finally come to terms with them.

There's not only a psychological but a spiritual reason for this trip: We can't slip through the finer and finer gossamer filaments on the way to the inner Self unless we're very light in our being, so we can't be carrying the dark, dense weight of the past with us. If there's any part of us that's still there, in our childhood, we can't be fully here, in our adulthood, getting our souls right, ultimately trying to achieve Self-realization.

By whatever means, including therapy, we try to finish our childhood and get to adulthood.

BACK TO THE PAST

And as the bombshells of my daily fears explode,
I try to trace them to my youth.

—Indigo Girls, "Galileo"

Donald, a forty-year-old electrical engineer, was in his third week of therapy. He suffered from anxious depression, "a slight drinking problem," and regular outbursts of tongue-lashing rage at his wife, his two children, and the subordinates in his office. His wife had encouraged him to seek therapy with me (she had been in therapy with me two years earlier), which he was willing to do, but with one condition.

"I don't want to go into any of that *psychological* crap," he said. "I'm willing to look at myself and the way I am, but I don't want to go back forty years and dig up my whole childhood and blame my parents for everything under the sun. I'm not into that 'inner child' garbage that my wife keeps talking about."

I admired his spirit. I thought it was great that Donald didn't want to avoid responsibility for how he is in the present by, as he put it, "whining" about what happened in his past. However, none of us can grow psychologically or spiritually unless we spend *some* time in the past, figuring out what happened then that keeps influencing how we are today. That time in our lives is like an electrical generating station that keeps feeding tremendous power into the repetitive and destructive patterns of thought, feeling, and behavior in our present lives. That's why those patterns seem to have lives of their own quite independent of our best intentions, our intelligence, and sometimes even our conscience.

We have to revisit those generating stations, to go back to our past and know it for what it was, good or bad or wonderful or horrible or a mix of it all. We need to expose our circuits and see the tangle of wires inside, trace them back to the generating stations, make sense of it all, and reconnect what has come loose. Often we have to clip some of the wires leading from our past to our present, bearing messages that don't serve us well. "I'm not the kind of person who can do that" . . . "It's just my nature and I can't change it" . . . "I'll always be stupid or ridiculous or unlovable"—and bearing with those messages, those powerful, recurrent, negative emotions that control and torture us from morning to night.

I think I spend half my time in therapy trying to convince otherwise intelligent people that the treatment they received in their childhood was not natural, or right, or acceptable, but traumatic and wrong and unacceptable. People tell me stories about their childhood as if they were reporting what they had for lunch, while I sit in a silent apoplexy of outrage at the many misdemeanors and downright crimes against innocent children I'm hearing about.

When my clients don't remember what it was like in their childhood, I say, "Trust your symptoms, and let your symptoms lead you back to your past. Based on the symptoms you're reporting to me, you're probably going to find some childhood experiences there that were pretty damn bad."

"It can't be as bad as all that," they say.

"Actually, it's probably worse," I say.

I know that sounds pessimistic, but I'm being up front about how easily we all minimize or rationalize away the most painful incidents of the past, hoping that by denying their power their energy will dissipate. However, the opposite is true: Admitting their power dissipates their energy. When our wires are covered by the insulation of denial, the pain of our past keeps flowing into our present.

Psychoanalyst Alice Miller says, "The individual psychological stages in the lives of most people are: 1. To be hurt as a small child without anyone recognizing the situation as such. 2. To fail to react to the resulting suffering with anger. 3. To show gratitude for what are supposed to be good intentions. 4. To forget everything. 5. To discharge the stored-up anger onto others in adulthood or to direct it against oneself." [2]

Looking honestly at our past is not easy. The forces of rationalization, minimization, repression, projection, denial, and straight-out amnesia make it hard work. Also, we still love our parents—they're our *parents* after all!—and we'll do just about anything to protect and defend them, including denying that they did anything harmful to us. The urges to protect and deny are so strong that we have to use the whole force of our desire to get better in order to look at it all. When we are supported and guided by a therapist or our partner or a friend who can remind us that we lived through many difficult moments, perhaps even a nightmare, we can remember the whole truth of it. With this honesty, we can make progress. Without it, the tangled wires from the past continue to transmit their destructive messages and feelings, and robotlike, we continue with the same old patterns that get us nowhere.

So while I hate to be the bearer of bad tidings, each of us *does* have to start our healing by going into that "psychological crap" and placing blame where blame is due, even if it's due to our parents. And sometimes we have to "whine," or "complain," or "gripe," or any of those other terms our culture has invented to shame its children to keep them from speaking the truth. Think of it as simply *knowing and reporting the truth of our childhood experience,* and realize that we can learn from it rather than getting stuck in it or using it to avoid responsibility for our present lives.

There are no excuses in our past, but there are facts we can't avoid. Once we face them we can finally snip those wires, reconnect with who we really are, and live in the present. That's when we can begin truly enjoying our lives.

Premature Exoneration
or
They Did the Best They Could . . .
and Sometimes It Was Pretty Bad

> *We often fail to recall events, and the feelings associated with them, that*
> *involve disappointment with our parents. . . . If we are to gain access to*
> *these facts about our lives, we simply must be willing to endure some of the*
> *pain of feeling disloyal to these loved, and inevitably imperfect, people.*
> —Augustus Y. Napier,
> *The Fragile Bond*

"They did the best they could." It's become a cliché, one that we feel pressured to parrot upon reaching adulthood: Our childhood and adolescence are over, and it's time to move forward and forgive our parents.

Not so fast.

Forgiveness is an important and loving act, but one that must not be rushed. Our parents may well have done their best and may deserve exoneration, but to give it prematurely is to cut short our own growth.

You cannot understand why you think, feel, act, hurt, and completely screw up your life the way you do as an adult without understanding what your parents did wrong to you as a child. Parents are supposed to do things right. When they do things right, children develop self-respect, inner peace, personal power, confidence, enthusiasm for the challenges of life, and the ability to love and be loved.

But parents don't always do things right, often because their parents didn't do things right to them. They pass on whatever neglect or abuse, inappropriateness or misunderstanding they received from the generations of parents before them. They can't help it. Nobody can. Nobody's really to blame. That's the way it works.

We're all damaged by this. Some of us are terribly damaged, some mildly damaged, but we're all damaged. In order to repair ourselves, we must figure out exactly how we have been hurt, which necessitates our going back and learning, in as complete and precise detail as possible, just how our parents were hurt. What childhood dreams of theirs were ridiculed and crushed? What broke their spirits? What pain did they go through that made them inflict pain upon their own children? We must look directly and long at the parenting that we and they received, and know it for the bad parenting it sometimes was, so that we can stop thinking *we're* bad for how we sometimes are. Part of the process of becoming an adult who can truly forgive our parents involves spending time looking fearlessly at how we've been failed by them. We have to stop covering for Mom and Dad if we are to see our childhood—and ourselves—clearly.

And ye shall know the truth, and the truth shall make you free.

Anything that gets in the way of seeing the truth about our parents is not useful. Denial is not useful, nor laziness, guilt, or self-blame, nor repression of memory, nor rationalization, nor misguided sympathy for them, nor any belief, feeling, or concept that protects our parents from our scrutiny. "They did the best they could" is such a concept. Get rid of it.

Get rid of it, even though it's totally true—because it's not useful right now. It's premature exoneration. Take the truth that "They did the best they could," seal it in an envelope, and place it in a time capsule. Do not open it until you've explored with your therapist, or with who-ever will listen to you with interest and compassion, the thousand and one ways that they totally blew it with you. If you're honest and fearless, you'll stay with that scrutiny until you know by heart and categorically how bad it really was, and you're not afraid to think so or say so.

But you never have to say so to *them,* if you don't want to. You will get to the point where what your parents did or didn't do to you doesn't matter to you anymore, and you go on with your life as an adult, inde-pendent of them. It's not about hurting them, or taking revenge on them. The work of looking at them, and knowing them, and being appropriately disappointed in them or angry at them can all be done with a therapist, or a friend, in the chambers of your heart. And when you're done with that work, you may find yourself able, and even want-ing, to just be nice to them for the rest of their lives, no matter what they did or didn't do to you.

Forgiving your parents doesn't come easy. You can't buy that forgive-ness cheap, and you can't buy it prematurely. You must buy it with the courage it takes to really look at your parents. Once you've done that, then you'll be able to say, "They did the best they could," except that this time, for the first time, you'll really mean it, and love them for it.

Who's Who?

Though they may outwardly appear to be adults, even successful adults, perhaps, the majority of "grown ups" remain until their death psychological children who have never truly separated themselves from their parents and the power that their parents have over them.

—M. Scott Peck,
The Road Less Traveled

A hurtful act is the transference to others of the degradation which we bear in ourselves.

—Simone Weil

When Nature set the game up, she made sure that children would be born dependent on their parents for everything, including their very lives, and would remain so for a long time. As a consequence, the parents' ways of thinking, feeling, doing, and being would, by proximity, example, and osmosis, permeate the child and become her own ways. Nature did this because she wanted each species to pass on to its children its collective knowledge and wisdom. It was a brilliant idea, and it works fine in every species but ours.

In the human species, the infinite ways we are royally screwed up also get passed down from the parents to the children. We get it all. We get their feelings, their thoughts, their prejudices, their obsessions, and their insecurities. We get their facial expressions, their tones of voice, the way they hold their bodies, and the way they live their lives. I even got my mother's *cough,* which scares the hell out of me. After a while most of us haven't a clue where Mom and Dad leave off and we begin. Who's who?

Separating ourselves from them—in other words, finding *our* selves—is a long process that we undertake in steps. The first step is to acknowledge that our parents moved this deeply into us. The second step is to develop the ability to recognize them when they make their appearance in us. The third step is to discriminate between the good that they imbued us with—values and qualities and feelings that serve us and the world—and the bad. The fourth step is to not want the bad stuff there anymore, and to start throwing it all out.

Many of the emotional energies inside us that we're not in control of are our parents making their appearance in us. Many automatic, compulsive reactions of ours, emotional or behavioral, are theirs, not ours. We can't help being this way, or so it seems.

Once when my daughter Greta was four and crying hysterically, I felt a rage rise up within me. I wanted to scream at her, "SHUT UP! SHUT UP OR I'LL KILL YOU!" I immediately felt that energy to be the energy that someone—my mother? my father? my sister? all three?—showed me when *I* was a child and crying hysterically. Fortunately, I had done enough work on myself by that point to be able just to feel the energy inside me without expressing it. That's an important accomplishment. Someday we may get our parents out of us altogether, and we should all be working on it, but they took a long time moving in, and it'll take a long time to get them to move out.

The Wanting and
Asking System

Ye have not, because ye ask not. Ye ask, and receive not, because ye ask amiss.

—James 4:2–3

Lillian, sixty-five, had finally been persuaded by her husband and children to enter therapy in order to deal with her chronic anxiety and feelings of inferiority. The family also wanted her to explore why all of them seemed to be so angry at her so much of the time, something Lillian could not, on her own, figure out. During one session, on a warm, humid evening in July, dabbing at her forehead with a crumpled tissue, she asked me, "Aren't you getting a little warm?"

"Are you?" I asked.

She looked surprised. "No, I was just saying that it seems to be getting a little warm in here." She dabbed at her forehead again.

"Are *you* warm, Lillian?"

"Well, I'm warm, but I was just saying—"

"Are you *too* warm?"

"No, I'm fine. I was just wondering if maybe it was getting a little warm in here."

"You're sweating, Lillian."

"Oh, don't mind me. I perspire. My mother would perspire—"

"You're sweating bullets, Lillian."

"It's a problem I have from my mother. I *schvitz*."

"So you're not warm?"

"I'm a little warm, but—"

"Are you asking for something?"

"Me? No."

"Are you sure?"

"No, I'm not asking for anything."

"Why not?"

"What would I ask for?"

"You could ask for the window to be opened or the fan turned on because you're uncomfortably warm tonight. Are you asking for that?"

"No, I'm fine."

"You're fine?"

"Well, maybe it's a *little* warm in here."

"Do you want to ask for something?"

"No, I was just saying—"

"You're always 'just saying.' What is all this 'just saying'?"

"I don't know what you mean."

"Ask for something, Lillian. Something to do with the fact that this room is hot as hell and you're over there soaked in sweat. I could open the window or turn the fan on or both."

"That would be good."

"Which?" I asked.

"What?"

"The window or the fan?"

"Whatever you like."

"*I* have nothing to do with this. This is about *you.*"

"What do you mean?"

"*Ask,* Lillian."

"For what?"

"For what you *want.*"

She dabbed at her forehead with the tissue. "What do you mean?"

"I mean I'm sitting here feeling furious at you, just as your husband and children have been furious at you for years. I know you're sitting over there uncomfortably hot and dying for the window to be open or the fan to be turned on, or both, but you won't say so. You won't ask. You've communicated your message to me without communicating your message to me, and I feel totally manipulated and powerless and crazy and furious at you. This is the effect you have on people when you won't ask for what you want."

"I don't follow you," she said, blotting at her neck with the tissue.

☽ ☽ ☽

Every human being is born with a healthy, strong wanting and asking system. The system *has* to be healthy and strong because our physical survival depends on our knowing our wants and asking for them from our caretakers.

Babies and children have lots of wants: *I want to be nursed . . . I want to be changed . . . I want that doll . . . I want dessert . . . I want to stay up . . . I*

want you to talk with me, Mommy . . . I want you to play with me, Daddy. . . .
And babies and children have lots of don't-wants: *I don't want you to go
now . . . I don't want to go to bed . . . I don't want to share . . . I don't want green
beans . . . I don't want you to do that to me.* A healthy and strong baby or
child uses whatever signals it can find to ask directly, repeatedly, cre-
atively, and loudly for exactly what it wants when it wants it.

A bad thing happens if our parents and other adults shut down our
wanting and asking system. They cut off our cries and protests. They
dismiss our clear, direct, powerful statements of want and need. They
make us feel bad for wanting anything from anybody and having the
gall to ask for it. We are called brats if we want something and spoiled
brats if we get it. It is an all-out, long-term, systematic adult campaign
against the right of a child and a human being to ask for what she
wants.

When this happens, we lose our loud, proud voice that asks for things
clearly and directly. We find we have traded it in, out of necessity, for a
mealy-mouthed mumble and a stutter that nobody can understand. We
have become self-effacing and docile, silent, and out of touch with what
we want. The fact that we're also furious at them for doing this to us usually doesn't kick in until our teens, when, pumped up by peers and
deranged by hormones, all hell breaks loose in our wanting systems,
and for a few years we go completely crazy, wanting everything in sight.

Having learned that asking for what we want doesn't get us anywhere, we develop a mutant way of asking. We silently begin to hope
for what we want, which over the years turns into silently expecting others to read our minds and give us what we want. Or we try to meet our
needs by overwhelming and overpowering other people, which for
some can even include terrorizing or even physically and sexually violating other people. Or we find indirect, passive-aggressive ways to ask:
Ostensibly, we are self-effacing, but in reality we are highly manipulative and very pushy, causing others to resent us, as Lillian's family
resented her.

When this is the case, the solution is to reempower your direct wanting and asking system. Reactivate the loud, proud voice; plug the power
cord in again. Take the risk of asking. Someday, you will be able to ask
directly for what you want without apology or intimidation or round-
about hinting. If she plugs in her wanting and asking system again,

Lillian will be able to say simply, "I'm hot in here. In fact, I'm *schvitzing* up a storm. Would you open the window and turn on the fan?" To which I, not feeling manipulated or pushed but asked and respected, will say, "Of course!" and immediately do both—and we'll all save lots of time and craziness.

No Trespassing:
The Boundaries of a Child

Thou has set them their bounds which they shall not pass.
—Book of Common Prayer

"I am so messed up in so many ways, I can't believe it," said Jerry, a forty-year-old computer store clerk who had repeatedly witnessed his father beating his mother and had himself been beaten by both of them.

"It's easy to believe because so many messed-up things happened to you when you were a child," I said. "Nobody in your family had *any* sense of appropriate boundaries with you. Again and again they broke your boundaries and they broke your heart."

☽ ☽ ☽

In the same way that children are born with hearts and livers and toes and noses, they are also born with boundaries. The boundaries are an invisible but real force field around the child, past which we cannot go without his permission and invitation. Posted around the perimeter of this force field are No Trespassing signs, the small print of which reads ALL VISUAL, VERBAL, PHYSICAL, AND SEXUAL ENCROACHMENT PAST THIS POINT IS PROHIBITED!

Visually, we must not show the child, or let the child see, inappropriate things. These include cruelty, violence, and all other forms of oppressive and threatening and disrespectful behavior.

Verbally, we must not yell or scream at the child. We must not insult the child or say unkind or sarcastic or impatient things to him. We must not call the child demeaning characterological names like "brat" or "crybaby" or "pest," or use adjectives like "selfish," "lazy," or "bad." We must not let the child hear abusive language said to others or sexual talk or sexual innuendo.

Physically, we must not do anything to the child's body with the purpose of intimidating or hurting the child. This includes pinching, slapping, grabbing, hitting, and spanking. It also includes certain forms of restraint, some forms of rough play, and tickling when it's used to overpower the child and render him helpless.

Sexually, we must not allow the child to see adult sexual activity, nor must we, in any way or to any degree, use any part of the child's body for our sexual titillation or pleasure.

A child whose parents have failed to protect—or themselves have violated—his personal boundaries will feel, deep inside, defenseless, terrified, and ashamed. As an adult, he will be subject to all the things that all other boundary-violated children are subject to: emotional stuckness at the age at which the violation occurred; eating disorders; sexual disorders; other behavioral and character disorders; compulsions and addictions; powerful, painful, and uncontrollable impulses and feelings; chronic anxiety; chronic depression; physical health problems; rage, sometimes violence, either to himself or others; and suicidal impulses. All these symptoms, traced to their roots, are attempts by a trespassed person to build a boundary between himself and a world that has proved to be out of control and therefore terrifying.

That's why Jerry was so messed up. His family messed him up when they trespassed his boundaries, and destroyed his sense of sovereignty and safety. They came in past where they should have come in; they said and did and touched things they weren't supposed to say or do or touch; and they left a great mess behind inside him. Our job in therapy was to help Jerry rebuild his boundaries and then communicate them with such clarity and power that people would respect them. Then he would no longer be transgressed upon, and he could begin to feel safe and strong in the world again. As his safety and strength increased behind those reconstructed boundaries, order and calmness would be restored inside him.

The Bridge to Adulthood

We are really fundamentally still children in grown-up bodies, and what we have to do is finish the task of growing up.
                    —Harville Hendrix,
                      the audiotape *Safety*

Too many of us receive neglectful, disrespectful, or abusive parenting when we are children. When this is the case, two things happen.

One, we are left with a heavy residue of bad feelings like anxiety, anger, sadness, and self-hatred, along with an assortment of compulsive, addictive, and self-destructive behaviors that we use to try to manage these bad feelings, and we have to spend a good part of our adult lives trying to clean up the whole mess.

Two, *we don't grow up*. We don't cross the bridge from childhood into adulthood because the construction material used to build that bridge is the parents' love and respect and attention for the child, which was never delivered. Without that love and respect and attention, there is no bridge, and there is therefore no passage for us from childhood to adulthood. Even though we grow a bigger body and we look like and sometimes even miraculously manage to act like we're adults, we're not adults, we're girls and boys gazing across a chasm where a bridge was supposed to be constructed over to adulthood, but there is no bridge. So when we're fifty-one years old and our eighty-three-year-old father, who in reality is just a cantankerous old guy whose health is slowly failing and whose opinion about our weight is totally irrelevant, mentions that we're putting on weight, we get furious, throw a tantrum, and run out of the restaurant. That's because we're still thinking of ourselves as children.

In the earlier years of my so-called adulthood, my wife and I used to have a standing bet. Every time we would visit my parents in Florida, we would bet on how many minutes it would take in their presence before I would turn from a relatively peaceful, happy, and grown-up man into a sullen, depressed, seven-year-old boy sitting slumped at the dining room table staring impotently into his potato kugel. The longest I ever made it was one hour and seventeen minutes, but that was because I only had my father to deal with because my mother was out playing bridge.

It is good to remember that it's a problem with *ourselves* now, and not with them. It may have been a problem with them thirty, forty, or fifty years ago, when we really were children, but it's with us now.

When will we grow up? When we've built the bridge for ourselves that our parents were supposed to help us build a long, long time ago. The materials we use to build that bridge are the love and respect we have for ourselves—which most of us have had to work a lifetime to develop—supplemented, if necessary and if available, by the love and respect of our partners and friends, with maybe a little help and guidance from our therapist thrown in. With these materials, and a little luck, can the bridge to adulthood be built? Can your father share his opinion about your weight while you, unperturbed, sit there enjoying your flounder? In other words, *can we grow up?*

Yes.

The Stowaway

I will listen to the terrors that tried you
Cold wind beating out of the past
I will cradle the child that breathes inside you
Hold on, I will stand fast.

—Fred Small, "I Will Stand Fast"

Leah, a thirty-three-year-old woman with three children, had come into therapy a year previously because, after seeing a television movie about incest, she had begun having flashbacks of her grandfather sexually abusing her when she was a young child. At first she was incredulous at this rediscovery. As her therapy progressed, however, the memories came back and she struggled to deal with the pain that had been buried in her subconscious. Her husband, Brock, who occasionally sat in on Leah's sessions to discuss the couple's issues arising from the recently remembered abuse, had been her anchor, offering strong support as she began to speak about the unspeakable. Now, however, his patience was wearing thin. He felt angry and alienated because Leah's interest in sex had vanished. Now even the thought of sex terrified and repulsed her. Leah and Brock's sexual life had always been a beautiful and powerfully bonding force in their relationship; now that it was gone, Brock felt cheated, and both of them were scared.

"I don't know who she is anymore," he said. "I married one woman who would make passionate love with me at the drop of a hat, and now there's this other Leah who's totally turned off by it. I feel blindsided."

꙳ ꙳ ꙳

Brock's feelings were understandable, but like so many people who are not the victims of abuse but the supporters of those who are, he had trouble maintaining his compassion. A part of him wanted a quick cure so that things could go back to what they had been. We all would like instant relief for our pain, or for that of our loved ones. Once something has been acknowledged, we think, Can't we just move on now? Unfortunately, it isn't that easy. Brock needed to accept the enormity of Leah's wound, and understand that it could be a long, long time before she would be able to fully embrace her sexuality again.

When Leah was being sexually abused by her grandfather, I explained, she was terrified, horrified, enraged, and repulsed by sex. Those feelings were enormously powerful and excruciating, but Leah couldn't safely express them to anybody. So she did what any normal person would do: She stuffed them deep inside herself and totally forgot about them.

Her ability to grow into an ostensibly sexually healthy woman was based on her ability to stow her early childhood feelings belowdecks, below memory, and to keep them there. The sexually abused child Leah, the carrier of all those feelings, became a stowaway deep inside the adult Leah. Nobody, not her husband, not even Leah, knew she was down there belowdecks all these years.

Then came the watershed moment—in Leah's case, viewing a TV movie about a sexually abused girl. Watching it from deep within Leah was the stowaway child, who, seeing her own childhood experience sympathetically portrayed, decided she was ready to come out now. So she did. After twenty-eight years as a stowaway, she came up blinking into the light. At first she was timid and told us her story haltingly, but gradually she became willing to tell more about the events that had driven her into the dark spaces below her consciousness.

Brock's challenge, and the challenge for anyone who wants to be supportive of someone who has been severely abused, was to be patient, to allow Leah the time she needed to slowly reveal the deepest wounds of her being. He needed to make every effort not to get angry with her, because she would perceive his anger as abandonment, and the wounded stowaway might very well decide to creep back into the darkness below, to the haven that had served her so well. Things had changed. Brock was no longer getting what he expected and wanted in their relationship, and his frustration was natural. But that's the way it is when there's a stowaway in a marriage. It's the responsibility of both spouses to receive and welcome the stowaway with love when she or he decides to come up. When the stowaway feels received and welcomed with love by the partner, when she feels he truly accepts her, the process of getting rid of her pain and mistrust can begin at last, and she can, over time, abandon forever the dark, hidden spaces below and live in the light.

The Subcutaneous Steel Plate

I like not only to be loved, but to be told I am loved.

—George Eliot, letter to
Mrs. Burne-Jones, May 11, 1875

Simon, a thirty-seven-year-old executive in a small software company, had rarely been appreciated, commended, or praised by his mother or his father. Instead, he had been constantly corrected, blamed, and, if his offense was big enough, hit. Consequently, although he was a success in his profession, a good provider to his family, and a good husband and father, he had very low self-esteem and a gloomy personality. He and his wife Penny were in marital counseling with me. Penny, although very much in love with Simon, was tired of his gloominess. Near the end of one of their sessions, I suggested that she spend a few minutes appreciating him.

"I can do that," she said, "and I'll mean it too, but it won't get through. I know him. He'll sit there stone-faced and not believe a word I'm saying."

"Do it anyway," I said. "It will help wear down his subcutaneous steel plate."

☽ ☽ ☽

Inside Simon, I told Penny, is a subcutaneous steel plate of disbelief and dismissal of anything good said about him. If anybody chances to say anything good to Simon, the words hit that steel plate so hard one can almost hear the clank while he just sits there wanly smiling and saying, "Thank you . . . thank you. . . ."

We all have this steel plate. We were born with it.[3] It goes by different names (poor self-esteem, guilt, shame, self-hatred, etc.), but it's basically just not feeling good about ourselves a lot of the time. If we were brought up by wise parents who treated us with love and respect, our steel plate will be thinner; if we were brought up by unwise parents who treated us badly, our steel plate will be thicker. In either case, thick or thin, the steel plate is hard to remove. The best way we can help each other remove it, in my opinion, is to wear it down with repeated messages of praise, gratitude, appreciation, admiration, and love. When I say "repeated," I don't mean two or three times. I mean two or three million times.

To wear down the subcutaneous steel plate in someone we care about, we must use every opportunity, every medium of communication, and every trick in the book to convey to him his wonderfulness. There are plenty of methods at our disposal: We can use notes on pillows and counters, letters in the mail, postcards, telephones, answering machines, fax machines, E-mail, and, if you can afford them, billboards, blimps, skywriting, and television commercials. Say those words in kitchens, bedrooms, across the table in dining rooms, and through the door in bathrooms. Praise him, appreciate him, commend him, tell him he's good, tell him he's wonderful, tell him you like him, tell him you love him. Tell him the *opposite* of what he believes about himself. Tell him that his moodiness is charming and his sullenness is sexy and his gloominess makes your life worth living. Figure out the one thing he hates the most about himself and tell him you love *that* most of all.

Now he won't believe a word of it, and *you* probably won't believe much of it either, but belief is not important here. If a believer in the rain steps out in the rain, he'll get wet; if a disbeliever in the rain steps out in the rain, he'll get wet too. So forget belief: Just say it. Say it because no matter how thick the subcutaneous steel plate is, there is someone inside it who listens through it and has been waiting his whole life to hear somebody tell him that he's good. The truth about Simon is that he's a totally wonderful man and husband and father and person to have on this earth. The one who listens inside is listening for *that*.

Engraved on that steel plate is the message "I'M BAD." Wear it down with messages of love, for love eventually wears down everything that is not love.

A Chalice for the Children's Tears

Suffer the little children to come unto me . . .
—Mark 10:14

The world is not a safe place. From the day of our birth to the day of our death, in a million different ways, the world scares and hurts and wounds us. This is the nature of the world.

If things are working right when we're children, we go out into the world and sometimes get scared and hurt and wounded by it, and then we come back home to the safety of our parents, whose love and care and attention to our feelings binds and heals our wounds. We can go confidently back out into the world the next time only if we've gotten each time the love and care and attention that we needed to renew our confidence.

What children need when they come home scared and hurt is the safety to feel their wounded feelings without being shamed for having them. Children will need to discharge those feelings, often by crying tears into the chalice of their parents' sympathy and love. The parents' job throughout the experience is to let their children know that, one, it's okay for kids to feel their emotions, and two, they will be there for their children, welcoming their emotions and supporting them with love.

When our daughter Greta was six, she, my wife Jane, and I were driving down to Long Island to visit Jane's parents. I was at the wheel, Jane was in the passenger seat next to me, and Greta was in back with her dolls. We pulled into a gas station and Jane went to use the rest room. I got out of the car to stretch my legs for a minute, with Greta still in the backseat. Suddenly the car started rolling! I had forgotten to pull up the emergency brake! I quickly jumped back in, yanked up the brake, and the car stopped. It had only rolled a few feet, no damage was done, and no one was hurt. In the backseat, however, Greta was screaming in terror. I mean, *screaming*.

Sitting in the front seat, I turned around and tried to comfort her by telling her that nothing had happened, that she was okay, and that it was all over, but it didn't work. She kept screaming. I began to feel a rage rising up within me in the form of the words "Nothing happened! You're fine! Stop crying!" but, knowing that all my male conditioning, not to mention the entire gene pool of untold generations of Alters, was in that rage, I restrained myself and sat silently in the front seat, white knuckles clutching the steering wheel while Greta kept screaming in the backseat.

Then Jane came back, heard Greta screaming, miraculously tuned into the whole situation, and without a word climbed into the backseat and held Greta, just quietly held her, while Greta kept crying and screaming. Five minutes went by. Greta's tears slowly subsided. Jane continued to hold her. Greta was now sniffling and catching her breath while Jane stroked her back. Then there was a silence. Suddenly, I heard Greta's voice, asking brightly, "Will there be bagels at Grandma's, Mommy?"

I turned around, surprised. Greta's eyes were glistening with excitement. Jane's face was smiling softly with love.

"Knowing Grandma, there'll be *thousands* of bagels, honey," Jane said, and we all laughed, and drove off.

And you know what? The fear that the rolling car brought out in Greta that day didn't get stuck inside her. It left her as the sympathy and safety of Jane's attention and love enveloped her. Greta didn't grow up with fears of backseats of cars, or moving cars, or rolling cars, or Mommy or Daddy getting out of cars, or being alone in cars, or gas stations, or rest rooms. The wound was *gone,* carried out of her system. And Greta was ready to face the world again, a world that, after another hour of driving, was indeed *bursting* with bagels.

The parents' job is to welcome their children back from a sometimes scary and hurtful world, to hold them and love them when they express their feelings about that world, and then send them back out to face it again, as we all must face it again.

TO SEE A CHILD

*The mother gazes at the baby in her arms, and baby gazes at his mother's
face and finds himself therein . . . provided that the mother is really
looking at the unique, small, helpless being, and not projecting . . . her
own expectations, fears, and plans for the child.*
　　　　　　　　　　　—Alice Miller,
　　　　　　　　　　　　The Drama of the Gifted Child

Deep inside, we all have self-esteem. We are, by nature, self-loving, self-respecting, and self-confident beings, with enormous enthusiasm and personal power. But in order for that self-esteem, self-respect, and self-confidence to be our actual experience of ourselves, our parents have the job of activating and nurturing it within us. They do it by sending into us a certain kind of energy throughout the years of our childhood. This energy has different names—recognition, acknowledgment, regard, appreciation, admiration, approval, and acceptance. The purest form of it, I think, is attention—a true seeing—and this attention is the purest form of love. Children who are loved in this way, who are truly *seen* in their deepest selves, grow up with self-esteem, self-respect, and self-confidence. Other children don't.

There is a kind of X-ray vision the parents must have to truly see a child; this vision sees through the outer layers of the child's being— what she looks or acts like—all the way into the moment-to-moment flow of her inner life, her thoughts and feelings, her moods and states, her *soul*. Otherwise, parents end up missing the child. When they say, "You look so pretty today, honey," they miss the child. When they say, "You're such a good little boy, Bobby," or "All A's? That's wonderful, sweetheart!" they miss the child. Once, when she was fourteen, my wife Jane brought home a test from school, on which she had received a ninety-eight. Her father looked at it, and said, "A ninety-eight! We're very proud of you, Jane." Then with a smile he added, "Maybe next time you could get a hundred, but this is well done." Jane took the test back from him, and went into her bedroom and closed the door, feeling disappointed and sad. Later that night, her father sat down next to her as she was reading in bed and said, "You know, I want to apologize for what I said to you this afternoon about your test. I've been thinking about it, and I realized that all I saw was the ninety-eight at the top of the paper, but I didn't see *you*. I didn't see my Jane and how hard you try to be perfect at everything you do. I didn't see you and how you tie yourself up in knots inside, trying to always do your best, and never being satisfied with yourself if you're not *the* best. So I just want to say that it's much more important to me that you be happy and carefree inside than that you get a hundred, a ninety-eight, or anything. I'm sorry I saw the wrong thing today, honey." Jane looked at the light streaming from her father's eyes and smiled. She put down her book, snuggled down into her blankets, closed her eyes, and went to sleep touched by his seeing of something about her she didn't know anyone else saw.

Parents have to look carefully at their child for a long time, pouring pure attention from their own faces and eyes through the child's face and eyes to the true self of the child within. I call that *respect*. Etymologically, "respect" means to "re-spect"—"to see again." Respect means looking at that child and then looking again, in a kind of permanently sustained double take, seeing over and over an authentic, singular, unique, inimitable, incomparable person. Parents are close to truly seeing the child when they glimpse innocence, goodness, and adoration of them in the child, and when they see God in that child.

In each interaction, in each moment, we must all greet and treat children with love and respect. Then we can truly see them. If we do not, they will grow up to be like many of us, relying on something or someone outside themselves to validate their worthiness. They will feel, like too many of us do, that they must prove themselves over and over instead of just being themselves. In some secret part of themselves, they will always be looking for their parents' approval of them, and they will never grow up.

If *we* want to grow up, we must see *our* parents as irrelevant now. Their time is past. We're not dependent on them or anyone to truly see us now. We all have to learn to see ourselves, and respect ourselves, and welcome ourselves, and love ourselves. With the inner eye that is opening in all of us who are working on ourselves psychologically and spiritually, we are learning to see what is there to be seen in the inner essence of our being. It is something to see. It's *us*. It's always been us. And, wonder of wonders, the somebody who finally sees us, the one who by that seeing finally confers on us the self-esteem, self-respect, and self-confidence that is our birthright, turns out to *be* us!

DROPPING THE DRAMA

There comes a time . . . when the "if only's" ring false and the "why me's?" are boring. To persist after that point is psychic death.
— Marion Woodman,
The Pregnant Virgin

Burton, a forty-six-year-old physician, had been neglected and ignored by his parents and frequently verbally and physically attacked by his schoolmates when he was a child. In four years of therapy, Burton had worked through much of that childhood trauma by bringing most of it into conscious memory and feeling the feelings associated with it. He still, however, had great difficulty in hearing criticism, and today he was angry at me for something I had said to him last week.

"I can't be having these reactions to correction and criticism anymore," he said, "but I don't know how to get past them. It's like I'm so damaged by my childhood that I can't help it."

"You can get past these reactions," I said, "but you'll have to do something big."

"What's that?"

"Drop the drama of what happened to you in your childhood."

He stared at me for a moment. "Did you say 'drama' or 'trauma'?" he asked.

"I said 'drama.' You're going to have to drop the drama of what happened to you in your childhood."

"*Drama?*" he said. He was fuming. "You call what happened to me '*drama*'?"

"I call what happened to any of us drama."

◡ ◡ ◡

If we want to get better, we have to spend some time—maybe a long time—going totally into the traumatic and wounding events of our childhood and remembering and reliving and re-feeling them.

Then there comes a point on this journey when it no longer helps to carry the wounds from our childhood around with us anymore. To get rid of them, once and for all, we have to stop thinking of our childhood as a bad, traumatic, wounding thing that happened to us—even though, on one level, it certainly was—and start thinking of it more as simply *what happened*. Once we can do this, we start to see it all as drama, and we can begin the project of dropping it. When we reach this level, what happened to us in our childhood doesn't matter anymore. True adulthood is when what happened to you in your childhood doesn't matter anymore.

Many people ask, "But *how* can I drop all that stuff?" Often I'll tell them this story, which I heard at a meditation workshop.

Once a man was walking through a forest thinking about his tendency to always feel angry.

"I just don't want to be angry anymore," he kept thinking to himself.

Deeper into the forest, he saw the wise sage of the forest standing by a tree—actually, the sage had his arms wrapped around the tree.

"O great sage," said the man, "can you help me? I've been plagued with anger all my life, and I just can't stand it anymore. Can you give me your teaching?"

"I can certainly help you," said the sage, "but first I have to wait until this tree lets go of me."

"But, sir," said the man, "the tree isn't holding on to *you, you're* holding on to *it.*"

The sage smiled. "That is my teaching," he said, and let go of the tree and disappeared into the forest.

2
THE MIND

The mind is its own place, and in itself
Can make a heav'n of hell, a hell of heav'n.
—John Milton, Paradise Lost

My dear,
is it true that your mind
Is sometimes like a battering
Ram
Running all through the city
Shouting so madly inside and out
About the ten thousand things
That do not matter?
—Hafiz, "Out of the Mouths of a
Thousand Birds"

The Eternal is not attained by rites and rituals, by pilgrimages or by
wealth. It is attained only by the conquest of one's mind.
—Vasishtha, Yoga Vasishtha

We may do all the work it is possible to do on what happened to us in our childhood, and completely put our childhood and our parents behind us. We may find and feel and express all our feelings, the ones from the past and the ones that come up in our present lives. We may lead virtuous lives, following all the legal and moral injunctions of our society and treating others with love and respect. We may be hugely successful in all worldly aspects of our lives, with clouds of achievements and admirers trailing behind us, but if we haven't solved the problem of the mind, we still have a problem, and we still have work to do.

The problem of the mind is that we have one, and that it has a natural tendency to spend a lot of its time thinking a steady stream of disturbing and distressing thoughts that make us feel bad about ourselves and our lives. When there's something inside us that spends a lot of its time making us feel bad about ourselves and our lives—and it's out of control, to boot—that's a problem.

The solution to the problem of the mind is to use the mind to understand and watch itself, to learn well all the ways and wiles of the mind, and to enjoy its play of thoughts. We must also gain control over the mind, purify and quiet it, and finally go *through* it to that place deep within us where we will find our own inner Self and the peace and happiness that is our true nature. To get our souls right, we have to understand the mind.

THE GOOSE IN THE BOTTLE

The mind, the mind, the mind—
This is the beginning and the end of it all.
The quality of one's life depends on
nothing but the mind.

—Buddha, the *Dhammapada*

"I'm feeling bad about my work today," said Murray.

"You always feel bad about something," I said.

"I know. Why do I feel bad about everything?"

"That's not the important question. The important question is, '*Where* do you feel bad about everything?'"

"I don't understand."

"Then I'll tell you a riddle," I said. "There's a goose in a bottle. It's a big, fat, healthy goose, and it's sitting at the bottom of one of those large bottles with a round bottom and a long, thin neck—a flagon, I think they call it.

"The riddle is, how do you get the goose out of the bottle without breaking, cracking, melting, vaporizing, or changing the bottle in any way, *and* without squeezing, squooshing, melting, vaporizing, chopping, or changing the goose in any way?"

Murray thought about it for a few minutes, then shrugged his shoulders.

"Make time go backward," he said, "until the goose is a gosling, or even an egg, and it'll be small enough that you can get it out of the neck of the bottle."

"Good try. But you can't make time go backward in this riddle, and besides, the neck is too narrow for even a gosling or an egg to pass through."

"Then I give up," he said. "It can't be done."

"Yes, it can. I'll give you a hint. I'll give you *four* hints. *Who* put the goose in the bottle? . . . and *when*? . . . and *why*? . . . and *with what*?"

He thought about it. "I don't know," he said.

"Sure you do. *Who* put the goose in the bottle?"

He looked at me blankly.

"You did. *When?* About two minutes ago. *Why?* Because I told you to. And *with what?*"

A flash of light came to his eyes, and he smiled.

"With my *mind!*" he said.

"Right. You put the goose *in* the bottle with your mind, so now take the goose *out* of the bottle with your mind."

He sat looking into the distance for a few seconds, smiled, then looked at me and nodded.

"Okay, it's out," he said.

"And the point of the riddle . . . ?"

He stared into space for an instant.

"It's my mind. The problem's not in my life, it's in my mind."

How many problems in your life are really in your mind? How many geese do you have in bottles up there? Take them out.

Now.

THE NATURE OF THE MIND
AND THE BIRDS ABOUT YOUR HEAD

*Of course, there is no mind without restlessness; restlessness is the very
nature of the mind.*

—Vasishtha, *Yoga Vasishtha*

In the quietest hours of the night, the worry swirls around in our heads,
keeping us awake despite our fatigue. We finally drop back to sleep, but
as soon as we awaken to start the day, the thoughts return. What could
go wrong today? How will I get everything done? Will there be enough
money? Why does Jimmy's teacher want to meet with us? What *is* that
thing on my back? Once, I heard the human mind described as a manic
monkey who's had too much to drink and who's just been stung by bees.
I felt relieved when I heard that, because I always thought it was just *my*
mind that was so restless.

Anyone who has spent much time looking at their mind has noticed
that the restless mind has three major tendencies: to be busy with
thoughts, to think a lot of negative thoughts, and to wander from
thought to thought.

Why do our minds act this way? We might as well ask why water is wet.
Just as it is the nature of water to be wet, it is the nature of the mind to
be busy, to be negative, and to wander.

Everyone with a mind, therefore, is in the same predicament.
Because of the three tendencies of the mind, we can't keep negative
thoughts from busily wandering into the mind. We can, however, keep
them from *staying* in the mind.

There is an old Chinese proverb: *That the birds of worry and care fly
about your head, this you cannot change. But that they build nests in your hair,
this you can prevent.*

The worried thoughts will come and come and come and come. You
have no choice over that. You do, however, have a choice once you
notice that they're there. You can stop thinking the negative, worried
thoughts, and start thinking other thoughts, the opposite thoughts—
positive thoughts, good thoughts. Or you can turn your attention away
from the thoughts—to your breath; to a soothing sound like music, or

prayer, or a mantra; to a memory of a serene place. Or you can *watch* the thoughts come and go in your mind without getting involved in them—you can watch the birds of worry and care fly about your head, but you don't have to let them build nests in your hair. You can do plenty of things with the thoughts in the mind. But first you have to notice that they're there.

In other words, you have to start watching your mind.

The Ten Things My Mind Was Doing While I Waited for Jane in Harvard Square

It is a thorny undertaking . . . to follow a movement so wandering as that of our mind, to penetrate the opaque depths of its innermost folds, to pick out and immobilize the innumerable flutterings that agitate it.

—Michel Eyquem de Montaigne,
Essais

Most of the time everyone's a mess. That's because everyone has a mind. The average human mind is a mess most of the time—that's the nature of it.

If we want to be happy, we have to clean up the mess in our minds. In order to do that, we first have to get a good look at the activities of the mind. I got a good look at the activities in my own mind three years ago when I was in Harvard Square.

I was meeting my wife Jane for lunch. Since I got there early, I sat down on some church steps to watch life go by. I like to sit places and watch life go by.

As I sat there, I had a revelation: I realized that life is a discontinuous series of discrete events happening in rapid, continuous succession, each instant a singular event, a still life, unconnected to the one before or after it except by this thin imaginary wire we call time. Each instant is like a single frame on a movie reel, and what we call life is the frames going by at a rapid clip, giving the illusion, as in a movie, of motion and continuity.

As I watched from my seat on the church steps, hundreds of these moments went by. A gray Volvo sat behind a blue van at a red light, while on the sidewalk near it a man and a woman holding hands stood looking into a store window. In the next moment everything was different. The light had changed, the Volvo and van were gone, the man and the woman had disappeared, and pedaling past me was a bicyclist whose sweat smelled like beer.

And each one of these moments was perfect. To say it most accurately, each one of them was what it was, and it was followed by another moment that was what it was, and so on.

The only thing that wasn't perfect was my mind, which was, unfortunately, having thoughts about all these moments. I say "unfortunately" because most of the thoughts it was having were negative.

So in addition to watching life go by in Harvard Square to see what life was doing, I also started watching my thoughts to see what my mind was doing. As far as I could tell, my mind was doing ten major things, each one of which was interfering with my experience of the moment, and all of which together were ruining my experience of the moment. In other words, my mind seemed to be making a complete mental mess of reality. Here are the ten things my mind was doing in Harvard Square that day:

It was *desiring*. I was experiencing attachment—and therefore frustration and sadness. A forest-green Jaguar stops at the light. I love forest-green Jaguars. I *want* a forest-green Jaguar. I want *that* forest-green Jaguar. I'm frustrated and sad because I can't have that forest-green Jaguar.

It was *disliking*. I was experiencing aversion. An old woman with white flakes of spittle caked on her lips is limping across the street toward me, pushing a shopping cart, looking my way. I look another way.

It was *judging*. A young woman is standing on the corner. She is dressed all in black, has spiked green and orange hair, jet-black lipstick, and a nose ring in each nostril. This is not the flower of femininity. This is not the rose of Sharon. I don't know what this is. I think this woman shouldn't be what she is. She's certainly not my idea of what a woman is. I'm judging her.

It was *being anxious*. A burly-looking drunken man is reeling down the sidewalk toward me. Will he engage me? Will he talk crazy to me? Will he ask me for money? Will he hurt me? I am anxious about him and the moment he might be bringing with him and inside I contract away from him.

It was *being impatient*. Where is Jane? I thought. She's late. I hate it when she's late. When will the moment be here when Jane is here? I am waiting for that moment, and am not in this moment.

It was *thinking of the worst catastrophes*. Where is Jane? She's never this late. Something terrible has happened to her. Something really terrible has happened to her. I should call the police to find out the really terrible thing that has happened to her.

It was *being angry*. A cute little baby smiles at me from the arms of a man who is waiting at the corner for the light to change. I am enjoying my eye contact with the baby. Then a heavyset man gets in between us. I can't see the cute little baby smiling at me anymore. I am angry at the heavyset man.

It was *comparing and envying*. A tanned young man wearing Tyrolean shorts and gargantuan hiking boots stands reading a magazine at the kiosk. He looks lithe, strong, handsome, bursting with testosterone. I am fifty-one years old, and I am none of those. I envy him, and feel lousy when I look at him.

It was *being intense about everything*. As if all of this *matters*! As if it's *important* what's happening for a few minutes on a Saturday afternoon in Harvard Square! As if each of these little events, all of which together are an infinitesimal fraction of the total number of events happening in the world at the same time, have important meaning that I need to have thoughts and feelings about!

It was *creating problems*. Whatever was happening, I somehow kept making it into a problem. There seemed to be an automatic mechanism in my mind that processed all experience into a problem, and couldn't rest until it had done that. Even then it still couldn't rest; it did it again.

Had it not been for my mind, I would have had a great time watching the continuous succession of discrete moments happening before me in Harvard Square. Instead, I was, as usual, making myself some version of mentally miserable in all those moments. But that didn't matter. I was also having an interesting time watching the continuous succession of discrete thought-moments happening in my mind. I actually ended up having a great time watching my thoughts go by and make me miserable in so many different and creative ways. As I say, I like to sit places and watch things go by.

I have heard it said that of all the things in the universe, the only thing that is not perfect is the human mind. I don't quite get that—there are many things in the universe, like plagues and famines and wars and things, that do not seem perfect to me—but I think I came closer than I ever have to understanding this idea on that day while I sat on the church steps in Harvard Square waiting for Jane.

REGROOVING

Always look for the good in yourself. Focus on that good, highlight it.
— Rebbe Nachman of Breslov,
The Empty Chair

Be ye transformed by the renewing of your mind.
—Romans 12:2

Eli, forty-two, owned a real estate management company that managed numerous commercial buildings, and he was exhausted from all the demands on his time and energy. He was also feeling terrible about himself.

"I don't do my job very well," he said. "I should know more. I should be better prepared. I'm *inept*!"

"Say that again," I said.

"I'm inept," he said.

"It has a familiar ring to it, doesn't it? I've heard you say it dozens of times before—about your work, your parenting, your lovemaking, even your bowling. I wonder why you say it so much."

"Because it's true," he said.

"The other possibility is that it's not true, but you just *think* it's true," I said.

☽ ☽ ☽

Imagine a hillside in which deep grooves, or gullies, have been cut by years and years of rain washing downhill. Now, whenever it rains, the water washes down the same grooves, each time cutting them deeper into the hillside. They are now permanently etched into the hillside and carry down all the water that falls on the hillside.

There are also deep grooves in your mind. They are the channels through which your thought-energy moves. They were cut in your childhood.[1] Now they're so deep that almost anything that happens to you in your adulthood will run down these grooves in your mind.

"I'm inept" is one of these grooves. When you were a child, every time your parents criticized something that you had just done as "shoddy," every time they pointed out that blemish on your face or in your character, every time anybody, including that stupid second-grade teacher of yours, told you, "You'll never amount to anything," the groove was deepened. Now it's there as a permanent feature of your mental landscape, and all your life experience and all your thought-energy runs down it.

As the Firesign Theatre said, you need regrooving.[2]

What you need to do—what we all need to do—is to etch new grooves in our minds. We have to go to that inner hillside of the mind, survey the existing channels, then dig new channels down which our thought-energy can start to run.

This regrooving can happen from inside us, slowly, or it can happen from outside us, sometimes quickly. Once when she was eight, my daughter Greta did a sort of instant regrooving on me. I was sitting on the edge of her bed tucking her in for the night. On an impulse, I asked, "Greta, do you think I'm a good daddy?"

"Yes," she said.

"How could I be better?"

"What do you mean?"

"How could I be a better daddy than I am?"

"You *are* a better daddy than you are," she said.

"What does *that* mean?"

"Wait . . . it means *something,*" she said, and lay staring at the ceiling for a moment. "Oh . . . right . . . you're a better daddy than you *think* you are."

I could almost literally feel a new thought-channel being cut in my mind at the instant of her response: "*I'm a better daddy than I think I am. . . . I'm a better everything than I think I am!*"

But to make a regrooving last, we always have to cut it deeper—on our own—from within. Instead of thinking "I'm inept," think "I'm an extremely capable person who tries my hardest at everything I do." Instead of thinking "I don't do my job very well," think "I do my job brilliantly." Instead of thinking "I'm so dark and dreary," think "I'm the light of the world!" Think it a thousand times. Think it a hundred thousand times. Don't worry that you don't believe it the first hundred thousand times you think it. That's not the point. Just keep thinking it and thinking it, cutting that new channel in the hillside. Use a toothpick, if that's all you've got, and cut inch by laborious inch down that hill. Just keep thinking it. You'll etch new grooves in your hillside, and your thoughts will start to flow in those new channels.

The Jewel in the Lake

Go find the gem hidden in your depths!
> —Jalaluddin Rumi,
> "Your Heart Is the Size of
> an Ocean"

Even if intellectually we accept the theory that inside us there's a place of peace and stillness and joy, and that that is our true nature, what if we've never experienced it? The only thing many people have experienced inside their minds is thinking. So where *is* all this peace and stillness and joy within? Where *is* our "true nature"?

Imagine a turquoise jewel resting on a black stone at the bottom of a clear lake. The jewel is lustrous and beautiful, but it is not visible because it's a windy day and the lake is choppy with waves, preventing us from seeing below the surface.

We could see the jewel, though, if we waited at the lake until the wind and the waves died down and the surface of the lake became placid and glasslike. All it takes is the stilling of the waves on the surface of the lake, and there it is!—the turquoise jewel!—resting on a black stone at the bottom of the lake.

The jewel is that place deep within us, the essence of our being, our innermost nature. It is that place of perfect peace and stillness and joy and love within us. It is who we are in our deepest inner Self.

But we can't see the inner Self, so therefore we don't really know ourselves. Our minds are choppy with waves, which we call "thoughts," that prevent us from seeing below our minds to the jewel of our true being. As long as our minds are disturbed with thought-waves, thought-waves are all that we can see, but when, through the practice of meditation and other self-awareness techniques, the thought-waves of the mind stop and the mind becomes still, we will be able to look below the placid surface of that lake and see the jewel of who we really are inside.

A Place of No Fear in the Mind

Those things that cause you inward peace, think upon deeply.
       —Thomas à Kempis,
        The Imitation of Christ

"It's been a rough couple of days," said Helen, a manager of a research and development team at a large computer company. "We heard there's going to be another round of layoffs at the end of the month, and this time I think it might be me."

"I'm sorry to hear that, Helen," I said. "Sounds scary."

"It's terrifying. But that's not all. My husband's company might be laying off too, which would *really* do us in, mortgage and all. So I worry. I'm always in fear. Wherever I go in my mind, there's fear, wall-to-wall, and I don't know what to do."

"Find a place of no fear in your mind."

Ꙩ Ꙩ Ꙩ

Find a place in your mind where you don't feel fear. If you can manage to get to this place, and remain there for any length of time, you can relax. Remember: You only need one such place in your mind, even if all the rest of your mind, and your life, is a complete catastrophe. I have a number of such places in my mind.

One place is the Twenty-third Psalm. It worked for David whispering it under his breath while he walked at night behind the lines of the Philistines, and it works for me. *Yea, though I walk through the valley of the shadow of death, I will fear no evil, for Thou art with me.* I repeat and contemplate those words, and keep trying to understand and believe them, for I know they're true. *Surely goodness and mercy shall follow me all the days of my life, and I will dwell in the house of the Lord forever.* Somewhere inside me I know that that's true too, and when I take refuge in this psalm, I am without fear.

Another place of no fear in my mind is a memory of a time in spring when I was about ten, standing, for some reason, on a garbage-can lid in my backyard next to the brick wall of my house. I can remember the rough, cool feel of the brick against the palm of my hand as I leaned against the house. It was lightly raining, though the sky was bright and blue—a sun shower! With uplifted face, I blinked up into the sparkling sky and heard a voice within me whisper, *April showers bring May flowers.* It was from a song. At that moment the sun was a song and the sun shower on my face was a song and the bright-blue sparkling sky was a song and my standing on a garbage-can lid next to the brick wall of my house was a song. In that moment and without words, I knew that everything was in harmony with everything else in this life and everything was and would always be okay. There's a place in my mind where I'm always a ten-year-old boy standing on a garbage-can lid in my backyard during a sun shower, and there's no fear there.

Another place I can go in my mind when fear comes is the day my daughter, who was nine at the time, saw me in one of my fearful moments sitting at the dining room table worrying. I get a certain stricken, deathlike look on my face when I worry. Seeing me in that state, my daughter came up to me, stood by my chair, put her arm around my shoulder, leaned up against me, and said, in her soft voice, and very slowly and deliberately, "This is just a moment, Dad . . . and in the future . . . there'll be . . . other moments . . . and in one of those moments . . . you'll be dead!" That cheered me right up. When I go to that place in my mind, to that great teaching whispered to me by my great daughter, all fear totally disappears.

Find at least one place of no fear in your own mind. Then, when fear comes, you can go there.

The Criterion of the Quiet Mind

There is a certain criterion by which you can judge whether the thoughts you are thinking and the things you are doing are right for you. The criterion is: Have they brought you inner peace? If they have not, there is something wrong with them.

—Peace Pilgrim,
   *Peace Pilgrim: Her Life and Work in
   Her Own Words*

A quiet mind cureth all.

—Robert Burton,
   The Anatomy of Melancholy

Rodney, a forty-one-year-old psychotherapist in private practice, wanted some advice. Should he or should he not declare on his tax form the $2,900 he had received in cash for therapy this year? It would be next to impossible for the IRS to trace it, he said, and he didn't like most of the uses the government put tax revenue to anyway. As far as he could tell, it seemed to be standard practice in the profession, and why should he play the fool by being overscrupulous? He knew he could "get away with it," but whenever he thought about it, it made his mind "kind of uneasy." What did I think?

☽　☽　☽

When faced with choices in my life, I use as my rule the criterion of the quiet mind. This means that when there are two or more courses of action possible for me, I take the one that will lead me to have a quieter mind, the one that will result in the fewest number of afterthoughts.

This criterion works for big choices and little choices. For example, I drive my car to the mall to do some shopping. I park it, get out, and start walking toward the mall. Halfway there, I realize I haven't locked the car. I have the impulse to go back and lock it, but I'm lazy, so the lazy voice inside me says, "You don't need to go back. Nobody'll steal your car here." I continue walking a few steps toward the mall. Then I remember the criterion of the quiet mind. So I think, "If I don't lock my car, will I, in the mall, have thoughts of what might be happening to my unlocked car?" The answer comes back, "Yes." Then I ask, "If I do lock it, will I have those thoughts?" The answer comes back, "No." I conclude that my mind will be quieter in the mall if I lock the car. So I overcome my laziness, walk back, and lock the car.

From experience I have learned that there are a number of activities and choices that lead not toward a quiet mind but toward an unquiet mind. They include:

Lying. "Oh, what a tangled web we weave, when first we practice to deceive," my wife is fond of quoting.[3] When we lie, we create more work for the mind, and then we have to create new lies to cover up the old ones, everything getting more tangled and mangled on our way to total mental agitation.

Gossip. If you want a *really* busy mind full of thoughts, think and talk about other people. Gossip! When it comes to other people, there's *so* much to think and talk about. There's no end to it! When you gossip about other people, whether your words are mean-spirited or kind-hearted, you're filling up your mental time with an inexhaustible supply of material, so you never get a chance to look at the material of your own life. The road to mental hell is *paved* with gossip.

Reading About, Hearing About, or Watching the News. If I do happen to be exposed to the news, it is all I can do to keep my mind from being crushed by the heaviness of it all, so I make it a practice to avoid the news. I use Thomas Jefferson and Henry David Thoreau as my models. Jefferson said, "I do not take a single newspaper, nor read one a month, and I feel myself infinitely the happier for it." And Thoreau said, "Read not the Times. Read the Eternities." If I have a half hour of reading time on a given day, I'd much rather spend it reading something enduring and uplifting—like the words of wise beings—than reading something ephemeral and dispiriting—like the news.

Intoxication. All kinds of drug- or alcohol-induced intoxication lead, either in the short run or the long run, to an unquiet mind. When I used to smoke marijuana, for example, there would be in my mind a veritable *explosion* of thoughts that would continue unabated for hours, and would leave me mentally and physically exhausted. With other drugs that seem to quiet our thoughts and feelings, they don't *really* do that, they just drive those thoughts and feelings deeper into ourselves, and they always show up later in noisier and more virulent forms.

Visual or Auditory Overstimulation. A few hours walking through stores at the mall, with all the colors and the voices and the people and everything in continual motion, requires a recovery period for me. I figure it takes me about half a day to quiet my mind after visiting a mall. And then there are video games, especially as they affect our children's minds and nervous systems. Don't even talk to me about video games.

Thinking About the Past. Between regretting one's past, being angry about the past, wishing the past had been different from what it was, and nostalgically hoping to repeat the past, there's a whole lifetime of thoughts about the past that can be thought.

Thinking About the Future. Between anticipating the future, guessing at it, fantasizing about it, and worrying about it, there's a whole lifetime of thoughts about the future that can be thought.

Thinking About Yourself. There are certain ways of thinking about yourself that lead to an unquiet mind: thinking about yourself negatively and judgmentally; thinking about yourself conceitedly and arrogantly; thinking about yourself comparatively, as either inferior or superior to others; thinking obsessively about the flux and fluctuation of events, experiences, or body or mood changes that make up your life; and taking everything personally, self-pity, and all other forms of egocentric self-absorption. These ways of thinking about yourself are all repetitive, endless, addictive, exhausting, and—when you come right down to it—*boring* for anyone, including yourself, who has the great misfortune to have to actually *listen* to it.

Thinking About Anything. As far as I can tell, based on my experience of my own mind, there's a whole lifetime of thoughts to be thought— if you want to think them.

Doing Anything Illegal, Unethical, or Immoral. Whether it's a small thing like not getting a license for the dog, or a bigger thing like taking something that belongs to someone else, or a really big thing like hurting another human being or any living creature, when I do *wrong* like that, when I violate the law of dharma—ethical behavior—it feels like the whole universe is thrown out of balance, including my mind, which reels with thoughts a long time after.

So is it wrong for Rodney not to pay all his taxes? The better question is, which choice will give him the quieter mind?

THE SLIDING-GLASS
DOUBLE DOOR OF THE MIND

If the doors of perception were cleansed, every thing would appear to us as it is, infinite.

—William Blake,
"The Marriage of Heaven and Hell"

Many years ago I was vacationing with my wife on Cape Cod. We were staying at a bed-and-breakfast on the beach. A sliding-glass double door led out to a wooden deck built over the sand, which led down the beach to the ocean. Through the glass doors, you could see the ocean rolling in.

One afternoon while Jane was napping, I took a shower. When I came out of the bathroom, the sliding-glass double door was all fogged up with steam from the shower. For some inexplicable reason I wrote the word **"YES"** in the steam on one of them with my forefinger, and the word **"NO"** on the other. Through the letters where my finger had cleared away the steam, peering closely, I could see the ocean rolling in.

Then I realized: When I look through the **"YES,"** there's the ocean rolling in, and when I look through the **"NO,"** there's the ocean rolling in, and it's the same exact ocean rolling in. Whether it's **"YES"** or **"NO,"** the ocean rolling in and my experience of the ocean rolling in are unaffected. The ocean just keeps rolling in.

Then it struck me. *This is my mind!* This is what my mind does to experience. It says **"YES"** to some things in my life and **"NO"** to other things in my life, but it doesn't matter: Things just keep rolling in in my life, and my life just keeps rolling in.

How thin and flimsy and insubstantial and comical this **YES/NO** mind of mine is compared to the vast ocean of life that keeps rolling in. What a ridiculous thing my mind is, and what a waste of time to keep dividing up experience into **"YES"** and **"NO"** when I could just be living in the present experience. What illusion! What ignorance! What arrogance!

So I took a towel and wiped off the steam from the doors. There was the ocean, rolling in. The narrow little view of it I had had through the **"YES"** and the **"NO"** had expanded. There was the vast ocean rolling in!

So when faced with seemingly unpleasant people or circumstances, try neither liking them nor disliking them, but just watching them rolling in as part of the ocean of your experience. Wipe off the **"YES"** and **"NO"** from the doors of your mind, open those doors, and greet all your experience.

3
MEDITATION

You gotta look inside yourself. You gotta look inside your inner self and find out who you are.

—from the movie *Analyze This*

Strive to close the eyes of the body and open those of the soul and look into your own heart.

—St. Teresa of Avila

Like oil in sesame seeds
butter in cream
water in the river-bed,
fire in tinder
the Self dwells within the soul.
Realize that Self
through truthfulness and meditation.

—*Svetasvatara Upanishad*

Meditation is very simple. It is an attempt to turn our awareness toward a place within ourselves that is continuously and unconditionally loving, peaceful, wise, and happy. This place exists within our own beings as the core and ground and essence of us. In some spiritual traditions, it is called the Self. Meditation is the quintessential act of Self-awareness.

I teach meditation in my therapy practice because I believe that the ultimate goal of therapy is to show people that there exists within all of us a loving, peaceful, wise, and happy inner place; that this place has never been disturbed or even touched by all the troubles and traumas that we've all gone through in our lives; that we can learn, with practice and over time, to direct the beam of our awareness to this place; that once we've learned to direct our awareness to this place, we start living our lives with more love, peace, wisdom, and happiness. The ultimate goal of meditation and all healing is to permanently establish our awareness in this place and finally realize who we really are. Once enough of us have realized who we really are, the world will become what it really is, a garden of paradise for our stewardship and enjoyment. I teach meditation in therapy because it is the supreme road to getting our souls, and the soul of the world, right.

After the first two or three sessions, once my clients have gotten comfortable with me, I introduce them to the practice of meditation by beginning each session with three to five minutes of it. Depending on the client's familiarity with meditation, sometimes I don't call it "meditation," but "going within," "centering," "prayer," or even just "relaxing" or "taking a breather." During that time, I dim the lights, and my clients and I close our eyes and go inside. If I'm moved to, or if the client requests me to, I sometimes do "guided meditations" during that time, talking my clients through the meditation to help them understand and experience it. At the end of the meditation, I ring a little bell and turn up the lights. Then we open our eyes and go on from there.

How to Meditate

Try to meditate regularly. That means once a day, every day, if you can. If you can't meditate every day, meditate almost every day. Find the time for it. We can all find the time for eating, sleeping, and grooming our bodies because we think those things are important and essential in life; and we should be able to find the time for meditation because meditation too is essential in life. And don't say you're too busy. We're all "too busy." There is a saying— "If you're too busy to meditate, you're too busy."

Meditate at any time of the day you can fit it in, morning to night. Make it a time during which you can be alone and undisturbed, in relative quietness. The best time is early in the morning, around dawn, because no one's up then and the earth is hushed. Another good time for meditation is at dusk, when again the earth is quiet. Some people meditate after everybody else has left the house for the day. Some people meditate in their cars in the parking lot before work, or during their lunch break, or during any kind of break, or on the subway, or in bed, sitting up, right before sleep. The best time for meditation is whenever you can fit meditation into *your* life.

Two times it is best not to meditate are right after you've eaten and when you're very tired. In both cases, you are likely to fall asleep. Sleep is pleasant and certainly necessary, but it's not meditation. If, however, the only time you have available for meditation on a given day is either right after you've eaten or when you're very tired, meditate then, and if you fall asleep, you fall asleep. Sleep can be especially sweet, restful, and revitalizing when entered through the doorway of meditation.

Meditate for an hour, a half hour, twenty minutes, ten minutes, or even for just ten seconds. Meditate for as many minutes or seconds as you can, and *will,* on a daily basis. Don't say you'll meditate for forty minutes every day and then, since you don't have forty minutes every day, you skip meditating every day; instead, say you'll meditate for ten minutes every day, and then do it. You may find that if you start with ten minutes, after a month or two you yourself will want to increase it to fifteen or twenty minutes, the experience of meditation being so satisfying to the soul that you start craving more of it.

If you can, create a place in your home—an extra room, an area in a room, a corner of a room, even a special pillow or chair you sit on—that is for meditation and only for meditation. Make this place clean and comfortable to you, and beautiful to your eyes. Some people set up a meditation table on which they'll have flowers, seashells, holy books, photos of loved ones, or any other thing that induces in them a feeling of love, reverence, and tranquillity. If, for whatever reason, you can't create a special place for meditation in your home, meditate wherever you find yourself at the time of meditation, in or out of your home, and by the very act of your meditating there it becomes a special place.

Meditate in clean, comfortable clothes. Since the peaceful vibrations of meditation build up in the clothes you wear for meditation, some people keep a special set of clothes that they use only for meditation.

Most people sit for meditation. People who, for whatever reason, can't sit for meditation either kneel or lie down. If you do sit, you can sit on a couch, a chair, or a pillow on the floor. If you sit on a pillow, you might want to lean your back against a wall for support, and cross your legs, and rest your hands in your lap or in whatever posture is comfortable for you. There are special pillows and benches that help one maintain a comfortable posture for meditation. Any regular physical exercise that stretches, strengthens, and tones the body helps one maintain a comfortable posture, and thus helps meditation. The stronger and more flexible your body is, the less its aches and pains will usurp your attention during meditation, and the more you'll be able to concentrate on meditation. If you sit on a chair, it is best to sit with both feet flat on the floor and your hands resting on your knees or lap. Wherever you sit for meditation, sit in an upright but comfortable posture, with your spine elongated and straight but not rigid, your shoulders relaxed and opened, letting go of any tension in your neck, jaw, and face. If you lie down, lie on your back with your arms extended, palms upward, slightly away from your body, and your legs extended with your feet about as wide as your hips. In whatever position you meditate, a disciplined yet relaxed posture will allow your body to settle down and become still, helping your mind to also become still.

Since meditation involves focusing one's awareness on a chosen object, you may want to choose an object or image to meditate upon that is engaging of, and worthy of, your awareness. For some people, it is a candle flame, a mental picture of a beautiful natural scene, a photograph of a holy person, a mantra or a prayer or other sacred or beautiful sound, the sound of your own breath, the name of God, or the nameless God.[1] Direct your awareness to this object, image, or sound, and try to keep it there as long and as steadily as you can. When your mind wanders, as it surely will, gently bring your awareness back to what you are meditating upon. Your repeated attempts to keep your awareness there as long and as steadily as you can *is* meditation.

Meditation is a journey, a long, inner journey of many, many years, and many, many things will happen on it. You will have many inner experiences: memories, feelings of every variety and intensity, more thoughts than you could imagine a single human mind thinking, physical sensations, unusual mental states, transcendental states, visions, the voice of your own wisdom, visits to divine inner realms, and other wonders that will inspire you to keep meditating. You will experience great clarity, intuitive understanding, timeless knowledge, perfect stillness, and sublime feelings. You will also experience restlessness, sleep, boredom, and physical discomfort. On the whole long journey of it all, it is best to remember that there is no *specific* experience or state that one is supposed to have during meditation, that *every* experience and state during meditation *is* meditation, and that the effort we make to meditate is the essence of meditation.

Meditation is its own guide as you continue the journey. It is a discipline, an austerity, a practice, a pilgrimage. It is a great comfort and a great joy, and it will allow you to discover who you truly are.

The Hurricane

All this talk and turmoil and noise and movement and desire is outside the veil; inside the veil is silence and calm and peace.
—Abu Yazid Al-Bistami

Imagine a hurricane on a weather map. Let's call it Hurricane You. Hurricane You has three parts to it. The outermost part is a ring of moving energy in the form of circling wind and rain. The middle part is another ring of circling wind and rain. The innermost part is the eye, where all is calm and still.

This is your very own hurricane. Your outermost ring is your life: the ever-moving, ever-changing, often unpredictable and seemingly random series of events and experiences that happen to you in your life. Some are big, some are small; some are pleasant, some are unpleasant. These events and experiences started happening to you at birth, are happening to you right this moment, and will continue to happen to you until you die.

The middle ring of Hurricane You is the ring of your thoughts and feelings and moods and inner states. From the moment you wake up to the moment you fall asleep, these circle around and succeed each other, morning to night, cradle to grave.

Sometimes the inner ring of our thoughts and feelings is connected to the outer ring of events and experiences, and the two rings circle together for a while. For example, if we get a raise or a hug or a new car or a new friend on the outer ring, on the inner ring we feel happy, we like life, we have pleasant thoughts and a pleasant inner state. Then we get fired or we get snubbed, or we get sick or get a scratch on the new car and we feel sad, upset, angry at life and have unpleasant thoughts and an unpleasant inner state. Our thoughts and feelings are in sync with external events.

And sometimes we have thoughts and feelings and moods and inner states that are totally independent of the events and experiences circling around us at the time. For example, we might be lying with our beloved on a beautiful beach on Aruba and still be in one of the darkest and foulest moods ever seen in the Caribbean. The two rings may circle at different speeds, even on different axes.

For most people the two circling rings are all there is, and they live their lives spinning along with them, and then they die. Some people, however, hear about the innermost part of the hurricane, the eye, and they start doing things in their lives in order to get to the eye. They learn how to go to a part of the storm that is not stormy, where they can just watch the storm, totally undisturbed by it, in a state of perfect peace and stillness. In the eye, at the very center of it all, we just watch, in pure unmodified awareness. This is where Consciousness, Awareness, the Knower, the Inner Witness resides.

Meditation is the effort to go to that place, and it's the state we're in when we get there.

THE FOUR STATES

There is a self-existent Reality. . . . That Reality is the Witness of the three states of consciousness. . . . That Reality is the knower in all states of consciousness—waking, dreaming, and dreamless sleep. It is the Self.
  —Shri Shankaracharya,
    The Crest-Jewel of Discrimination

At the end of our three-minute meditation at the beginning of the session, Dominic reported that he had had so many "thoughts, feelings, and scenarios" playing through his mind during it that he "couldn't meditate at all."

"How do you *know* you had all those thoughts, feelings, and scenarios playing through your mind?" I asked.

"What do you mean?"

"*Who* knows, and is able to report to me, that you had all those thoughts, feelings, and scenarios playing through your mind?"

"I don't know what you mean."

"Are you confused right now?"

"Yes."

"How do you *know* you're confused? *Who* knows that you're confused?"

"I do."

"You *know* that you're confused?"

"Yes."

"And who's reporting it to me?"

"I am."

"And what are you reporting that you know?"

"That I'm confused."

"Who's 'I'?"

"I am."

"And you're confused?"

"Yes."

"I thought you just said you're the one who *knows* that you're confused."

"I do."

"Well, which is it? Are you the one who's confused or are you the one who knows he's confused?"

"I am confused, but I also know that I'm confused."

"Then you're two beings. You're what you are, which right now is confused, and you're also something inside that seems to *know* what you are, and that *knower* is *not* confused."

He paused for a moment, staring at me.

"Now I'm really confused," he said.

☽ ☽ ☽

In order to understand meditation, we have to understand the four states of consciousness.[2]

The first state of consciousness is the *waking state*. In this state we go about our business for many hours a day, moving around, acting, reacting, relating, speaking, thinking, and feeling. When we get tired from all this business, we go to bed and fall asleep and enter the second state of consciousness, which is the *dream state*. In this state, we're sleeping and dreaming, with images and sounds being projected by our consciousness onto the inner screen of our consciousness. Then we move into the third state of consciousness, the *deep-sleep state*, during which nothing is happening in our consciousness, just a still, silent, velvety womb of total darkness in which we are nourished by deep rest.

The fourth state of consciousness is called the *witness state*. The *witness state*, as its name implies, *watches* the three other states. It knows what we're experiencing in the *waking state*, and it also knows what we're dreaming in the *dream state* and often reports that in the morning to whoever will listen. The *witness state* also knows when we're in the *deep-sleep state* and reports, "I slept like a log last night. I was dead to the world." Like the operating system in a computer, the *witness state* is the state *behind* all the other states. It is always awake. How else could we know, for example, that we had a dream unless there was someone who was awake to watch it and record it and report it back to us in the morning?

Walt Whitman describes the *witness state* in *Song of Myself:*

Apart from the pulling and hauling stands what I am,
Stands amused, complacent, compassionating, idle, unitary,
Looks down, is erect, or bends an arm on an impalpable certain rest,

Looking with side-curved head curious what will come next,
Both in and out of the game and watching and wondering at it.

Henry David Thoreau describes the *witness state* in the "Solitude" chapter in *Walden:* "[I] am sensible of a certain doubleness by which I can stand as remote from myself as from another. However intense my experience, I am conscious of the presence . . . of a part of me, which, as it were, is not a part of me, but spectator, sharing no experience, but taking note of it, and that is no more I than it is you."

Meditation is something we do every day to strengthen our identification with the "spectator," or witness, within. It is our daily attempt to realize that we are not *what* we're witnessing in our lives and in our bodies and in our minds, but we *are* the inner witness watching all of that from a state of perfect peace. The ultimate goal of meditation is to know at all moments that you are the inner witness—"I am the one inside who is watching all of this; *that's* who I am." Once you know that you are the witness of what happens, and you never forget it no matter what happens, you have achieved total inner peace. Total inner peace is the goal of meditation.

That means that if you are having thoughts, feelings, and scenarios playing through your mind during meditation, it doesn't matter. They come and go. Let them come and go; from the place of the witness, *watch* them come and go. You have nothing to do with all that coming and going, and it has nothing to do with you. *You* are the witness of it all.

THE FLASHLIGHT OF AWARENESS
or
WHO ARE YOU ANYWAY?

Meditation is an unbroken flow of awareness toward the object of concentration.

—Patanjali, *Yoga Sutras*[3]

Oh, how wonderful!
I am Awareness itself!
No less!

—Ashtavakra, *Ashtavakra Gita*

If you don't understand how awareness works, you don't understand how you work; and if you don't understand how you work, you won't understand who you really are.

Who are you anyway? A woman, a man, married, not, baby boomer, thirtysomething, black, white, gay, thin, a Baptist, a Buddhist, a typist, a loving mother of three great kids—any of these might be who you think you are. But are you aware of who you *really* are?

Deep inside us there's a place of pure, unconditional happiness. Dante describes it in *The Divine Comedy* as "joy past compare, gladness unutterable, unmeasured bliss." Jesus calls it "the Kingdom of God," and says it's "*within* you." All the great sages and saints and mystics and meditation masters speak about this place and point us within to find it: Our very nature *is* happiness, they say.

So why aren't we happy? If our very nature is pure, unconditional happiness, why are so many people running around frantically looking for happiness in their lives? Because even though our very nature is happiness, most of us are not *aware* of it. What's the use of the beautiful sunset over the ocean if we don't look at it? What's the use of the fifty terrific stations coming in on my radio if I don't tune in to them? Only the things we're aware of can exist for us.

Awareness is like the beam of a flashlight: It is a flow of illuminating light toward an object. If we walk into a pitch-black room carrying a flashlight, there might be a dozen pieces of furniture in the room, but not one of them exists for us until we illuminate it with the beam of light from our flashlight. We cannot make use of that comfortable couch in the corner of that room until we become aware of it by shining a light on it.

In the same way, we can make no use of our own inner nature, which is pure, unconditional happiness, until we become aware of it by illuminating it with the flashlight of our awareness.

In meditation we learn to direct the flow of our awareness, just as we point the beam of a flashlight toward a chosen object. Most of us spend most of our time directing the flashlight of our awareness toward the world and the sensory experiences that fill it, and toward our minds and the thoughts that occupy them. That's why we're so unhappy most of the time: We always seem to have our awareness pointed in the wrong damn direction!

If we could learn, by discipline and practice, to direct the flashlight of our awareness toward that place inside us that is pure, unconditional happiness—toward the truth of our nature—we would be purely, unconditionally happy all the time. Everything we want and have ever wanted is right there, right *here*, inside us. All we have to do is become aware of it.

Let's practice awareness. Close your eyes, please . . .

Notice that as soon as you close your eyes, the beam of your awareness, which up to now had been flowing *outside* you through your senses to apprehend and negotiate the world, now starts to flow *inside* you. Take a moment and experience that . . .

If you're like most people, when you close your eyes and your awareness starts to flow within, it immediately goes to your mind. If that happens to you, just sit there and be aware of what's going on in your mind . . . there are lots of thoughts in your mind . . . the flashlight of your awareness is pointed now at your mind. . . .

Now take the flashlight of your awareness and point it at your left foot. You don't have to open your eyes, just move your awareness to your left foot from inside. . . . You are now aware of your left foot. You now know if your left foot is hot or cold, tense or relaxed, cramped or comfortable. You've illuminated it. You're *aware* of it. It's always been there, but now you're *aware* of it. . . .

Now move the flashlight of your awareness to the inside of your mouth. . . . Notice that as soon as I say that, you are instantaneously and almost effortlessly able to move your awareness where you want to move it, and you can hold it there for a while. Someone inside there seems to be in control of your awareness and can make decisions about where to point it. With your awareness now pointed at the inside of your mouth, you now know if it's moist or dry, sweet or sour. . . . You are illuminating the inside of your mouth with the flashlight of your awareness. . . . It's always been there, but now you're *aware* of it.

Now move the flashlight of your awareness to the sounds surrounding you . . . the creaking of the house . . . the birds outside . . . the cars going by . . . your own breath. . . . Notice that, once again, you are instantaneously and almost effortlessly able to move your awareness where you want to move it, and you can hold it there for a while. Once again, someone inside there seems to be in control of your awareness and can make decisions about where to point it. These sounds now exist for you because you have pointed your *awareness* at them. . . .

And now move the flashlight of your awareness to your breath and simply be aware of your incoming and outgoing breath. . . .

Breathing in . . . breathing out . . . breathing in . . . breathing out . . .

Notice that you are able to do that. You can point all of your awareness at your breath, and you can keep it there for a while.

If you can keep the beam of your awareness flowing to your breath for a long while, the movement of your breath, or, rather, your steady, prolonged *awareness* of the movement of your breath, will take you down into the deep places of your being, where, underneath all the other parts of your being, pure, unconditional happiness dwells as your essential nature.

See if you can go there right now by pointing the flashlight of your awareness at your breath . . . breathing in . . . breathing out . . . breathing in . . . breathing out . . .

Keep breathing . . .

Deep inside your being is the truth of your being—your inner Self, happiness!—and you can find that truth by illuminating your breath with the beam of light of your awareness. You *are* that light. Meditation is the experience that you are the Light of Awareness.

The Two-Step

Guide our feet into the way of peace . . .

—Luke 1:79

If meditation involves gaining access to the Inner Witness who observes all our feelings, but therapy involves getting in touch with our feelings, which is more important—to observe or to feel our emotions?

Both.

When we walk we step first with one foot and then with the other; alternating between the two feet, we go forward. In the same way, on this journey of self-transformation we must alternate between two feet. One foot is meditation. Through meditation and other techniques of self-awareness, we establish and keep strengthening our identification with the Inner Witness, the eye at the center of our storm of feelings, the one inside who's watching our feelings in a state of perfect peace. The other foot is the feeling of those feelings. Because there is nothing hidden that shall not be revealed on this journey—and that includes all our emotions—we must sometimes go into that storm and be willing to feel the feelings that are whirling about in it. That's a major step in overcoming them.

It takes a brave person with a strong and steady consciousness to walk into that storm and face the swirling buffets and blasts of the primal energies that are our feelings. Stepping with one foot, we walk into the storm and feel the feelings in it. Stepping with the other foot, we walk out of the storm, into its center, and watch it peacefully from there. Like the systole and diastole of a heart, pumping in and out, or like the high and low tides of the ocean, we engage in a back-and-forth process. Stepping first with one foot and then with the other, feeling our feelings, watching our feelings, we go forth, we propel ourselves forward, to the Self.

ON THE BEACH

Sit in reverie and watch the changing colors
Of the waves that break upon the idle seashore of the mind.
—Henry Wadsworth Longfellow

Some people practice meditation on and off for years, but never quite develop an enthusiasm for it because they are unable to stop their minds and experience inner quiet. Paradoxically, what they are doing wrong is *trying* to stop their minds. Yes, quieting those buzzing thoughts is the purpose of meditation, but you can't quiet them by trying to quiet them.

Spend any amount of time with your mind and you learn to respect the sheer power of it. It has the power of the ocean. In the same way that wave after wave of water arises from the ocean in an unceasing arising of waves, wave after wave of thought arises from the mind in an endless arising of thought-waves. What we call the mind is this continual succession of thought-waves arising and subsiding inside our poor little heads.

Total immersion in the ocean of the mind is the normal state of almost everybody. We're all like fish in that ocean, so totally surrounded by and immersed in mind that we can't even conceive of there being anything *but* mind.

Meditation involves climbing out of the ocean of the mind and going to sit on the beach to watch the waves of that ocean arise and subside, arise and subside. When we're sitting on the beach, the specific size, shape, speed, sound, or color of each individual wave doesn't matter. What do we care? We're not *in* the waves, we're just watching them.

In meditation we don't try to stop the mind. We just learn how to watch it. Once we learn how to watch it, we don't need to stop it. It remains what it is, and we remain what we are, the watcher of it.

There will be moments in meditation, and sometimes whole meditations, when the thought-waves stop altogether and the ocean of the mind becomes calm and still. We also become calm and still. Nothing moves anywhere, not even time. There is complete peace.

Sitting on the beach, in deep meditation, we are able to stare at the ocean of perfect stillness within us.

The Railroad Station
or
Stop This Thought!
I Want to Get Off!

Often I am not where I am, but where my thoughts lead me.
—Thomas à Kempis,
The Imitation of Christ

If your mind races, return to the place you were before the thought. Return to the site of oneness.

—The Kabbalah

In your mind's eye, imagine that you are standing at a railroad station in front of empty tracks. You are all alone. It is one of those small outdoor stations—like you see in movies about the old west—with a wooden platform, a single set of tracks, and a view of a broad valley ringed by mountains. It is quiet and peaceful there, and you are quiet and peaceful. Nothing is going on in your mind, you are just standing there on the wooden platform gazing at the empty tracks. There is great stillness around you. All you can hear is a high, steady wind in the valley and the sound of your own breathing.

A soft rumble, far in the distance to your left, gets gradually louder, and you can feel a slight vibration in the platform. The rumble grows, the vibration increases. You look to your left, and in the distance you can see a train puffing toward the station. It gets closer and closer, looming larger and larger, and now it's pulling into the station hissing and squealing.

A sign on the front of the train says, **A Thought!**

The train comes to a stop in front of you. The passenger car is directly in front of you, and as the door opens a sign above it flashes, **I Am One of Your Thoughts! Think Me! Get On!**

The rapid flashing of the sign is insistent, so you get on. You step onto the train and the door closes behind you, and the train starts to pull out of the station. You're thinking that thought now, it's picking up speed, you're taking a ride on that train of thought, farther and farther from the station. In fact, you completely forget about the station.

Keep taking the ride on that train of thought for a few moments. Think that thought, and its successors. And see where they take you . . .

Now . . . *stop* thinking those thoughts. Stop the train. Pull the cord. Feel the train stop. The door opens. Get off the train. Walk back to the station. It's closer than you think. Actually, it's right there. You haven't gone anywhere.

There you are, once again standing on the wooden platform at the quiet, peaceful train station. You are all alone, gazing at the empty tracks. Nothing is going on in your mind. There is silence and stillness all around you—in front of you, the empty tracks. All you can hear is the high, steady wind in the valley and the sound of your own breathing.

Listen to that for a few moments . . .

Suddenly you hear another rumble off in the distance to your left, and it gets louder and louder, and then you can see it, another train getting nearer, looming larger and larger, and pulling into the station with a hissing and a squealing, and you see it bears a sign that says, ANOTHER THOUGHT!

The train pulls in front of you, stops, and the door slides open. Above the door is a flashing sign, I AM ANOTHER ONE OF YOUR THOUGHTS. THINK ME! GET ON!

The rapid flashing of the sign is insistent.

You stand there. You have a choice this time, and you know you have a choice. You pause, but you're kind of intrigued by the thought, so you decide to get on. The door closes behind you, and off you go.

Ride that train of thought. There you go again . . . farther and farther from the station.

Now stop the train! Stop thinking that thought. Pull the cord. Feel it stop. The door opens. Get off the train. Walk back to the station. It's closer than you think. It's right there. You haven't gone anywhere.

And there you are again, once again standing on the wooden platform at the quiet, peaceful train station. You are all alone, gazing at the empty tracks. Nothing is going on in your mind. There is silence and stillness all around you—in front of you the empty tracks. All you can hear is a high, steady wind in the valley and the sound of your own breathing. Listen . . .

Now comes another train rumbling in the distance, getting closer and closer, looming larger and larger, and now pulling into the station in front of you. The sign on the front of the train says, **ANOTHER THOUGHT!** and the flashing sign over the opening door says, **I AM *ANOTHER* ONE OF YOUR THOUGHTS. THINK ME! GET ON!**

You stand there. You have a choice. You choose not to get on. You're tired of riding train after train of thought, so this time you stay at the station. You don't move a muscle. The sign flashes, the open door beckons, but you stay at the station.

The train door closes. The train pulls out. You are not on it.

You are standing at the station on the wooden platform, in silence and stillness, contentedly gazing at the empty tracks. Trains continue to come and go, but you don't get on, for you are meditating.

The Clutch

Do you know how to drive a standard-shift car? If so, you understand how the clutch works—and how meditation breaks the attachment between us and our minds.

According to my rudimentary automotive understanding, the way a car works is that the pistons inside the cylinders in the engine go up and down, and this up-and-down motion is transferred to the crankshaft, which spins, and the spinning of the crankshaft is transferred through the transmission and the drive shaft to the axle, which spins and causes the wheels to spin, thus moving the car.

On cars with standard transmissions, the clutch is a major transfer point in the series of transfers from the pistons to the wheels. When the clutch is engaged, the two clutch plates are connected to each other and spin in conjunction with each other, thus transferring the spinning motion of the crankshaft through the transmission to the driveshaft, and from there to the wheels. When the driver disengages the clutch by pushing in the clutch pedal, the two clutch plates separate so that the spinning motion of the crankshaft and engine is not transferred through the transmission to the wheels. When the clutch is disengaged, the engine can spin all it wants and as fast as it wants, but it doesn't move the car. The car sits still, its engine idling, until you release the clutch pedal, engage the two clutch plates, and connect the whole thing back up again.

That, loosely speaking, is the way a car with a standard shift works.

The way *you* work is: Your mind spins, in the form of your incessant thinking and feeling, and the spinning of your mind is sometimes transferred to your tongue, which starts spinning in the form of your speaking, and it's sometimes transferred to your body, which starts spinning in the form of your performing actions in the world. In other words, the moving of your mind is your engine, moving all the rest of you.

That can be unfortunate because it means that you're moved by something in you—your mind—which, as we all know, is often out of control and is sometimes more compelling than your intelligence, your conscience, or your love. It would be good if by an act of will you could stop the out-of-control, thinking-and-feeling mind, but you can't yet— the mind's too powerful, and you can't just turn it off like you would the ignition of a car. So you do the next best thing, which is just as good. You throw the clutch in. If you're driving a car with an automatic transmission, you throw it into neutral. You practice meditation.

Meditation is when you sit down and close your eyes, and for a specified amount of time you watch your mind move without doing anything about it. By watching your mind move without speaking or acting from it—in other words, by not being moved by the movements of the mind—you have, in effect, thrown the clutch in. You have disengaged the thinking and feeling part of yourself from the speaking and acting part of yourself. In meditation, we just witness the motion of the thinking and feeling part of ourselves while the speaking and acting part of ourselves remains motionless. In other words, we *idle*.

The practice of meditation is the daily attempt to idle by throwing the clutch in between our minds and ourselves. By doing that, we are no longer being driven by the mind, but by our intelligence, our conscience, and our love, which is our true nature.

Going Below

Do not try to stop your thinking. . . . When you try to stop your thinking,
it means you are bothered by it. Do not be bothered by anything.
                    —Shunryu Suzuki,
                        Zen Mind, Beginner's Mind

I think of my mind as a wandering psychopath who has somehow taken up residence in my attic and spends all his time up there crashing around muttering strange, incomprehensible things to himself. He doesn't really disturb me, though, because I'm down in the living room lounging.

I think of my mind as an energetic and somewhat manic kid playing upstairs in his bedroom, making lots of noise, babbling and yelling and having long, animated conversations with his imaginary friends while I sit quietly downstairs in the den dozing.

I think of my mind as the surface of the ocean, wave after wave rising and rolling, ever restless, ever moving, with endless energy, while I, in a diving bell, sit on the bottom rocking in the slow, undulant currents there.

Who cares if you can't stop your mind? It's above you. It has nothing to do with you. Be below it. It's peaceful below it. In meditation, we don't try to stop the mind, we go below the mind.

CHINESE BOXES
or
WATCHING THE WATCHER

The Soul should always stand ajar.
>   —Emily Dickinson

On one level, there are some things that are better to watch than others. It is better for our nervous systems, for example, to watch a beautiful sunset than a violent movie. In meditation it is better to watch our breath than our mind. That's because it is better to watch something with soothing energy than to watch something with unsoothing energy, because what we watch we become.

On another level, it doesn't matter what you watch in meditation, since the purpose and goal of meditation is to break all identification with what is watched and completely identify yourself with the Watcher. So whether you're watching a sunset, a movie, your mind, your breath, or your anxiety, it's all the same to the Watcher. On this level, it is as meditative and as beneficial to watch your anxiety as to watch your breath, just as long as you don't forget you're the Watcher.

If you're completely stabilized in the Watcher, you can play Chinese boxes with yourself. Chinese boxes are those boxes where in each new box you open, there's a smaller box inside.

In the same way, once you're stabilized in the Watcher, you can watch the infinite regression of your mental states. If you're anxious, you can just watch your anxiety; and if you're angry about being anxious, you can just watch yourself being angry about being anxious; and if you feel tired of feeling angry with yourself for being anxious, you can just watch yourself being tired of feeling angry with yourself for being anxious; and then you might feel proud that you're able to be such a good Watcher of everything, so you watch your pride; and then you might think that this whole Chinese-box-watching thing is stupid, so you watch yourself thinking that this whole Chinese-box-watching thing is stupid—and so on, ad infinitum, until you hit the point where you're the Watcher watching the Watcher watching everything there is. And as you merge into that Watcher, you have reached the goal of meditation: You sitting there watching *You—God!*—watching.

The Realm of Amazing Wonders[4]

The stations and stages of yoga constitute a fascinating wonder.
—Vasugupta, *Shiva Sutras*

What wondrous experiences await the meditator?

In the twenty-five years I've been meditating, I have had many experiences of the realm beyond the mind. These experiences are so deep, so enchanting, and so outside the boundaries of my normal experience that I find myself strongly drawn to our meditation room every day for the sheer adventure of it. Some of these experiences are outside the boundaries of language, so they're kind of hard to describe, but I'll do my best.

In many meditations I have become so established in the Inner Witness, the pure Perceiver, that my thoughts seemed to be happening in a faint, faraway place way on the periphery of my consciousness, and were clearly other than who I am. I have become so quiet and still in meditation that I wondered if I was still breathing. I have settled slowly down into a profoundly peaceful velvety darkness—what you'd imagine outer space to be like, but this was inner space!—in which there was no movement of any kind, including no movement of time. Once, all movement of thought stopped in my mind, and a vision of a candle flame, completely steady in a windless place, appeared before me. Another time, my mind abruptly emptied of all thoughts and opened up to a dimensionless "space," which I cannot describe but I remember hearing myself whisper, "Oh my God, this is infinity!"

Often during meditation there come spontaneous psychological insights into other people and myself, spiritual insights into the workings of the universe, knowledge of the past and future, answers to life's questions, and practical solutions to my everyday problems. These come not *from* my mind but *into* my mind, from some seemingly vast store of knowledge deep in my being.

I have felt the pains and sorrows of a thousand lifetimes being gently removed from my heart. I have heard God's soothing voice reassuring me about my fears and anxieties. I have felt utterly calm and content about everything.

I have felt understanding, kindness, respect, and love for all beings, including myself. I have had moments of knowing that we are all one Consciousness—God's Consciousness!—dancing and sporting in different bodies in a universe that is itself a play of God's Consciousness. I have felt the supreme goodness and perfection of this universe, and the supreme goodness and perfection of myself.

I have felt a great tenderness in my heart for my family and friends and all the people in my life. One time I felt for them a love that was so pure and perfect—so connected and yet at the same time so detached—that I knew that if I died that moment and never saw any of them again, I would be fine.

I have experienced unimaginable joy as wave after wave of pure bliss rose from deep within me. I have felt my heart well up with enormous gratitude to God for all the blessings in my life. I have felt an aching longing that all I wanted to do in my life—*really*—was to serve God.

I have experienced my body as a temple of God. I have experienced my body as made of tiny points of scintillant light. I have seen, in a misty distance, a city of shimmering light. I have seen a pure azure light, an effulgent golden light, and a white light that was astonishingly bright, yet soothing to my eyes.

I have seen visions of saints sitting cross-legged underneath beautiful trees with jewels sparkling in the earth all around them. I have heard sages chanting ancient mantras. I have heard angelic voices, celestial instruments, and the roar of waterfalls. I have smelled sudden intoxicating fragrances, and have seen peacocks spread their plumes and dance in ecstasy. Once, repeating my mantra, all my limited ideas of who I am dropped away, and I experienced my oneness with God.

There is truly a realm of amazing wonders beyond the mind, in the inner world. I feel that I have just begun to tap into them. It is so intoxicating to remember them and to speak of them. Regular meditation opens up this inner realm, full of many adventures and mystical experiences. These experiences are among the many mansions in the supreme abode of the Inner Self. Whether we visit them or just sit quietly in a very ordinary way, it doesn't matter; the power of meditation is immense, and pervades our daily lives with serenity and happiness.

4
THE INNER PLACE

There is an inmost centre in us all where truth abides in fulness.
—Robert Browning, "Paracelsus"

The clear bead at the center changes everything.
—Jalaluddin Rumi, "No Wall"

Within each of us there's a place that has been known and named by every authentic spiritual tradition, by all the saints and sages and mystics and masters throughout history, by the great poet-saints like Mirabai and Kabir and Rumi and Hildegard of Bingen and Dante. Most people have experienced it at some level, and it always exists within us whether we're experiencing it or not.

All the world's great spiritual traditions, in their essence, are paths to and prescriptions for finding this inner place. In the mystical branch of the spiritual tradition I grew up in, Judaism, this place is called Ye'chidah.[1] In the religion of the Lakota Sioux it is called Nagila. In Christianity it is called the Kingdom of God. In Hinduism it is called the Atman; in Buddhism, the pure Buddha nature; in mystical Islam, Qalb. I have also heard it called God within, Consciousness, Awareness, the Heart, and the Self.

This place is both inside us and outside us. It is so far outside us that it is nonlocalized in space and time, and it is so deep inside us that it dwells in, and *is*, our very core. It is not the mind, and it is not the body. It is not our feelings, our opinions, our moods, or our personalities. It is not any of those, yet it is all of those. It is a place inside us that both transcends and contains them all.

In this place we're very peaceful. We're powerful. We're clear. We're happy. We love. We *know*. We see design and beauty and intelligence and love in all things. We have compassion for all things. We understand that we're not running life and we have no desire to run it because God is running it just fine. There's no need to think too much about anything, so our minds are quiet when we're in this place. Perfect quietness *is* this place. When we're in this place, we're experiencing the highest state it is possible for a human being to experience, our true state, our essential innermost nature. To get the soul totally right is to become established in this state.

There are experiences in this state that I cannot talk about in my own words because I have not yet had those experiences myself, but the great beings who have realized this inner state have for centuries described it and have taught us how to get there. To the best of my ability, I will try to describe aspects of this place, as I do for my therapy clients.

THE INNER GUIDE

Why should we ever go abroad, even across the way, to ask a neighbor's advice? There is a nearer neighbor within us incessantly telling us how we should behave.

—Henry David Thoreau,
in a letter to Harrison Blake,
December 19, 1854

The highest revelation is that God is in every person.

—Ralph Waldo Emerson, "Fate"

There's a place inside us that has the answers to all our questions and the solutions to all our problems. This place is where God dwells within us. It is the home of what we call the inner guide, the inner knower, the inner Self, intuition, instinct, insight, innate wisdom, the voice of truth, the voice of the heart, the soul, spirit, conscience, and a lot of other names. It is the voice of God within us. The inner guide *is* God.

The inner guide has many powers, one of which is that it always knows the exactly right thing to do or say in any situation. It tells us the perfectly appropriate thing to say or do whether we are facing big decisions, such as what job to take or whom to marry, or small decisions, like what to say to the person who just cut in front of us at the check-out counter. A doctor can make medical decisions from this place, a lawyer can make legal decisions, a writer can make writing decisions, a parent can make parenting decisions, and any other person can make all the practical and ethical decisions that arise every day in his life and make up a life.

This place is the abode of the inner voice, and this voice always tells the truth.

The tricky part is to be able to distinguish this voice from all the other voices that are making such a ruckus inside us. And there are *lots* of other voices inside us.

That's why, when I'm asked a question about myself, I'll often think, Who do you want to talk to in here? And then the fun starts, as I try to identify all the different voices speaking within me. For example, if a client were to ask me if I wanted to be sitting in my office doing therapy with her at that moment, I could go inside myself and hear many voices.

The professional psychotherapist voice inside me would say, "Of course. You're paying me to perform an important service for you, and I will perform it to the best of my ability."

The inveterate helper voice inside me would say, "Yes. I seem to have a certain ability to help people, and my therapy office is one of the places where I can use it, and I am honored to be able to help you."

The businessman voice inside me would say, "Yes. By sitting here with you, I'm earning a living for myself and my family."

The grandiose, egomaniacal voice inside me would say, "Yes! I *have* to be here because what *I* have to say to you WILL CHANGE YOUR WHOLE LIFE!"

The lazy voice inside me would say, "Are you kidding? I'd much rather be upstairs lying on the couch watching the Red Sox," and the long-suffering Red Sox fan inside me would say, "Spare yourself the pain, pal."

The ashamed, self-doubting, self-denigrating voice inside me would say, "No. I can barely handle my own sorry life and have no right to be meddling in yours or anybody else's. I don't even know why anybody comes to me."

We have a whole chorus of voices inside us; how do we know which one to obey? Among all these voices, how do I find the voice that's my inner guide?

Different people have different ways of hearing the voice of their inner guide. I *wait*. I try to become very still inside, and I listen for a particular voice to start speaking. When it begins to speak, I listen hard. I *have* to listen hard because the voice of *my* inner guide speaks always in a whisper. It is, in me, "a secret, hushed voice, a gentle intercourse of heart to heart, a still small voice, whispering to the inner ear."[2] So if a client were to ask me if I want to be sitting there doing therapy with her, the whispering voice of my inner guide would respond, "It doesn't matter what I want. The fact that I'm here means that God wants me here, so there's nothing else to do but to be fully, joyfully, enthusiastically here, doing the work that God has assigned me to do."

Perhaps your inner guide speaks in a command, a shout, a song, a picture. Maybe it's "the bright and clear inward voice" described by

Hermann Hesse in *Siddhartha*. Or maybe it's a whisper in you too, or words from a whirlwind. Whatever it is, listen for it, learn to recognize it, and when you hear it, trust it and do what it's telling you to do. It's your inner guide. It knows and speaks the truth, and it lives in the core of you.

The Seer of Truth

The soul is the perceiver and revealer of truth.
We know truth when we see it.

—Ralph Waldo Emerson,
"The Over-Soul"

Lionel, a thirty-four-year-old radio announcer, had been in therapy with me for two years, working on getting out of an addictive relationship with his emotionally unavailable, sexually unfaithful, verbally abusive boyfriend, Henry. During one session, he reported to me that, after three weeks of "abstinence" from him, neither seeing him nor calling him nor answering calls from him, he had broken down and called him over the weekend and invited him to spend the night with him, which Henry did, and then ended up, once again, verbally abusing him.

"Why did you do that?" I asked.

He became silent and stared at the floor—for an uncharacteristically long time.

"What's going on, Lionel?" I finally said.

"I feel you're mad at me," he said. "I feel you're judging me for what I did."

"Why do you think that?"

"I could just feel it."

"Do you trust your feeling?"

"Sort of."

"Trust your feeling, Lionel."

He looked up at me. "Does that mean you *are* mad at me?"

"I promise I'll answer your question, but before I do, take a moment to close your eyes and go inside to that place we've been talking about, the place inside where you *know* things, you just know them even if you don't know *how* you know them. Bring your attention to that place. Breathe in and out of it. Quiet your mind down inside, and just breathe in and out of that place. It's a very quiet place. It's in your heart. It has intuitions about things. Go there. Hang out there for a moment with your breath, and then, when you're ready, open up your eyes and ask me the questions you want an answer to."

He sat with his eyes closed, quietly breathing, for a few moments. Then he looked at me with eyes that were very clear and still.

"Are you mad at me, Robert? Are you judging me for what I did with Henry?"

"No, I'm not angry with you. And no, I'm not judging you." I paused for a few seconds. "Now, Lionel, just keep breathing in and out of your heart, the place where you know the truth about things, and take my answer into that place. Was what I just said the truth, an untruth, or a half-truth?"

"Half-truth," he said quickly.

"How do you know?" I said. "And so quickly?"

"I just know. It was instant."

"Do you trust this knowledge?"

"Yes."

"So, if you can recognize a half-truth, you must know the full truth. What's the full truth?"

"I think the full truth is that you believe that I made a mistake by calling Henry, and I think you believe that that wasn't good for me. I think you're not judging *me* but you are judging my behavior as a mistake."

"Now say it all again, but this time take out the three 'I think's'—to hear what this inner place sounds like when it speaks what it *knows* to be the truth."

Lionel took a deep breath. "The truth is that you believe I made a mistake that wasn't good for me. You're not judging me, but you are judging my behavior as a mistake."

"Is that the truth?"

"Yes."

"Do you know it?"

"I know it."

"If you know that, maybe you also know my motive for telling you only a half-truth before."

He paused for a second, staring at me. "I know that too," he said. "You're somewhat protective of me, and you didn't want to hurt my feelings."

"Is *that* the truth?" I asked.

"Yes."

"How do *you* know *my* inner feelings?"

"I just know. Am I right?"

"Absolutely. Is it okay with you that I feel that way about your behavior with Henry?"

"It's fine. That's what I think too."

"Then we both think the same thing."

"Right."

"We both know the same truth."

"Right. That's amazing."

"It *is* kind of amazing."

☾ ☾ ☾

Truth is the sum of things seen and known with the physical eye (and our other senses), the rational mind, or the intuitive heart. Between the eye, the mind, and the heart we can know *all* of reality. From the densest form of energy, physical matter, which we perceive with the physical eye, to a more subtle form of energy, intellectual and moral truth, which we perceive with the rational mind, to the *most* subtle form of energy, spirit and spiritual truth, which we perceive with the intuitive heart, all of reality is available to our perception and cognition.

That's why Lionel and I both knew what I was thinking and feeling about his night with Henry. That's why he was thinking and feeling and knowing the same thing I was. Between our physical eye, our rational mind, and our intuitive heart, we all can see and know physical truth, emotional truth, intellectual truth, moral truth, and spiritual truth. We are all seers seeing the same truth simultaneously. *That's* amazing.

THE CLEAR PLACE

Blessed are the ears that do not heed the voice sounding without, but hear clearly the voice within teaching the truth.

—Thomas à Kempis,
The Imitation of Christ

Laila had been away on business for two weeks, during which time Frederick, her husband of eight years, had done "some important thinking" about their relationship. I asked him to share his thinking with Laila. He did so, with a lot of nervousness, hesitation, and obliqueness, so that when he was done, I had no idea what he had just said. I asked Laila if she had understood him.

"Not really," she said.

"By the time I was done, I didn't either," Frederick admitted.

I asked Frederick to sit up straight and to hold his head up, taking up his full height in the chair. He did. I asked him to take a deep breath, exhale fully, and continue breathing deeply, watching his breath. He did that for a moment. Then I asked him to "ask inside" what it was he wanted to say to Laila about their relationship.

"And after you ask inside," I said, "just sit quietly, eyes open or closed, and *wait*—do nothing—just wait and listen for a voice to start speaking inside. When you hear the voice, repeat out loud and *verbatim* what you're hearing it say."

Frederick sat silently for a moment, gazing at the floor. His eyes closed for a few seconds. Then he raised his head, opened his eyes, and, looking straight at Laila, said to her, "The goal of our relationship should be to love and help each other and to be joyous in life together, but both of us have so many childhood wounds that we need to do a lot of healing, individually and together, to get to our goal. If we don't do that, we will not get to our goal, and we will live together unhappily for the rest of our lives, or we will separate."

Laila stared at him.

"Where did that come from?" I asked.

"I don't know," he said. "From someplace inside me. I didn't even know I could speak like that."

"What does that place inside you *feel* like?" I asked.

He thought for a moment.

"It feels clear," he said. "It's a clear place."

◡　◡　◡

Inside all of us is a place of truth, a clear place, and from this place comes a clear voice. With this voice, we speak the truth in concise, precise, powerful words.

Sometimes a person will start speaking from her clear place and her words come out strong and true, but then she loses heart. She doubts, she fears, she sees the person she's talking to lose interest, or disapprove, or get angry or hurt, and she collapses. The connection with her clear place breaks, and from then on the words that come out of her mouth turn into mashed potatoes. When that happens, the truth that she is trying to communicate does not get communicated, and no teaching, learning, growing, or changing can take place in her or in her listener.

Statements from the clear place can be recognized because they are usually short, direct, pointed, declarative sentences with proper periods at the end of them. They are free of qualifiers and mollifiers like "maybe," "kind of," "sort of," "perhaps," "it seems," "in my opinion," "for what it's worth," "I think," "I believe," "I feel," "I guess." When we speak from the clear place, we do not have opinions or think, believe, feel, or guess—we know. We do not say, "I think there might be sort of a chair over there, in my opinion." We say, "There's a chair over there," and are done with it. When we speak from this place, we don't whine or complain or argue or plead or get defensive or confused. We *know*, and we know that we know, and we say what we know.

In order to attune to the inner knower who speaks from the clear place, we do not need to *think* as such. There is too much effort in thinking, and the effort itself interferes with the signal from the clear place. In order to be attuned to this place, we direct our awareness to our heart. We patiently breathe in and out of the heart, quietly wait, humbly listen. In time comes a voice.

When you hear this voice, listen to it, and repeat out loud what it's saying. Repeat it sentence by sentence. If the sentences stop, go back inside . . . breathe . . . wait . . . listen . . . and, when they start up again, repeat out loud what you're hearing from within. It's as easy as taking dictation. When you speak from your clear place, it is a beautiful sight to behold. People know they are in the presence of truth, and they become quiet and listen to you. You yourself are also quietly listening to you, listening to words of truth coming out of you.

I am a strong knifeblade word,
not some if *or* maybe *dissolving in air.*

—Jalaluddin Rumi,
"All Rivers at Once"

How forcible are right words!

—Job 6:25

Megan and Paul, both in their early thirties, had been married for six years. One of the issues they were working on in therapy was Megan's jealousy when Paul habitually stared at other women while with her.

"What do you feel when he does that?" I asked her.

She cleared her throat. "I don't know. I guess I don't like it too much. It bothers me a little."

"If you were asked to take everything out of those three sentences that diluted and weakened your statements and masked your real feelings, what would come out?" I asked her.

"What did I say again?" she asked.

"When I asked you, 'What do you feel when Paul looks at other women?' you said, 'I don't know. I guess I don't like it too much. It bothers me a little.'"

She thought for a moment. "'I don't know' would come out. So would 'I guess' and 'too much' and 'a little.'"

"Leaving what? Megan, what do you really feel when Paul looks at other women?"

"I don't like it. It bothers me."

"Why didn't you say that in the first place?"

"I don't know."

I turned to Paul. "What do you think of Megan's real feelings, Paul?" I asked.

"I don't see why she gets so upset. It's just the way a man looks at women. I don't mean anything by it."

"What's your response to that, Megan?"

She was silent for a moment. "I don't know why I get so upset. It's this jealousy thing. I just know I don't like it when we're in a restaurant and he's looking at other women."

"Does it make you mad?" I asked her.

"A little."

"Just a little?"

"I don't know. Maybe a lot. I don't know."

"If you were asked to take everything out of those three sentences that dilutes and weakens your statements and masks your real feelings, what would come out?"

She thought for a moment, then laughed. "Everything but 'a lot.'"

"So it makes you angry *a lot* when Paul looks at other women when he's with you?"

"Yes."

"Let me ask you, Megan, do you think it's okay for a husband to stare at other women when he's with his wife?"

"I don't think so."

"You don't think what?"

"I don't think it's okay for a man to do that."

"Is that something you *think* or something you *know*?" I asked.

"It's something I think."

"Pretend that you don't *think* it but you *know* it. How would your sentence 'I don't think it's okay for a man to do that' change?"

"It would change to 'I know it's not okay for a man to do that,'" she said.

"Do what?"

"Stare at other women when he's with his wife."

"Make a full sentence of it."

"I know it's not okay for a man to stare at other women when he's with his wife."

"Now see what the sentence sounds like if you put the 'I think' back."

"I think it's not okay for a man to stare at other women when he's with his wife."

"Which is stronger?"

"'I know.'"

"So say it."

"I know it's not okay for a man to stare at other women when he's with his wife."

"Now take out the 'I know' and try it again," I said.

"Why?"

"Because if you really know something, and you have conviction, you don't even have to say you know it, you just know it, and you say it."

"It's not okay for a man to stare at other women when he's with his wife," she said.

"Say it one more time, and this time put Paul's name at the end of it, sit up, look him straight in the eye, don't jiggle your leg like you were doing, take your hand down from your chin, don't blink, don't sniff the words back in through your nose when you're done, and when you're done, keep looking him straight in the eye, as if, after saying the truth, you're pushing it a little farther into his mind with your eyes, like setting a nail."

She put her hand on the arm of the chair, straightened up, cleared her throat, and took a deep breath.

"It's not okay for a man to stare at other women when he's with his wife, Paul," she said, looking straight at him.

"Is that your opinion or is that the truth?" I asked.

She laughed. "I *feel* it's my opinion, but I *know* it's the truth."

"Do you have any doubt about that?" I asked.

She thought for moment. "No."

"So it's not okay for a man to stare at other women when he's with his wife."

"Right."

"And it's not okay for Paul to stare at other women when he's with you?"

"Right."

"Is that the truth, Megan?"

"Yes, it is."

"Tell Paul what you want him to do about it, Megan," I said.

"I want you to stop looking at other women when you're with me."

"For how long?" I asked.

She laughed. "Until we die."

"Now change your want into an instruction—a command."

"Paul, stop looking at other women when you're with me."

"Now say it as if you're absolutely sure that what you're saying is right and true and he should therefore obey you."

She slowed it way down, and stared him hard in the eye. "Paul, stop looking at other women when you're with me."

"Do you have any doubt about what you're saying, Megan?"

"No. I just doubt that he gets it, or will stop doing it."

"Tell him to get it then."

"Just get it, Paul."

"Take out the 'just.'"

"Get it, Paul."

"I hope he gets it, Megan," I said.

She looked strong and calm, staring straight at Paul, who was staring back at her, half-smiling.

"One last question, Megan," I said. "Do you know the *absolute truth* on this issue?"

"What do you mean by 'absolute truth'?"

"I mean the universal law that pertains in this case."

"I don't know."

"Think about it."

She thought for a few moments. "I do know. It is not right for a human being to knowingly do something to another human being that is hurtful to that other human being."

I turned to Paul, who was still half-smiling and eyeing Megan curiously. "Paul, what do you think of all this?"

"I actually like it. I'm seeing a new Megan."

"What's the name of the new thing you're seeing and liking in Megan?" I asked.

"Power." He was looking at her with a mixture of surprise, affection, admiration, and caution.

"How do you feel now, Megan?" I asked.

"Powerful. And peaceful."

BIFOCALS

Everything is perfect, but there is always room for improvement.
—Suzuki Roshi

Andrew, a thirty-eight-year-old insurance agent, in therapy with me for five years, was habitually negative about himself, always focusing on his weaknesses, shortcomings, and mistakes. During one session, I interrupted his litany of self-debasement and told him that, contrary to what he believed about himself, I saw him as "a smart, courageous man devoted to the truth and persistent in your journey to it."

He smirked. "Are you kidding? I'm undisciplined and lazy and too fat and totally scared to death half the time," he replied.

"I see that too," I said.

☽ ☽ ☽

On the journey to the truth, we need bifocals. One focus needs to be on our weaknesses, our shortcomings, and our mistakes—all that is imperfect about us that we know only too well—because that's what we need to work on until it's worked out.

But don't stay too focused on it all. Remember to also stay focused on the part of you inside where there's total perfection. In that deep, inner place, you are totally pure. In that place you already *are* that which you are striving to become. Everything you ever wanted to be, everything you've ever beaten yourself up for not being, every good thing there is to be is inside you, in this deep, inner place. Don't forget to keep looking in there.

We should never ignore or deny our weaknesses, or tell ourselves we don't have to work on becoming better or stronger. But we should also, and simultaneously, see right through it all to the perfect one inside. We must put on our bifocals and see both parts of ourselves because together, both parts of ourselves constitute the full truth about ourselves.

The Eyes of the Heart

Hafiz, there is no one in this world
Who is not looking for God.

—Hafiz, "I Follow Barefoot"

So many of the clients I see feel deep anger and cynicism about people. They summarily dismiss some for not meeting their expectations, and constantly put down others for their "trivial" concerns and "stupid" pursuits. In their anger and frustration, they do not see that they must change the way they see their fellow human beings if they are to release their own pain.

When you look at others with the part of you that is feeling bad about yourself, you tend to see other people as bad. I see like that sometimes. When I'm feeling bad about myself, I see human concerns and pursuits that go way beyond trivial and stupid all the way into completely incomprehensible. I can see all that stuff. There is a lot of it to see in people—if you're into seeing it.

If you're not into seeing it, you might want to periodically travel to that part of yourself that isn't feeling bad, which is the heart, and start seeing the world with the eyes of the heart. The eyes of the heart don't see bad in people, except with the compassionate desire to comfort and alleviate their pain. The eyes of the heart see the brave and beautiful search of other human hearts looking for happiness, truth, peace, love, and God. Every human being is a seeker of the truth of her own self and of the truth of the universe. When we know that we're all on this journey together, we no longer concern ourselves with who's bad and who's good, who's stupid and who's smart, who's ahead and who's behind, we just take the journey, following the same searching heart that everybody else is following.

"Make your eyes pure," says St. Hildegard of Bingen, and they will see only purity.

So the next time you look out the window and see the multitudes marching into their next round of trivial and stupid pursuits, immediately change your vision, see with your heart, see them all as the pure, searching human heart looking for happiness, truth, peace, love, and

God in the best ways they presently know how to do this. Fall in love with them all for doing that. Fall in love with them all, period. They're heroes and saints and gods and goddesses in magnificent disguise. See them as truth looking for truth, as love looking for love, as God looking for God, and you'll be seeing truly. "The world is as you see it," says the sage Vasishtha, so when you see with the eyes of your heart, you see the whole world on a journey to the heart.

A Revolution of the Heart

I can say without the slightest hesitation, and yet in all humility, that those who say that religion has nothing to do with politics do not know what religion means.

—Mohandas K. Gandhi,
An Autobiography

When I was in college in the sixties, I, and half the rest of my generation, thought that the huge change we wanted to see in the world—the ending of violence and war and the dawning of equality, justice, and freedom for all human beings—would come about by our actively protesting against what we called "the Establishment." We debated and demonstrated and mobilized and marched, right up the steps of the Pentagon. We hoped for—even expected—an imminent political revolution in our society, a revolution that was going to overthrow the old order, an order based on greed and privileged power, and usher in a new order based on love.

It turned out to be a slower, longer, and more internal revolution, a revolution of the human heart. It is going on today all around us and within us. You say you want a revolution? You've got one. We're all living in the middle of it!

The revolution that is happening in the world in our day is political, psychological, moral, and spiritual all at the same time. Actually, there is no difference between political, psychological, moral, and spiritual. It's all the single process of the collective human heart opening, and expressing its love.

I have come to believe since the sixties that true revolutionary change—and by "revolutionary change" I mean change in the way human beings feel about themselves and others, change in the way human beings are treated on this earth, and change in the way the resources of this earth are distributed and used to serve human beings—is going to happen only when the hearts of human beings have changed. As the human heart continues to free itself of fear and the mutant forms of fear—intolerance, arrogance, avarice, cruelty, and violence—this kind of radical change will continue to happen.

When the human heart is freed of fear, it will become what it really is, which is love. When human hearts on this earth are only love, they will be able to feel and do only love, so the world will be filled with love. That's the political, moral, spiritual, and political change I'm talking about. When I think of this kind of change, I think of Thoreau[3] and Gandhi and Martin Luther King and Chief Seattle and Elizabeth Cady Stanton and Mother Teresa. It's a change toward love. Since the sixties, I have come to believe that no other change will work.

True and lasting change happens first in the heart, then from heart to heart as the love in the human heart expands outward (as is the nature of love) and spreads around the globe. True and lasting and revolutionary change happens when we all awaken the longing for truth and love—for God!—in our hearts and in the hearts of others. All that needs to be done for the people of this world—the providing of food, shelter, clothing, health care, and comfort, the vast amount of selfless service that will be needed to lift humanity into an era of peace and security and happiness—will be done by people whose love for themselves, each other, and God has been awakened. Then we'll all be serving each other gladly, with love.

The part of me that was deeply and forever transformed by the sixties, my consciousness so changed that it never changed back, that part is still here, alive and well, still sitting on the steps of the Pentagon, and still conscience-bound to help solve all the problems of the world. I want to help solve the problem of poverty, and the problems of violence toward women and cruelty toward children and animals, and the problems of Rwanda, Kosovo, Oklahoma City, and Columbine High School. And I am hopeful because the solution to it all isn't complicated, but simple: The solution to all the problems in the world is in purifying our own hearts and helping others do the same. That's the revolution of the heart.

THE UNABUSABLE PLACE:
AN EASTER STORY

Father, forgive them; for they know not what they do.
—Jesus of Nazareth,
Luke 23:34

In the course of his three years of therapy with me, Carl, a thirty-year-old laboratory technician, had discovered in himself an intense anger toward his parents and older sister because, as the youngest and weakest member of the family, he had been emotionally and verbally abused by them, and sexually abused once by his sister. He had worked through a lot of his anger in therapy and had managed to get to a place where he could be civil and cordial to his parents and sister over the phone, and maintain some measure of equanimity when at family gatherings.

Now he had a decision to make. His parents were inviting him to join the family at home for Easter. He didn't really want to go because he knew he would be asked sarcastic questions about his somewhat unconventional life by all of them, and would be generally criticized, even ridiculed, by them.

"Is there any part of you that *wants* to go?" I asked.

He thought about it for a moment. "Yes. There's a part of me that thinks it's the right thing to do."

"Why is that?"

"My family wasn't the best family in the world, but they're basically nice people, and I know it would mean a lot to them to have the whole family there for Easter," he said.

He paused, staring into space for a few moments. "But I just can't deal with the abuse anymore," he said with a mixture of firmness and sadness.

"If you really want to go," I told him, "if you really think it's the right thing to do, then go. The only thing you have to do in order to go is to protect yourself from being abused. There are lots of ways to protect yourself from being abused, but the best way—because it involves no one but you and obviates any confrontation or conflict with anyone—is to move from the outer, abusable level of your being to the inner, unabusable level."

On the outer, abusable level of Carl's being, he perceived his family as the perpetrators of mistreatment of him, and that was the truth. On that level, Carl's family had abused him all his life, and would probably continue to hurt him on Easter. That also is true.

On the inner, unabusable level of Carl's being, which is the level of the heart, he was in touch with his family's heart, and saw a family that, despite its dysfunction, was still trying to come together in love. On the level of love, he was in touch with their love. On that inner level, it's *all* love.

Our inner level has never been abused. No matter what was done to us and by whom and for how long, there is a place in us that was never touched by any of it. I imagine that this is the place from which Jesus, while being nailed to the cross, asked God's forgiveness for the soldiers who were pounding the nails into him. We are not talking about enablement of abuse here. We are talking about power, and the stopping of abuse. We are talking about Jesus and Gandhi and Martin Luther King. We are talking about spiritual power. We are talking about love.

This strong, clear, powerful, peaceful place inside you is your center. When you are centered there, you are so absorbed in peacefulness that everything else happening in your environment, including abuse of you, is happening on a level of no disturbance of your inner state. That's where Jesus was at the crucifixion.

You can go there. You've been there, in meditation or in life, you've focused your awareness on that inner place. Go there because by going there you will be able to do what your heart is telling you it's right to do. Sometimes your heart tells you you should leave abusive situations, especially the really horrible ones—because *Who needs it?!*—but sometimes your heart tells you to go to an inner place in your being where you're not affected by them. Go to that inner place because when you're there, pain, hurt, and abuse can't touch you. Go there because that's where we're all eventually going anyway, and it would be good for the planet if we could speed this process up a little bit.

In this place is an imperturbability so profound that nothing can get to it. In this place is quietness and peace, indomitable power, and a very humble love. It's the place that Easter celebrates by celebrating the life and death and apotheosis of the great Master who, in his words and actions, showed us how to get to that place and how to love from that place.

5
FEELINGS

*Facing our emotions can be very challenging, but it is also very
strengthening. It is the first step in overcoming them.*

—A sage

*Emotion is the chief source of all becoming conscious. There can be no
transformation of darkness into light . . . without emotion.*

—Carl Jung,
*Psychological Aspects of
the Modern Archetype*

*Where am I going? he said.
To joy, I said.
How am I getting there? he said.
Through all your other feelings, I said.*

—Adrian Brooke,
"Notes from the Inner Office"

*You're invisible now—
You've got no secrets to conceal.
How does it **feel**?*

—Bob Dylan, "Like a Rolling Stone"

One of the major challenges of getting the soul right is that the journey
invariably takes you through all your feelings. There's no way to get
there from here *except* through your feelings—in the same way that
there's no way to get to the clearing in the woods without walking
through the woods—so you have to be ready to face all your feelings,
including the painful ones, if you're serious about experiencing your

inner Self. In fact, most people come into therapy because they are beginning to feel—or are fed up with feeling—painful feelings within: feelings about themselves, about their relationships, about their lives, feelings they don't like, don't understand, and don't know how to get rid of. Some of these emotions are caused by present-day events in their lives (the loss of a loved one, for example), but most have their roots in the past.[1] Wherever they're coming from, we spend a lot of time in therapy talking about—and feeling—*feelings*.

The Human Heart Is a Package Deal

If you can't feel pain, you can't feel anything.
            —from the movie *Ordinary People*

Every human heart contains all human feelings, from rage to loving kindness, from unbearable sadness to unfathomable joy. Some are pleasant, some are unpleasant, but they are all there, part of the same package.

We are born with the capacity to feel all human feelings, including the unpleasant ones, but our society is phobic about the unpleasant ones, and we acquire this phobia in a long, complex, and relentless process called growing up. Disapproval, ridicule, threat, punishment, and violence from those around us teach us to squelch our anger, our jealousy, our fear, our melancholy—any of the emotions that we deem unpleasant. In order to become a full-fledged member of this society, we have to go through a long initiatory rite, performed mainly by parents and ably assisted by schools, religions, and the mass media, at the end of which we will be, at best, embarrassed by our unpleasant feelings, and, at worst, totally clueless that we have them.

We do have them, because the unpleasant feelings don't go away. They don't leave when they're not wanted. They just sit and fester inside, way down deep below consciousness, and give off an emotional effluvium that seeps up into consciousness and feels like generalized, nonspecific, chronic anxiety or chronic depression, guilt, or unworthiness.

Rick, a thirty-six-year-old executive in a large HMO, told me he had *no* feelings. "I can't even tell you in all honesty that I love my wife and children," he said. "I know I'm supposed to, and I probably do, but I don't *feel* love. I don't feel sadness either. Or happiness. I just go through the motions. The most I ever feel is anxiety about everything, if that's a feeling. Even all that anger you keep telling me I'm supposed to have toward my parents, I think I *have* it, but I don't *feel* it."

Numbness of the kind Rick was experiencing isn't due to an inability to experience emotion. It's just that we cannot selectively shut down some of our feelings and retain the capacity to feel the others. That's not how our hearts work. Our capacity to feel our pleasant feelings, like happiness, joy, enthusiasm, and love, is tied to our capacity to feel our unpleasant feelings, like anger, fear, sadness, and shame.

The human heart is a package deal.[2] If you want to reclaim your capacity to feel, you've got to go into that heart and open it up. At first, it's not the most pleasant process in the world—actually, it sometimes feels like an exorcism—but if you want to feel happiness and joy and enthusiasm and love, and all the other pleasant and even ecstatic feelings waiting to be felt in the human heart, you have no choice but to feel *all* your feelings. You must reclaim the dark feelings and face them in the light, or remain wooden and numb. It's tempting to play it safe, because the intensity and magnitude of some of those emotions can be very scary, but, since the human heart is a package deal, you really have no choice but to open the package and see *everything* that's in it.

Down the Cellar Stairs

I must go down! I must go down deeper than ever I descended—deeper into pain than ever I descended. . . . Thus my destiny wants it. Well, I am ready.

—Friedrich Nietzsche,
Thus Spake Zarathustra

Angela, a thirty-one-year-old physician, was plagued by insecurity. Every time an attractive woman entered her husband Dante's life, whether it was a coworker at his company, a waitress in a restaurant, or an actress on a magazine cover, the same sickening feeling would come over her. Fueled by her insecurity, she would interrogate, accuse, and verbally batter her husband, sometimes flying into rages at him, and once even physically attacking him. She was sick of feeling this way, but how could she escape it?

☽ ☽ ☽

With feelings, you have to get to the bottom of things. Chronic feelings, like insecurity, are not the bottom of things, and actually keep us from getting to the bottom where more intensely painful feelings dwell.

Underneath most of the feelings we experience, including insecurity, is fear. For example, Angela and Dante are sitting in a restaurant. A pretty woman is sitting at a table nearby. Dante glances at her. She glances back. At the moment their eyes meet, and hold, a small bond is formed between them, and Angela feels fear—*terror!*—because in that moment the bond between her and her husband is broken, he being momentarily occupied in the bond with the pretty woman at the nearby table. So in that moment Angela is all alone, and it's terrifying to be all alone.

The human fear of being alone is the human infant's fear that all warmth, nurturance, sustenance, safety, and love will suddenly leave it forever and it will, literally, die. The sudden sinking, hollow dread that grips Angela's stomach when Dante and the woman glance at each other in the restaurant is the fear of that abandoned infant who, left loveless, will die.

That's down at the bottom of things.

Sitting in the restaurant, having witnessed the momentary bonding between Dante and that woman, the infant's fear of death rises up and becomes panic in Angela's chest, which rises higher and becomes anger: "What are you looking at her for?! What's going on between the two of you?!" By the time the words come, the fear of death has completed its mutation to aggressive anger, which is what Dante sees and hears.

With feelings, and especially with chronic feelings, you have to get to the bottom of things. You must go down the cellar stairs of yourself. You can't stop at the first or second or even the third landing down, you have to descend farther, to the damp dirt floor of yourself where the light is dim and the air dank. You must shine the light of your awareness there, look around in the corners and the cobwebs, and see what's really there.

Like Angela, we must go below the insecurity, the anger, the blame, and the accusations, go below the fear of betrayal and abandonment. We must even go below the panic. Keep climbing down those stairs until your feet hit dirt. That's emotional paydirt. No one will be there—just you, all alone, with no love and afraid you'll die. Bring *that* to consciousness, and bring *that*—not the insecurity or anger or accusations— to your partner or friends. Tell them about the floor of your cellar; let them come down there with you. You need someone down there with you—to help you see what's there and bring stuff up.

THE UNDERGROUND STREAM

Go burrow underground.
And there hold intercourse
With roots of trees and stones,
With rivers at their source . . .

—Elinor Hoyt Wylie,
"The Eagle and the Mole"

Once when I was hiking in the Maine woods I was following a stream down a wooded mountainside when it suddenly disappeared into the ground. I kept walking, and in a few moments forgot all about the stream. Then, in about a half mile, continuing to walk down the mountainside, I saw another stream trickling out of the ground and flowing down a bed of sand and small rocks. I stopped and watched it for a while. Then I realized it was the same stream that had disappeared into the ground a half mile back. The water had a more reddish tint, but it was definitely the same stream.

In the same way, things that happened to us years and years ago when we were children will often go underground, disappear for a short or a long while and then reappear when we're adults. Having been underground for so long, they may reappear looking slightly or entirely different from when they disappeared, but it's the same stream, and if you do the thinking about it, you can recognize it.

Becky, a twenty-seven-year-old journalist, wife, and mother of two young children, came into therapy because of her fear of riding in the passenger seat in cars, and her obsessive fear that her children would be kidnapped whenever they left her presence. She wanted to understand "where it all comes from." I told her that it came from her parents.

"But they weren't afraid of riding in cars or of us kids being kidnapped," she said.

"They were both alcoholic," I said.

"What does that have to do with it?"

"It's about control."

◡ ◡ ◡

When Becky was a child, at any given moment, seven days a week, one or both of her parents was drunk, which means that she grew up with parents who were either potentially or actually out of control all the time. Because they abdicated their parental responsibility of being in appropriate control—in this case, by being drunk most of the time—Becky naturally became committed to, and often was obsessed with, control.

That's why Becky does just fine when she's in control, when she's writing a story or cleaning her house or driving her car or playing with her kids in the den. Even if she's not truly in control, at least she has the illusion of it, so she is fine. But in the passenger seat of a car she cannot maintain the pretense of being in control. In fact, one is totally out of control in the passenger seat, which is why, in this situation, Becky's emotions go totally out of control. And when her children are out of her sight, they are out of her control, which means Becky panics. That panic is the same panic she felt as the child of alcoholic, out-of-control parents, but didn't know she felt. The stream of her panic went underground for a number of years and reappeared when Becky became an adult, tinted differently and looking like head-on collisions and lurking kidnappers instead of drunken parents.

We all have these underground streams that wind and disappear and reappear. We lose track of their trail, and their origin, but they are continuous streams. Once we recognize that, we can begin to understand why we are the way we are.

The Crack in the Wall

For there is nothing covered, that shall not be revealed; neither hid, that shall not be known.

—Luke 12:2

Every human being has every human feeling inside. Many of us, especially men, were told at a very early age to stuff vulnerable feelings deep inside and build a thick defensive wall around them. In some of us, the wall is so thick that it blocks us not only from expressing our emotions but from even knowing that we have them. Many of us take our feelings with us to the grave, all our lives wondering why we're just always kind of in a bad mood.

Some of us get lucky though. Something happens in our lives. We get hurt. We get sick. Someone else gets sick. There's a divorce. *Something* happens, usually a loss or a crisis, and a crack appears in that wall we've built around our feelings. From that crack the emotional energies we've been holding in all our lives seep into our consciousness, and those energies feel foreign, painful, and powerful.

Recently, my wife was very sick for many months with a viral inflammation of her thyroid gland. During the worst weeks of her illness, she looked like one of those survivors of the Nazi concentration camps that you see in World War II documentaries—emaciated, exhausted, unspeakably sad, weak, fragile, and frightened, with sunken, dark-circled, half-dead eyes and a tentativeness of movement and speech that was shocking to see. But there it was—there *she* was—this strange, scared human being, looking both very old and very young at the same time, gliding like a ghost through the house. One evening, looking at her as she sat slumped on the bed staring blankly into space, *I got it*—this thyroid thing was the crack in *her* wall, and the full emergence from behind that wall of the trauma victim, the little girl who, for many years, *had* lived in the concentration camp of her great-uncle's sexual abuse of her. We had always known about that little girl as a fact of Jane's history, and had certainly had glimpses of her over the years, but this was *really* her, fully manifest, small and frail and defenseless and terrified and heavily burdened for all our eyes—especially mine, I think—to see.

When a crack opens in us or in a loved one, we're supposed to see who walks through it, to *really* see her or him, and learn as much as we can about them before the crack tries to close again. It's a revelation, a coming out. That crack is life giving you the opportunity to see, for a time, the most deeply hidden feelings of a human being. So look well at those feelings when they come out, and act well. To act well is to acknowledge and move toward and greet and embrace the human being, yourself included, who's been carrying and hiding those feelings all her life; to gently and tenderly minister to her and her feelings; to compassionately understand what she's been through and what she's up against; to be the chalice into which her feelings can now pour as she finally lets them out and lightens the tremendous burden of her past. To act well is to encourage your loved one and yourself to feel those feelings, to remain a loving witness while that which has been hidden for so long is revealed, and to welcome your loved one and yourself into the present. To act well is to use the crack in the wall to finally break the wall.

The Pot of Self-Loathing

If you bring forth what is inside you, what you bring forth will save you.
If you don't bring forth what is inside you, what you don't bring forth
will destroy you.

—Jesus of Nazareth,
The Gospel of Thomas

James, a forty-four-year-old medical equipment salesman, had had a bad week. As he sat in my office, his body was slumped, his voice lifeless, his glazed eyes staring at his shoes. I asked him if he would like to go deeper into his feelings tonight. He shrugged a halfhearted assent. Dimming the lights, I invited him to talk about his week. After a short silence, he did.

"I blew it with two customers," he said. "I always blow it. I've blown everything my whole life. My whole life adds up to shit. I'm sorry I ended up this way. I don't make enough money, so my wife has to work so hard, and she looks so *tired* sometimes. [Here his voice broke.] I shouldn't be sad and depressed so much. I spread my sadness like poison over everybody. . . . I feel like I'm poison. I feel disgusting. I feel sick, and old, and ugly. . . . I'm a lousy everything. I'm a lousy salesman and a lousy father and a lousy husband. It seems all I do is disappoint people. . . . I've let everybody down. . . . "

He kept talking. The words seemed to have a life of their own, as if, once begun, they couldn't stop coming out from the place he had opened up inside. After a while, he began to cry. He cried for a long time.

When he was done, he sat in silence for ten minutes, his eyes closed, the muscles of his face relaxed and smooth. Then he opened his eyes and looked up at me.

"What was *that*?" he said.

"What was what?"

"Those words I said."

"That was the pot of self-loathing tipping over inside you."

☽ ☽ ☽

The pot of self-loathing is that place inside that says "I'm horrible, I'm worthless, I'm unlovable, I'm repulsive, I'm all alone, I deserve nothing, and I hate myself." It is the place where our deepest depression lives, and despair, and utter isolation, and suicidal feelings. It is the place where we feel totally alone in the universe, and broken, and unfixable.

As we work on ourselves, we must all recognize this pot of self-loathing inside, and bear witness to it when it tips over and spills through our consciousness. Many never come to know about it because it's both gilded with compensatory feelings like superiority, arrogance, anger, and judgment, and it's camouflaged pretty well with worldly goodies like youth and health and success and pleasure. But woe to the person whose pot of self-loathing is struck by an outside event like a rejection or a failure or a loss or a disease, causing its camouflage to disappear or its gilding to get scratched, exposing the darkest imaginable feelings inside. At this point, the pot reels and tips and spills over into consciousness.

I believe that we all have this pot. If the parenting we got was really, really good, making us feel really, really loved and welcomed to this earth, we may have grown up with a relatively small pot that leaks out a little self-judgment, unworthiness, and feelings of imperfection from time to time and doesn't give us too much other trouble. But if we got the parenting that many of us got, a parenting with large amounts of neglect, disrespect, and shame in it, we grow up with a large pot of self-loathing from which all the mutant forms of self-loathing, including self-negation, self-abuse, and self-destruction, drip like acid on our hearts. When that pot tips over, it fills our minds and mouths with words sounding like the ones James poured out.

When that pot of self-loathing tips over, it's important to stay present. Feel it spill into your consciousness. Speak its words and cry its tears. Let all that sewage spill out, and then you will feel lighter, cleansed, more peaceful.

The pot of self-loathing will still exist, however: It will fill again, and spill again, periodically, until after a long time of filling and spilling, it's all emptied out—or you die or you smash it. The easiest way to get rid of it is to smash and destroy it. You can do that by learning to love yourself unconditionally. This smashes the pot to smithereens, and the self-loathing inside it will just evaporate.

How can you love yourself unconditionally when you have a pot of self-loathing inside? Start by loving yourself for having it, and then go on from there.

A TALK THING

Talking with one another is loving one another.
       —Kenyan love poem,
        African Love Poems and Prayers

For men and women to live in harmony with each other, we have to understand that there's a big difference between us: Women have been trained to talk to other human beings, especially about their feelings, and men have not. Women understand this "talk thing." They understand that connection requires communication.

On one level, feminism is an attempt by the human species to start talking to itself as a way of creating a cooperative, collaborative, loving relationship between all human beings. Women are saying more and more, and more and more insistently, to their men these days, "*Talk* to me," but often their pleas go unheeded. The man looks away, at the television, at the newspaper, at anything but her, and becomes immobilized—and stays silent!—while the woman gets more and more frustrated.

It may be the hardest thing for men to do: to come out from behind the five-thousand-year-old wall of serious and stern male silence, perk up a little, and actually start talking to women. In my personal life, I myself have the hardest time talking of any man I know, so when I talk about talking, I know what I'm talking about. But men are good at doing hard things, and, besides, it actually begins to feel good because it's so liberating. We are so used to holding in our thoughts and feelings that when we let go and start talking about them to our partners we feel an unfamiliar but remarkable feeling of freedom and connection.

This was a lesson Reggie had yet to learn. As he sat slouched in his chair, his wife told me that he hadn't spoken to her for two days. "On some level," she said sadly, "he hasn't spoken a word to me in fifteen years. I can even stand there saying directly to his face, 'Talk to me!,' and he won't. How can anything get better if he won't talk to me? We have these horrible fights, and they just go on forever because he won't talk to me."

"Reggie," I said, "talk to Janet right now. Say anything you want to her, but just talk to her."

Several long minutes passed. Then he lifted his head and looked at her.

"I hate our fights," he said quietly. "I *hate* them. I don't want to fight with you anymore, Janet."

Janet's eyes immediately teared up. Another minute went by.

"Thank you for saying that, Reggie," she said. "It feels good to hear you share your feelings with me."

His face softened at her encouragement. Hers was streaked with tears.

"Keep talking, Reggie," I said. "Just talk. The words will come. This relationship thing is a talk thing."

Though they may come haltingly at first, and talking may feel foreign to the point of impossible to us, the words come more easily after a while, and once we get the hang of it, guys, talking to our partners—sharing our feelings and listening to theirs—actually becomes kind of *fun*.

The Ebb and Flow

Just as you breathe in and breathe out
Sometimes you're ahead and other times behind
Sometimes you're strong and other times weak . . .
　　　　　　　　　—Lao Tzu, *Tao Te Ching*

My strength is made perfect in weakness.
　　　　　　　　　—II Corinthians 12:9

B.J. came into therapy one day upset because his two-year-old son Benjamin had fallen out of his high chair the night before while drinking a glass of juice and had cut his wrist on the broken glass. The cut was so deep that the median nerve had been partially severed. Benjamin was in the hospital with his mother, Claire, awaiting surgery. B.J. had spent the day with them.

About halfway through our session, while B.J. was describing how small Benjamin looked in the big hospital bed, he broke down and started crying, which soon turned into deep sobbing. His abdomen heaved and he buried his face in his hands. He sobbed for a long time while I sat silently. When it was over, he rested, bent forward in his chair, the heels of his hands supporting his forehead. Then he leaned back and looked at me.

"I've got to be stronger than *this*," he said, sniffling.

"No," I said. "You've got to be *precisely* this *in order* to be strong."

☽ ☽ ☽

Nature is waves: crest and trough, summer and winter, ebb and flow. Nature is circles: day and night, evaporation and rain, turn and return. Nature is made up of seemingly opposed but actually complementary energies that alternate and wax and wane like the moon.

This principle also operates in human nature. There is happiness and sadness inside us, love and hate, openness and closedness, faith and fear, strength and weakness.

During a crisis like B.J.'s, we know that it's our job to be strong for our loved ones. "Strong" means being intact and available and together enough to support and serve the person who has been injured, like

Benjamin. In physical, emotional, and spiritual ways, Benjamin needed B.J. to support and serve him in the days to come. "Strong" means being intact and available and together enough to support those who are primary caregivers, like Claire. And "strong" means being together enough to think clearly and make the right decisions in the situation.

It will take so much strength to do all this that you'd better remember that, like nature, you too must ebb and flow, wax and wane. To be strong, you will need to be "weak" sometimes. You'd better make sure to fall apart now and then. Falling apart allows you to keep it together. So you might have to periodically break down and cry and be scared and feel sorry for yourself. A counselor or a therapist's office—or a minister's or a rabbi's—is a good place to do that. The arms of your partner is also a good place to do that. On the phone with your brother or aunt or friend is a good place to do that. If no one is available to be there for you when you need to fall apart, do it alone and be there for yourself. Cry your eyes out—give yourself *permission* to be "weak"—so that then you can turn around and be strong.

You Make Me Feel

You make me live!
You make me die!
You make me laugh!
You make me cry!

—Celine Dion and Luciano Pavarotti,
"I Hate You, Then I Love You"

Nobody makes anybody feel anything. If we're feeling an emotion, it is because that emotion exists inside us in its potential state, and it's only been activated, or triggered, by something outside us. When that something is marriage, which is the most intimate human relationship on earth, the person to whom we're married is cosmically custom designed to trigger all our emotions. That triggering is actually a favor to us, because not until we have looked at those feelings coming up in our being can we begin the work of moving through them in order to experience the core of our being, which is beyond all feelings but love.

David, a psychotherapist, was lambasting his wife, Carole, for running out of gas on the Mass Pike and stranding herself and the children for over an hour.

"You make me feel so guilty!" Carole yelled. "You make me feel like the biggest criminal in the world!"

"I don't *make* you feel anything!" David yelled back. "If you feel guilty, *you* feel guilty! Nobody makes anybody else feel anything!"

"It's not quite that simple, David," I interjected.

He turned to me, his eyes sharp.

"In marriage we do make each other feel certain feelings, and we don't," I said. "It's one of the paradoxes of marriage, a koan of marriage. You're not going to be able to either deal with your feelings or get past them until you understand that your partner both makes and doesn't make you feel them."

In David and Carole's case, David doesn't make Carole feel guilty or like a criminal—he *helps* her feel it. In order for Carole to not have that feeling drifting around in her being, she's got to see it and feel it and get beyond it. Then, and only then, can David say anything he wants to her and she won't feel guilty or like a criminal. She will be completely unaffected by his words. There is a story that illustrates this state of detachment:

A warlord once captured a town where there were many monks. The warlord had a reputation for torturing and killing monks, so all the monks fled into the mountains as the warlord approached. One monk, however, did not flee. He meditated in the monastery temple. The warlord was enraged to hear this and marched straight to the monastery and into the temple. He ordered the monk to come out of his meditation and stand up. The monk opened his eyes and stood up, and the two men faced each other. The warlord pulled his sword from his scabbard and touched the tip of it to the monk's stomach.

"Don't you know who I am?" the warlord sneered. "I could run my sword through your stomach without blinking an eye."

The monk looked back at him, his face serene.

"Don't you know who *I* am?" he said. "I could have your sword run through my stomach without blinking an eye."

Nobody makes anyone else feel anything. Not even in marriage. That is true.

And it's not true. It's especially not true in marriage. In marriage two people are so emotionally tied to each other that the one can't blink without the other noticing. *Her* blink made *him* feel abandoned for a second, which made him angry, which made him talk sharply to her, which made her scared, which made her talk sharply to him, which made them both start fighting, which eventually made them both feel like jumping off the nearest bridge, on opposite sides. Let's face it, our partners make us feel *everything*!

And they don't *make* us feel anything.

Welcome to marriage.

RIGHT HOLDING

When you hug someone, you want it to be a masterpiece of connection.
—Tess Gallagher, "The Hug"

One of the things we can certainly make our partners feel is *good*; and one of the ways we can make them feel good is by holding them when they need to be held. Holding heals our hurts. When we are in the safe haven of another's embrace, when we have *physical* knowledge that we're not alone our hurts heal.

How we hold is also important. The Buddhists talk about Right Livelihood, Right Speech, Right Effort, Right Understanding, etc. I believe there is also something we can call "Right Holding."

Always ask permission to hold. Without permission, holding can be experienced by the one being held as violating a boundary, as an imposition.

If you get permission, then find out, either instinctively or by asking, *how* the other would like to be held. She may want your arm around her shoulder, or your hand on her back, or on her forehead, or holding her hand. She may want the pressure of your hand to be heavy, or light. She may want to put her head on your shoulder or on your chest. Or she may not. Find out. Hold her the way she wants to be held.

If possible, sit together on a couch or the floor—anywhere where your two bodies are not restricted to a particular place or position and can touch and hold freely and fully.

Be fully involved. Hold her with *both* your hands. Don't put one on her shoulder and drop the other into your lap, then inspect its nails. The one who is being held will perceive that kind of half involvement as inattention, which it is. By not practicing Right Holding—which means attentive holding—you will diminish and often destroy the healing effect of the holding.

The hand or hands that are touching his body should be still, not patting or rubbing or tapping or stroking. All of these movements are picked up by the one being held as *your* nervousness, which they are. Unless otherwise instructed by his words or his body, keep your hands and body still. Much of the healing of being held comes from the stillness of the holder.

The healing stillness should be sent not only through your still hands and your still body but also through your still mind. While you're holding him, don't be thinking of other things. As a matter of fact, don't be thinking. Just be holding. Direct the pure, undivided beam of your mental attention solely to him.

Harmonize your breathing with hers. Pay such focused attention to her while you hold her that you breathe in as she breathes in, and you breathe out as she breathes out. She will experience your breathing with her as pure attention, true joining, and deep healing. I once knew a woman who belonged to a volunteer organization that would go into hospitals and nursing homes to be with the dying. I asked her about the things that she did with the dying, especially the ones too weak to talk, or in a coma. She said that she would most often just sit with them, hold their hand or touch their shoulder and silently breathe with them.

If the one you're holding is sighing, crying, sobbing, screaming, or otherwise uttering words or sounds of pain and distress, do not say "Ssshhh" or "Hush" or "There, there" or "What's wrong?" Nothing's wrong. He's letting the pain come out of his body through those sounds. The sounds are not the pain, they are the healing of the pain, so let them come out and encourage them to come out. You can encourage them either by remaining silent while they're coming out or by making those little compassionate "Mmmm" sounds in your throat as they come out. Whatever you do, do not ask questions, comment or make suggestions, interpret, or share your own feelings. Basically, shut up and let what's coming out come out.

On pain of death, let there be no sexuality in your holding. Touch no sexual part of her body, and do not touch her body in a way that she might interpret as sexual. Let there be no sexuality in your mind either. Banish the thought, if it occurs, that this holding will lead to more than holding. The moment sexuality enters the energy, either in your body or in your mind, she feels it, and gets so alert inside, so apprehensive and angry, that all healing comes to a screeching halt.

When we're being held, we're being assured, deep inside, of the one thing that human beings want to be assured of: that we're not alone. Knowing we're not alone helps us feel safe. If our bodies know that we're safe because they're being touched and held by another body, on some deep level of our beings, deeper than the hurt and the pain, we're fine.

When my daughter Greta was seven, Jane and I took her to an amusement park, and Greta and I went up on the Ferris wheel. On one of its revolutions, the wheel stopped, with Greta and me at the very top, gently rocking back and forth in our little green car. Way below us Jane was sitting on a bench eating an apple, looking up at us and waving.

I had my arm around Greta's waist, holding her tightly to my side while she leaned forward over the metal bar, looking down and waving back at Jane. She leaned farther forward over the bar. The car tipped forward a little and my arm tightened around her.

"Aren't you scared, Gretty?" I said.

"Of what?" she said.

"Of falling out," I said.

"No," she said. "Are you scared, Daddy?"

"You bet. How come you're not?"

"Because I have *this,*" she said, and patted my arm that encircled her waist.

THE CHAIRS

During the first week of my junior year in college, my girlfriend
Candace informed me that on her trip to Florence, Italy, over the summer, a museum guard at the Uffizi Gallery had come up behind her and
stuck his hand down her blouse as she stood gazing at Giotto's *Madonna
Enthroned*, and one thing had led to another, and . . . well, she was breaking up with me.

The next couple of weeks were hell for me. Mostly I lay in bed in my
apartment struggling with my feelings. I experienced lots of feelings—
disbelief, loneliness, anger, self-pity, self-hatred, depression, resigna-
tion, a kind of grim resolution, lots of nostalgia, a wry sense of the
existential absurdity of the whole situation, and a weird, detached feeling that somehow everything was still fine in my life. There I'd lie staring into space, night after night, cigarette after cigarette, beset by all
these feelings that seemed to be voices having a conversation inside my
head.

So I decided to write the conversation—which actually turned out to
be a one-act play. In the play, it is night, and I am lying disheveled in bed
in a haze of cigarette smoke, staring into the semidarkness. The bedroom door opens and in come a dozen or so characters, all dressed differently and each carrying a folding chair. They set up their folding
chairs in a three-quarter circle around the foot of my bed, sit down, and
begin talking. The characters are my different feelings. My anger is
dressed in a bright red tunic. My depression wears a black turtleneck.
My sense of the absurd is dressed like a harlequin, and my sense that
everything is still fine wears a white robe. They sit on their chairs talking
among themselves while I lie in bed smoking Marlboros. They don't
come to any conclusion or solution, they just talk. At the end of the play,
I fall asleep and they fold up their chairs and *exeunt*.

Artistically speaking, it's probably the worst one-act play ever written, but psychologically speaking, it was great for me because for the first time in my life I realized that there was a "me" separate from my feelings, that this "me" was a kind of wakeful, watchful consciousness that did not fluctuate with the fluctuations of my feelings but simply watched and listened as my feelings came and went. The fact that "I" was not my feelings but was the unmoving witness to my feelings was a huge serendipitous discovery for me, and was, I think, my first introduction to meditative consciousness. That meditative consciousness—that wakeful, watchful "me" lying in bed—was the *true* me, and even though I had just lost my girlfriend to a sexually enflamed museum guard at the Uffizi Gallery and was having plenty of painful feelings about that, the feelings were just characters sitting in folding chairs around my bed talking, and *I* was fine.

At times, feelings come to visit us. They carry in and set up their folding chairs and say their lines and then after a while they pick up their chairs and leave. That's the play, a play of feelings, and we're watching it.

The Pain of the World

They all belonged to each other: the lament of those who yearn, the
laughter of the wise, the cry of indignation and the groan of the dying.
They were all interwoven and interlocked, entwined in a thousand ways.
And all the voices, all the goals, all the yearnings, all the sorrows, all the
pleasures, all the good and evil, all of them together was the world.

—Hermann Hesse, *Siddhartha*

Somebody's got to cry some tears
I guess it must be up to me.

—Bob Dylan, "Up to Me"

Ella sat across from me, tears beginning to course down her cheeks as she retold her story. In therapy, she had been dealing with the pain of having been physically tortured by her cruel alcoholic stepfather from when she was five until she was nine. When Ella was eight, she had just begun to tell me, her stepfather had, in a drunken rage, cut the throat of the family parakeet in front of her. As the pain came forth, her crying heaved through her.

"Keep crying, Ella," I said. "Whatever the memory is that brings the tears, remember it . . . keep remembering it. . . . "

I put on a tape of quiet classical music as Ella's heart erupted.

"Keep going, Ella. Keep remembering. Keep going."

And she did. She cried and cried. After a while, she was doubled over on her chair, clutching her stomach, rocking back and forth and groaning. Then, jackknifing slowly forward, she fell to the floor, ending up on her knees, rocking back and forth, still clutching her stomach.

"Let it all come out, Ella . . . everything that's in there . . . all your pain. . . . "

"There's so much!" she whispered.

"It's okay to feel it," I said softly.

Ella spent the next half hour on the rug, crying, whimpering, sobbing, screaming, rocking back and forth, finally falling on her side, still clutching her stomach, and rolling from side to side while words and tears poured out of her, with the classical music still playing quietly in the background.

"Stop it . . . Leave me alone . . . Ow! . . . It hurts! . . . It hurts! . . . Stop it! . . . Please! . . . Stop! . . . Ow! . . . Please, Daddy! . . . Please, Daddy! . . . Oh my God! . . . OH MY GOD! . . . NO! . . . OH MY GOD! . . . All the pain! All the pain! . . . I can't stand it! . . . I can't stand it! . . . It's all over! . . . It's all over! . . . IT'S ALL OVER! . . . "

"All over your body, Ella? Is the pain all over your body?"

"It's all over the world! The pain is all over the world!"

I sat for a moment in stunned silence. Then I leaned forward in my chair.

"Go ahead, Ella. Channel the pain of the whole world through your body. Channel all the suffering, the grief, the horror. Let all the pain of all the world come through you."

'There's so much of it!" she whispered hoarsely.

"It's infinite," I said. "And it's all inside you. It's all inside all of us. We can feel it."

She did feel it. She opened to the scream of the world. It came as a scream, again and again, her mouth open in a wide oval with bared teeth, screaming, and it moved through and up and out of her as a wall of pure unbroken ululating sound, followed by long sobbing. She had crossed the line between her personal, finite pain and the infinite suffering of humanity. They had become one pain, and she let it move through her. When it was over, she lay still for a long time, holding a throw pillow, staring into space.

"I don't know what just happened," she said.

"What did it feel like?"

"It felt . . . complete. It felt complete."

"I think you just let the complete pain of the world pour through you," I said.

There was a short silence. "I feel different," she said. "Cleansed. Everything feels quieter now. I can breathe better. I feel good."

She was quiet for a long time, lying on her side with the pillow, curled up, her eyes closed, her face giving off a faint amber light. There was nothing left in her, no movement of any kind, just her slow and almost imperceptible breathing. The classical music continued. Her breathing changed after a few moments, and I realized she was sleeping. She slept, and as she slept, looking down at her serene face, I felt a great peace, for an instant, come over the whole world.

6

ADDICTIONS, COMPULSIONS, AND OBSESSIONS

I started out on burgundy
but soon hit the harder stuff.
Everybody said they'd stand behind me
when the game got rough.
But the joke was on me
there was nobody even there to bluff.

—Bob Dylan,
"Just Like Tom Thumb's Blues"

There is a basket of fresh bread on your head, and yet
you go door to door asking for crusts.
Knock on your inner door. No other.

—Jalaluddin Rumi,
"A Basket of Fresh Bread"

Whatever problems my clients might be having in their lives, I have never had a client without an addiction. By addiction I do not mean just chemical dependency, but *any* dependency. The addiction might be to food, sugar, chocolate, alcohol, coffee, cigarettes, marijuana, cocaine, prescription drugs, pornography, sex, relationships, shopping, television, videos, computers, work, accumulating money, spending money, or any of the inexhaustible supply of sensations and stimulations out there in the world.

An addiction is an attempt to find happiness, peace, love, and enchantment outside ourselves. They can't be found outside ourselves, but we don't know where else to look, or we're too lazy or addicted to look elsewhere, so that's where we keep looking.

Happiness, peace, love, and enchantment are found inside ourselves. On some level of our beings, we all know that, and are just avoiding it. We've been deeply conditioned by our culture to look outside ourselves, and it requires an independence, a patience, and a courage to look inside ourselves that not many of us think we have.

One evening a man was looking for something under a street lamp in front of his house. His neighbor came over and asked him what he was looking for.

"I'm looking for the keys to my car," the man said.

"Where did you lose them?" asked the neighbor, bending down to help the man look.

"Inside my house."

"*Inside* your house? If you lost them inside your house, why are you looking out here?"

"It's *dark* in there," he said.

An addiction is the last stop we make outside ourselves before going inside ourselves to look for the happiness, peace, love, and enchantment that is our nature. When we have gotten our souls right, we are completely free of addictions.

THE ESSENCE OF THE ADDICTION

Look to the essence of a thing . . .
—Marcus Aurelius, *Meditations*

There are many reasons people continue to smoke when they know it's bad for them, or to use drugs when they know they are screwing up their lives, but I believe that to really break an addiction, it is good to get to the *reason of reasons,* the meta-reason of the addiction, to understand what the *essence* of the addiction is, and what the essential wound or need or drive or pleasure in it is.

I believe that the essence of the addiction to cigarettes is the drawing in of a wonderfully satisfying and therefore soothing deep breath.

The essence of the addiction to food, including sugar, is the search for the fullness, peace, bliss, and beatitude at the mother's breast.

The essence of the addiction to alcohol and all mood-altering drugs is the attempt to feel positive emotions instead of the negative ones we're feeling at the moment.

The essence of the addiction to caffeine is the need for a lift out of fatigue and depression.

The essence of the addiction to love, sex, and relationships is loneliness.

The essence of the addiction to television and other forms of visual and auditory sensation and stimulation is loneliness.

The essence of the addiction to attention, recognition, praise, and adoration from others, including the attention attracted by immoderate and immodest self-display, is loneliness and self-hatred.

The essence of the addiction to gambling is the desire to numb and deaden intolerable chronic anxiety with intermittent acute anxiety.

The essence of the addiction to hurting others is revenge against those who hurt you.[1]

The essence of the addiction to acquisition and possession of material things is a feeling of inner emptiness.

The essence of the addiction to work is the inability to rest, driven by anxiety—driven, deeper down, particularly for men, by the primal fear of the starvation and death of you and your family if you don't protect and provide for them.

The essence of the addiction to all irrational behavior involving money, including the endless accumulating, hoarding, and/or stealing of money, and including all forms of cheating with money, is greed, and greed is a form of fear.

The essence of *all* addictions and all addictiveness is fear, and the essence of fear is the feeling that you are totally alone in the universe. When we reach for that bottle, that bonbon, or that body, we are trying to not be alone and scared anymore by reaching out for a *relationship* with something. What we are essentially reaching out for is love. When, with the help of our supporters, we learn to reach *in* for it, our addictions end.

FILL WANTED

There is nothing here in this world which can lead you to the state of fullness.
　　　　　　　　　　　　—King Janaka

God said to Abram, go to your Self, know your Self, fulfill your Self.
　　　　　　　　　　　　—The Kabbalah

Until we reach Self-realization, human beings are dependent beings, especially when we're children. If we were lucky when we were children, our parents understood and welcomed our dependency on them and devoted themselves to providing what we were dependent on them for: food; shelter; attention; protection; nurturance; acknowledgment; encouragement; appreciation; praise; respect; love; and a general enthusiastic welcome of us to the world. If we received all these from our parents, if they filled us with everything they were supposed to fill us with, we got to grow *out* of being dependent children and become adults. An adult is someone who was allowed to feel and show her dependency needs as a child, and to get most of those needs fulfilled by attentive, loving, nurturing parents, thereby outgrowing her child dependencies, and not carrying those dependencies around with her for the rest of her life in the gargoyle forms of her compulsions, obsessions, and addictions.

If we were not so lucky when we were children, our parents didn't understand or welcome our dependency needs and did not fill us full with all the things that parents are supposed to fill their children full with, so our dependency needs, never having been met, traveled with us into our alleged adulthood, as the set of compulsions, obsessions, and addictions that we somewhat euphemistically call our "life." Fundamentally unfulfilled in childhood, we enter adulthood with invisible FILL WANTED signs hanging around our necks, and it's just a question of time before some addiction the size of a truck rumbles along to try to fill us.

You'd think by now we'd wise up and see that all those people stuffing their faces full of fries and their bellies full of beer and their lungs full of smoke and their veins full of drugs and their pockets full of money and their closets full of clothes and their houses full of house-wares and their blankets full of lovers—you'd think by now we'd see that all of that just doesn't work, doesn't fill the unfulfillment inside, and we're crazy to keep doing it!

So what does fill the unfulfillment?

Love, happiness, peace of mind, quietness of heart, a purpose in life, faith in God, and self-respect.

And where do we look for those?

Not from our parents. It's too late for them. You can't go home again. And not from our partners and lovers either. It doesn't work like that. Or in Bloomingdale's or in Dunkin' Donuts. It *really* doesn't work like that.

So where do we look for love, happiness, peace of mind, quietness of heart, a purpose in life, faith in God, and self-respect?

Inside. All the things we're looking for are inside us, as our very own Self. We *are* all those things. We are already full.

And how do we look?

By going inside. Through meditation and other practices of self-awareness, we make the effort—a steady, persistent effort over a long period of time—to go inside.

And what happens when we find what we're looking for?

An amazing thing. We feel full, from inside. At that point, the FILL WANTED signs drop off our necks, and addictions drop out of our lives.

Whoso commiteth adultery with a woman lacketh understanding.
—Proverbs 6:32

Leave all women, save your wife, alone.
—Liberian love poem,
African Love Poems and Prayers

Jules, a twenty-six-year-old commercial artist, was married and having his second clandestine affair. The first affair had ended an important long-term relationship three years before, and this one was well on its way to ending his marriage. In addition, he compulsively stared at women across streets and parties, flirted with them at every opportunity, and fantasized about them constantly.

"I've got a problem with women," he said.

"I'll say," I said.

"I'm tired of it. It's ruining my life."

"The fact that you know that and can say that is a good sign."

"It feels hopeless to me. Women are just so damn *beautiful* to me."

To some men, women are like a kind of drug—exciting, intoxicating, and irresistible. The woman might be one of those "Dear-god-give-me-a-break" women in bathing suits on beaches, or any woman anywhere. When these men see a woman, they become crazed inside and can't keep themselves from looking at them or from sexually pursuing them in the hope of possessing them. Many men are addicted to looking at and sexually pursuing women. Even when they want to stop, even when it's completely messing up their lives, these men can't stop looking at and sexually pursuing women. This is addiction, even though in our culture we don't call it addiction, we call it "normal," as in, "Boys-will-be-boys, ha-ha-ha!"

Underneath the adrenaline rush, the ego rush, the phallic flush, and the thrills and chills of men's sexual addiction to women, there is pain. All that looking at, desiring, approaching, pursuing, and possessing women are forms of suffering. You have to look hard and clear and long at it, and be really honest with yourself, to see that it's suffering, but it is.

To relieve the suffering, a man has to travel through seven levels, or degrees, like seven concentric circles, of sexual addiction to women. Moving through the circles from the outer circle toward the inner one represents moving away from addiction and toward the heart of yourself, your own core where there is no more addiction and no more suffering.

In the seventh circle, the farthest one out, there are no controls at all on your sexual addiction to women. You see a woman . . . what you see, you're attracted to . . . what you're attracted to, you want . . . what you want, you approach . . . if you have to, you pursue . . . if you get what you pursue, you act, and then you buckle up your belt and leave her, with no sense of obligation or connection to her. There are no restraints, no rules, no boundaries, no morals. There are hardly any thoughts when you are in this circle. If you have a career, there is no career. If you have a high and responsible position, there is no position and no responsibility. If you have children, there are no children. If you have a wife, there is no wife. There is no consideration of consequences at all. For men who are acting out in the seventh circle of sexual addiction, there is only the addiction.

When you're done acting out in the seventh circle of sexual addiction, you might move to the sixth circle. In the sixth circle, you see her, you're attracted to her, you want her, you approach her, you pursue her, you get her, and you touch her, but you now have one rule: no intercourse. You don't fornicate with her. You restrain your touching to kissing, holding, patting, petting, and the ten thousand other forms of sexual touching that stop short of intercourse and sometimes even pretend *not* to be sexual touching, as in, "Would you like a back massage?" In the sixth circle, you'll touch her, but you've gotten some control of yourself and you can now draw a line.

When you're done acting out in the sixth circle of sexual addiction, you might move to the fifth circle. In the fifth circle, you see her, you're attracted to her, you want her, you approach her, you pursue her, and when you get her, you'll talk to her, but you won't touch her. There she is, across the room at a party, a bar, a bookstore, a faculty tea. You go over to her and start talking to her. If you're successful, she talks to you. You get to know her, draw her out, gaze deeply into her eyes, use a lot of words. The two of you have engaged the gears of your two sexualities, and they're turning on talk. The fifth circle is the flirtation circle. In our culture, it's a *very* crowded one. If you're good at deluding yourself, you can feel relatively innocent in this circle, but there is sexual attraction and sexual intrigue every step of the way. Many men have a hard time knowing when they're flirting with a woman, they call it "just being friendly." If you're a man and you want to know when you're flirting, ask your wife or girlfriend, who usually has to stand there silently witnessing the whole sorry scene, feeling like screaming and/or killing you.

When you're done acting out in the fifth circle of sexual addiction, you might move to the fourth circle. In the fourth circle, you see her, you're attracted to her, you want her, but you won't approach, pursue, or talk to her. The only thing you'll let yourself do is look at her. In the fourth circle, the addiction is in looking. You'll look at her, stare at her, eye her, ogle her, furtively glance at her, and get a big thrill every time you catch her glancing back at you over the cheese dip. Sexuality is played out with your eyes. The fourth circle is a relatively benign one, but like all the other circles, it's seductive and addictive, and still makes your wife or girlfriend, who is again silently witnessing the whole thing, feel like screaming and/or killing you.

When you're done acting out in the fourth circle of sexual addiction, you might move to the third circle. In the third circle, you look at her, you're attracted to her, you feel the familiar wanting of her . . . so you don't look at her again! You couldn't help the first look—that's usually involuntary, an accident, a twist of fate—but you don't allow yourself a second look. You look away. You look down. You leave the room. If necessary, you leave the conference, or the country. Your eyes are under your control now. You've got the addiction contained inside your own being now. In this circle, you might still think about her, or fantasize about her, both of which are forms of looking at her in your mind's eye, but you can't look at her with your physical eyes anymore because you know it's not right and you don't need that anymore. Then you'll be like Jalaluddin Rumi: "For years I gave away sexual love with my eyes. Now I don't."[2]

When you're done acting out in the third circle of sexual addiction, you might move to the second circle. In the second circle, when you happen to look at her, you still notice her physical appearance as an interesting phenomenon in your visual field . . . and that's the end of that! You don't even think about her after that. She was just a figure on the far horizon of your consciousness, a momentary flashing forth of a familiar cognition of no great importance inside you. You witness the brief flashing forth inside and you witness its cessation.

When you're done with the second circle of sexual addiction, you might move to the first circle, which is the innermost circle and the cessation of the addiction. In the innermost circle, you look at her and you see her as a human being among five billion other human beings on the planet. You see human beings as human beings now. Their size, shape, age, and gender has ceased to matter to you. Whoever happens to make their cameo appearance in front of your eyes, your response is the same: In your heart you are loving, in your words and actions and eyes you are respectful and appropriate, and in your mind you are quiet. You're home now. After a long journey in from the outer circles, you have gotten to the innermost circle, which is your heart. In your heart, there is love, happiness, peace, respect for women, and freedom from all addiction, including the sexual one. All you have to do to get there is to bring all the parts of your body under the control of your understanding. All you have to do is to see everybody, including women, as human beings—to see everybody, including women, as *God*.

Come into the innermost circle as quickly as you can. It's the only one where there's true love and respect for women and there's no suffering anymore for men.[3]

John Ingersoll's Orchard
or
Keep Good Company

Bad company is loss, and good company is gain. In company with the wind, the dust flies heavenwards; if it joins water, it becomes mud and sinks.

—Tulsidas

In the early seventies, I used to work for a farmer, the late John Ingersoll of Sheffield, Massachusetts, one of the kindest, ablest, most hard-working men I have ever met. He was one of my mentors in life, a man who operated a beautiful apple orchard named Sky Farm that grew on a high foothill in the Berkshire Mountains. One of my jobs was to tend the saplings in John's orchard.

When you first plant a sapling, its bark is very soft and tender and vulnerable to being nibbled by field mice and other animals, so you must protect the sapling by wrapping a strip of heavy plastic around its base so the animals can't get to it. When the sapling becomes a mature tree with tougher, thicker bark, it is no longer vulnerable to animals and you can take the plastic off.

In the same way, anyone with an addiction he or she is beginning to address is a sapling on the path of recovery and is still vulnerable to bad influences. One of the primary ways bad influences gain access to us is through bad company: our drinking and drugging buddies, the friends who encourage us to take a spin around the mall or indulge in a rich dessert just this once. They may be our friends, or even our family, but if we want to break our addiction and stay on our path, we must keep away from bad company and its temptations. The best way to keep away from bad company is to surround ourselves with good company.

What is good company?

Twelve-step meetings are good company. So is the Big Book of Alcoholics Anonymous. So is your sponsor. So is your spouse or child. So is any friend of yours who doesn't drink or use drugs or shop till she drops. So is your therapist. So are inspirational tapes. So is your place of worship. So are prayer and meditation. So are positive, uplifting thoughts. So is anything that reminds you of the sober truth and helps you live it.

There is a Sanskrit word, *satsang*, which means "the company of the truth." Anything that reminds you of the truth and helps you live it— any person, place, book, thing, thought, or activity that keeps you on the path of the truth—is *satsang* for you, is good company. Anything else is bad company.

Drinking and drugging buddies may be good people, but they're bad company—*miserable* company—because they use and they want you to use, because misery loves company. As long as we're still saplings in this orchard, we need to protect ourselves from bad company.

I Didn't Straighten the Pillows!

All change is a miracle to contemplate.
—Henry David Thoreau, *Walden*

Joyce, a twenty-nine-year-old art curator, had come into therapy because anxiety permeated her life, from her fear of driving to her compulsive housecleaning. Over the past couple of months, we had been talking about her compulsive housecleaning and the problems it caused for her husband and two young children. Typically, she would come home from work at around six P.M., perfunctorily greet her children, barely say hello to her husband, and with a quick "I just have to do a few things" to them all start straightening up, always starting with the throw pillows in the living room. By the time she was done, two hours had passed and she was too exhausted to play with her children, who were being shepherded off to bed by her furious husband.

One day Joyce came into the session with a big smile on her face. She'd been using some of the relaxation techniques we had worked on the previous week, and as a result, when she'd gone home the night before she'd felt able to spend about a half hour with her husband and children.

"I didn't have to straighten the pillows as soon as I walked in the door!" she proudly reported.

"Is that a first?" I asked.

"Yes," she said, and laughed. "I know it sounds silly—"

"I think that's wonderful, Joyce!" I said.

"I *looked* at them though," she said. "Repeatedly. The compulsion to straighten those pillows was there the whole half hour." She sighed. "And then I couldn't stand it anymore and spent the rest of the evening cleaning."

"It's still wonderful," I said.

She smirked and shrugged and waved me off with her hand.

"Be careful there, Joyce," I said.

"What do you mean?"

"You have to make sure to continually congratulate and celebrate yourself on this journey. It may seem minor now, but you have to take the time out to enjoy even the smallest victories. If you don't, you don't get where you want to go.

"The journey of change is like a steep stairway with many steps—each one of them difficult to take—and your legs need strength and spring to climb from one to the other. The strength and spring for the next step comes, in part, from the inward acknowledgment, appreciation, congratulation, and celebration you give yourself for the step you just climbed. If after climbing to one step you shrug, smirk, wave it off, or blow it off, not permitting yourself to bask in the light of your own self-praise, it is harder to take the next step.

"So you didn't straighten the pillows when you came home last night. Did I hear you say you spent *a whole half hour* with your family before starting to clean?! Did I hear you say that you actually *resisted* the impulse to clean your house *for thirty full minutes*?!"

"Yeah . . . "

"Wow! That's *so* great! You're changing! Your work on yourself is paying off! You're doing battle with your compulsions, and winning! You didn't straighten the pillows! You only *looked* at them! You stayed with your family! You played with your children! *Good* for you! I bet they loved it! I bet your husband was so pleased! I bet they were *all* so pleased!"

She stared up into space for a second, as if recollecting.

"They were, actually," she said, a smile spreading across her face.

"So no more dismissing your small victories. Because the biggest successes don't come out of the blue—they're built on the little ones."

Joyce laughed. "Like resisting the throw pillows!"

"And conquering our compulsions and crazinesses a half hour at a time."

THE STRAIT GATE

The externals are simply so many props; everything we need is within us.
—Etty Hillesum, *An Interrupted Life*

Harland, a thirty-two-year-old recording engineer, was interested in spiritual disciplines such as meditation and prayer, but was also addicted to marijuana and (when they were available) hallucinogens. In this session I confronted him with his drug addiction, urging him to give it up if he was serious about the spiritual path.

"But drugs do the same thing for me that meditation does for you," he argued. "You say you get to a place of clarity and confidence and happiness and inner peace with meditation. I get to the exact same place when I smoke weed. And it's a lot easier."

"Maybe so," I said, "but with your drugs, do you ever get to *stay* in that place?"

☽ ☽ ☽

The place of clarity, confidence, happiness, love, and peace inside us is like a magnificent interior castle, as St. Teresa of Avila called it, and whether we know it or not, we're all spending our lives trying to get into it.

Our interior castle is protected by a high wall, though, and is not easily entered. The challenge of our lives is to find a way in.

Drugs are a way in, there is no denying that. You smoke a joint or snort a line or pop a pill and suddenly you're catapulted high over the castle wall, into the courtyard. For a little while, you're happy. It's great. You explore the castle and see some of its treasures. Then the drug wears off, and you're thrown out of the castle, just like that, lobbed back over the wall, and you crash with a thud outside.

In the sixties and seventies, drugs catapulted a whole generation into their interior castle, and showed them many treasures there. Some of us even glimpsed the supreme treasure—the experience of our true inner nature as beings of vitality and intuition, so full of joy and love and peace that it passes understanding. I was one of those. The first time I took LSD it was in Ithaca, New York, on a warm, sunny Saturday afternoon in the spring of 1965, and I was a sophomore in college. I felt the contentment, exhilaration, wonder, love, and perfect mental clarity that was at the core of me. Without a shadow of a doubt, I knew that those feelings were not coming *from* the drug but were aspects of my own nature made available to me *by* the drug, and I knew, from that day on, my path in life. I would search for that experience—for the truth of my own nature, using any means necessary—until I found it.

For a few years, I used drugs. They did put me into the castle, but over time they wore me out, physically and emotionally. I ended up dependent on drugs and depressed in the dungeon of the castle, so I stopped using. But having experienced getting inside those castle walls, I knew I had to find another way in. I had to find the *gate*. And I did.

Strait is the gate, and narrow is the way.

The way into the interior castle is a small, strait gate—more like a tunnel actually—almost hidden in the wall. To walk through that gate requires intelligence, courage, patience, discipline, stamina, a sense of humor, and time. While you're walking through the gate, you'll find yourself thinking about your psychological self a lot, you'll practice meditation and other techniques of self-awareness, and you'll find yourself coming to know your innermost spiritual Self.

There is no other way into the interior castle. Drugs don't work. They're just a round-trip ticket into and out of a castle you can never stay in. Eventually they're a one-way ticket to physical and emotional hell. The real trip to the Self is through the strait gate, through your self. When you get into the castle that way, you get to stay.

The Drain vs. the Gain of Power

Insanity is doing the same thing over and over again, but expecting different results.

—Rita Mae Brown, *Sudden Death*

Any person who's addicted to anything is fooling herself if she thinks she has power. She doesn't have power. She has given her power over to the substance or the activity or the person or the emotion she's addicted to, and they never return that power. When you're addicted to something, you pour your personal power down the drain of that addiction, and you never get it back.

In order to conquer an addiction, you must first acknowledge that you have poured your personal power down the drain of it, and then you must give that power over to another—a higher—power. That higher power might be your sense of responsibility to yourself or your family, your sense of responsibility to the world, your fears for your life or health or career or reputation, or God. You can use any or all of these as a higher power, but you must use *something*, or your addiction is the highest power in town and you're a goner.

Once you accept the fact that you need a higher power, you might as well save yourself some major time and go right to the top, to the Highest Power. This Highest Power, sometimes called God, is the Source of all the power in the universe. By entering into a relationship with this Power, you receive Its power (also called grace), and by continuing in that relationship over time, surrendering your power up and receiving power down, you eventually gain enough power to overpower your addiction.

Like a gardener, you sow the seed of your personal power into the Source of all power, and you pour your energy into the budding plant, nurturing it. What's returned to you is a huge crop of power—enough to conquer an addiction.

The twelve-step programs, and any programs like them, work. They help you to break addictions. They work because they connect you with the Highest Power, eventually causing you to see that the Highest Power and your own power are one and the same, and that's more power than *any* addiction has.

The Altar of the Heart

Many people in our society are being driven to addictions because there is no collective container for their natural spiritual needs. Their natural propensity for transcendent experience, for ritual, for connection to some energy greater than their own, is being distorted into addictive behavior.
—Marion Woodman,
Addiction to Perfection

Addiction is the far-off remembering of our true nature, our pure state. It's a nostalgia that periodically rises up into our consciousness in the form of a sharp craving for that state. It's the same hunger that has clutched every human breast since the beginning of time.

Our true nature is spiritual. It is joyous and loves to have fun. In fact, one of the reasons we go to our addictions is because they're fun. That buzz off that drink or drug is *fun*. That surge from that coffee is *fun*. That pizza and that pastry are *fun*. Buying everything in sight at the mall is *fun*. Sex is *fun*. We indulge in them because they partially and temporarily satisfy our craving for fun, which is a spiritual craving.

Our true spiritual nature also loves order. It loves structure, regularity, routine, rhythm, ritual. The whole universe, spiritual and material, is one huge ritual that we are all participating in with every breath we take. Our true spiritual nature knows that it's all ritual and therefore impels us toward ritual in our daily lives. Since we live in a time of human history when all our other rituals—familial, communal, social, cultural, and spiritual—have broken down, we turn to the rituals of our addictions because they're the only rituals we've got. Look at yourself or anyone when engaged in any addiction—look closely, and look repeatedly—and you will see ritual: the martini with two olives, shaken not stirred; the dressing up for the mall spending spree; the settling into the couch with chips and beer and the remote for a day of uninterrupted football.

Our true spiritual nature is a state of pure peace, and we turn to our addictions because they mimic that state, each in its own way. The passed-out drunk on the floor, the junkie nodding off in the corner, the overeater sleeping off a heavy meal, the workaholic crashing at the end of an eighteen-hour day—they've all taken their addictions as close as they can get to peace. Unfortunately, the closest an addiction can get to peace is a coma. True peace comes when we find our true spiritual nature because our true spiritual nature *is* peace.

Our true spiritual nature is a worshipful nature. Worship is its *essential* nature and its heart's desire. There is an altar in the heart, and we must place something on it as our object of worship because until that altar in our heart is occupied, our worshipful nature has nothing to worship and we cannot rest. There are lots of things we can place on the altar of the heart for our worship: God, Truth, Love, Righteousness, Service to Humanity, Spirit, a spiritual master, our own deepest and highest Self. They all work, and they're all the same. Whatever we call it, we must place it on the altar of our heart and spend the rest of our days worshiping it through our thoughts, words, and actions because if we don't, if that altar stays empty, an addiction will eventually land on it. Then the worshipful energy of our spiritual nature will flow to the addiction instead of to the Spirit.

All of the energy at the core of addiction is spiritual energy flowing in the wrong direction. What we have to do is to get it flowing in the right direction. In order to break an addiction, we need to worship Spirit, whatever name we give to Spirit, on the altar of our hearts and bow our heads to it every day.

To Break an Addiction

The point in life is to know what's enough.
—Gensei,
"Poem Without a Category"

Many people come to the realization that it is time to break an addiction because it is ruining their lives. They have finally found a powerful enough incentive to kick their habit.

To break an addiction, you definitely need incentive. It can be rooted in the fear of future consequences, an aversion to your own physical or emotional pain, an unwillingness to cause pain to other human beings, or a surrender to an authority that you recognize as higher and greater than yourself. If you can't find one incentive that's strong enough, remember that there's strength in numbers, so use a number of them together. Whatever the incentive is rooted in, it should be some variation or version of *self-interest*, something *you* want for the sake of your own life, health, mind, conscience, sentiments, or feelings. Enlightened self-interest is the only soil that incentive roots well in; all other soils—guilt, shame, "doing it for somebody else"—are dust.

In addition to incentive, there are other tools you will need to break your addiction . . .

Understanding

You can't recover from what you do not understand.
—Lillian Hellman, *Maybe*

You need to understand as much as you can about addiction itself and the whole complex of cultural influences, childhood wounds, feelings, thoughts, impulses, choices, and actions that result in addiction. To understand something is to take a big step back from it. At the root of all addiction is some form of misunderstanding about the nature of true happiness.

Honesty

Hence with denial vain, and coy excuse.

—John Milton, "Lycidas"

You need honesty. Sometimes I call it self-honesty because it's being honest with yourself about yourself. When trying to break an addiction, watch out most for lack of honesty—for denial—for it is a total cul-de-sac, and you must get out of it before you can even hope to address your addiction. Look at the facts of your life and what they're telling you to do about your addiction.

Help

You need more help than you know.

—Jalaluddin Rumi,
These Branching Moments

To break an addiction, you need help. You may need the help of your partner, your family, your friends, a therapist, a twelve-step program, some other kind of program, your place of worship, the right books, and/or God. Whatever kind of help you need, seek it, find it, and use it. Use it for as long as you need it, even if you need it your whole life. There's nothing wrong with needing help. We all need all the help we can get.

Love

We are to live so that no harm or pain is caused by our thoughts, words, or deeds to any other being.

—Patanjali, *Yoga Sutras*

To break an addiction, you need love. You need to want to stop hurting and injuring people—especially your family, and yourself—by saying and doing things that harm them. Your addictions harm people—especially your family, and yourself—and you need to love people too much to be able to do that anymore.

DISCIPLINE

For the very true beginning of wisdom is the desire of discipline.
—King Solomon, the *Apocrypha*

You need to understand how the universe works: by order and discipline. Seasons are in their order, planets are in their orbits, parents care for their children, bodies are born and eat and grow and die—all things are held by order and discipline. We too must be held by order and discipline. We must know our limits and stay within them. We will only begin being happy when we come under discipline. To break an addiction, we must come under discipline.

MEDITATION

Solve all your problems through meditation.
—Paramahansa Yogananda,
Autobiography of a Yogi

You need meditation. Meditation gives you the ability to *watch* your thoughts, as opposed to *acting* on them. That is an important ability to have when you're trying to break an addiction because an addiction is, at its root, nothing more than an agitated thought that arises in the mind, followed by a craving for a substance or an activity that will soothe the agitation, followed by an action we then do in the world to satisfy that craving. If we could only hold the thought there—as nothing more than a thought (and then a craving) that arises in the mind—and not allow it to become an action that we do in the world, we'd be fine. Meditation, by giving us the ability to watch a thought without acting on it, protects us from addiction.

PATIENCE AND SELF-FORGIVENESS

I learn it daily, learn it with pain to which I am grateful: patience is everything!

—Rainer Maria Rilke,
Letters to a Young Poet

You need patience and self-forgiveness. The breaking of addictions takes time. Sometimes there are stumbles and bumbles, backslides, setbacks, and all manner of lapses and relapses along the way. The essence of patience is self-forgiveness. You need lots of self-forgiveness to break an addiction, and the longer it takes to break it, the more patience and self-forgiveness you need.

HUMILITY

Mental health requires that the human will submit itself to something higher than itself.

—M. Scott Peck, *People of the Lie*

You need humility to break an addiction because addiction is, at its core, arrogance. It's not that an addict "has no will of his own," it's that his will *is* his own, and *only* his own, which means he does exactly what *he* wants, and he wants his addiction. In that sense, his addiction is a little fiefdom in which his own will rules. Humility is the end of addiction because humility is the willing acceptance of a will other than your own, outside that fiefdom, and the voluntary surrender of your will to it. Many people experience this other will as outside them, as God's will; some see that it is also inside them, as the voice of their own deepest truth. Wherever you locate it, doing what the truth wants you to do instead of what *you* want to do, is humility; and by practicing humility, you eventually end up not only *doing* what the truth wants, but *wanting* what the truth wants, at which point your individual will has merged into that other and higher Will and your addiction is over.

SELF-KNOWLEDGE

Rama, you are already a liberated being: live like one!
—Vasishtha, *Yoga Vasishtha*

And last, you need to know who you really are. In your essential nature, you are pure spirit, blissfully happy, supremely free, not addicted to anything. Really, deep inside, you're not addicted to anything. The struggling, addicted part of you is a *part* of you, but it's not You. You need to know that.

7
THE TWO OF US

For one human being to love another human being: that is perhaps the
most difficult of all our tasks, the ultimate, the last test and proof, the
work for which all other work is but preparation.
                              —Rainer Maria Rilke,
                                    Letters to a Young Poet

The meeting of two personalities is like the contact of two chemical
substances: if there is any reaction, both are transformed.
                              —Carl Jung

And the closer I'm bound in love to you
The closer I am to free.
                              —Indigo Girls, "The Power of Two"

All the people who come into therapy with me are having problems in
their relationships. Even problems that seem to have nothing to do with
relationships—like addiction, anxiety, depression, identity crisis, or other
forms of life crisis—always lead back to relationships. People have problems with their coworkers, colleagues, bosses, and employees; with their
roommates, neighbors, and friends; with their parents, children, and, of
course, romantic partners. Our partners are the focus of this chapter.[1]

Problems exist in relationships so we'll be forced to deal with the
problems in ourselves that cause the problems in our relationships. The
constant need for communication and cooperation with our partners—
in other words, the constant pressure to be healthy human beings—
shows us the ways in which we're still wounded human beings.

In addition to exposing our wounds, relationships also heal them.
They don't heal all of our wounds, especially not the wound of
wounds—not knowing our own Self, our own divine nature, which we all

have to heal on our own—but relationships can heal many of them. They're especially good at healing the wounds of our childhood.[2]

The closer and longer the relationship, the more thoroughly it reveals the places inside us where we still need to work on ourselves. In getting my own soul right, the deepest and most intense work I've ever done on myself—and am still doing—is in my thirty-year-long marriage with Jane. And in my therapy practice, I watch couples going down to the deepest parts of themselves and making incredible changes in order to make their marriages work.

There's a rumor floating around our culture that says that marriage goes bad after a few years; that the interest and the passion for each other grows stale and dull over time; that the sex grows routine and after a while you're not making eyes at each other, or passes, and before you know it, sex is gone and you don't even try anymore; and that the talking about anything except who's picking up the kids stops after a while, and the vast marital silence descends until death descends. After a decade or two, says this rumor, it's empty nest and empty eyes, empty arms and empty hearts. The divorce rate, which is about 50 percent these days, seems to support this rumor. Even young couples, just married or about to be married, believe it.

I don't. I think that people in bad marriages have given marriage a bad name. I'd like to give marriage a good name. I'd like to call it one of God's greatest gifts to humankind; a form of heaven on earth; a lovely abode, a green and leafy bower, for two people who simply love being with each other; a sanctuary in a sometimes scary world; a secret, private place where two people are open and honest and comical and tender with each other for the rest of their lives.

I believe in this kind of marriage because I'm in this kind of marriage. I believe in the possibility on this earth of a stable, faithful, passionate, compassionate, loving, happy, and lifelong relationship with a partner who is your lover, your comforter, your nurturer, your teacher, and your very best friend all in one. My wife and I are all these things to each other. I believe that that kind of relationship is the essence, goal, and divine purpose of marriage, but it takes a lot of work to achieve it. In my therapy practice—and in this book—I try to teach couples the work they have to do to reach it. I believe that the work is teachable, and therefore that marital happiness is reachable.

THE WORK ON YOURSELF AND THE JOURNEY TO THE HEART

> *. . . we are married*
> *until death, and are betrothed*
> *to change.*
>
> —Wendell Berry, "The Dance"

> *The purification of the intellect and the heart from year to year is the real*
> *marriage, foreseen and prepared from the first, and wholly above their*
> *consciousness.*
>
> —Ralph Waldo Emerson, "Love"

Eduardo, thirty-four, and Aretha, thirty, both social workers, had been married for seven years and had two children, ages five and three. Tonight was their first session.

"Why are you here?" I asked.

They looked at each other, each waiting for the other to speak. Finally, Eduardo cleared his throat.

"We're in trouble," he said. "We hardly speak anymore, except to work out the logistics of our lives. We don't look forward to seeing each other anymore. We bicker a lot. We hardly have sex anymore. We don't have much of anything. Just a lot of silence now."

I asked Aretha if she agreed.

"Yes," she said sadly. "We can't go on like this."

"What happened to you?" I asked. "How'd you get like this?"

They told me they had met ten years before when Aretha was a new clinician at the agency Eduardo had been working in for years. Whenever she could, Aretha would observe Eduardo's therapy sessions from behind a one-way mirror.

"I had a lot of respect for the way Eduardo did therapy," Aretha said.

"It was more like reverence," said Eduardo.

By the end of the year they were in a romantic relationship and then, after another year of dating and living together, marriage.

At first they had been very close, loving to be with each other, playing together, making love, having fun.

"It *was* fun," said Eduardo, "but there was something wrong with it. Something was rotten in the state of Denmark."

"What do you mean?" I asked.

"There was a way she looked up to me so reverentially, and a way I supported her and took care of her and advised her, that, even though it felt good, in a way, at least to me, it wasn't right. It was unequal."

"I was always trying to please him," said Aretha. "Eduardo is very exacting, very judgmental and critical. Nothing is ever good enough for him. I'd try, but he'd always be angry at me. He'd yell at me. He scared me. I kept trying to please him so he wouldn't scare me. I can't do that anymore now. I've stopped trying."

"Good," I said.

Aretha's eyebrows raised. "What do you mean?" she asked.

"The something that was rotten in the state of Denmark is really putrid now and needs to be buried. The old way of doing the relationship is dead. That's good. Now you're here to look for a new way for the two of you to relate."

"How do we find that way?" Aretha asked.

"By being willing to work at it," I replied.

"And the work?" asked Eduardo. "What's the work?"

◡ ◡ ◡

The work is hard and long; it's intriguing and fun and not fun; and it's do-able. It's the work of understanding yourself and your partner so completely that all that's left in you is respect and compassion and love and service for each other. It's the work of purifying yourself of anything in you that isn't respect and compassion and love and service. The work will take you into the youngest, deepest, darkest, most damaged parts of yourself, parts you put away a long, long time ago and haven't heard from in years. You'll hear from your partner's deepest and darkest parts too. The work will also take you into the most tender and innocent and sweetest parts of yourself, and into the highest, purest, most spiritual part of yourself—the loving heart.

The work is really a journey to the heart. It's a journey you take together, each taking your own and each other's journey. Wherever one goes inside her being, the other must also go there, and what one sees inside his being, the other must also see. The work is to go everywhere inside both of you and see everything: the faded and curled old family photographs, the wounds and scars, the lost and frightened child, the hope and aspiration, the sweetness and light, the god and the goddess in there. And then the work is to respect and care for all that is in both of you throughout the journey. It's a complete piece of work, this journey of relationship. It takes you every place you ever wanted to go and a lot of places you don't.

The good news about the work is that it's a journey toward the marriage of your dreams, a beautiful and peaceful lifelong marriage between two pure and loving beings. The bad news is that there's going to be some pain along the way. During these painful times, it is good to remember that you are being purified, so that all that's left in each of you, eventually, is respect and compassion and love and service for each other. At that point, you will be living in your hearts, and in marital harmony.

THE TOTEM POLES

I am large; I contain multitudes.

—Walt Whitman, "Song of Myself"

Relationship, as I understand it, has to do with the exquisitely tuned harmonics between two people who are attempting to become conscious of their personal psychology.

—Marion Woodman,
The Pregnant Virgin

A successful marital relationship is like two totem poles standing side by side. All our different "selves" are on these totem poles, and we all carry many selves. A successful marital relationship happens when each partner is aware of, and accepts, all the different selves on the other's totem pole. When that awareness and acceptance exists, then love makes possible a crossing-over to meet whichever of the other's selves needs to be met at a particular time.

Chris, forty-two, and Dan, forty-one, were going to be married in four months, each for the second time. They had come into therapy to "smooth out some rough spots" in their relationship so they wouldn't repeat the mistakes and failures of their first marriages. Their roughest spot was Dan's inability to be nurturing to Chris when she was feeling frightened and lonely. Instead, Dan judged her and criticized her and wanted her to "just grow up." Again and again they got stuck here, Chris wanting Dan's gentle nurturing when she was feeling scared and lonely, and Dan off in another room waiting for her to grow up. The clash between their needs was causing them great pain.

What they needed to learn was how to use the totem pole to complement each other. Sometimes Chris will be her wounded and frightened baby-girl self, down at the bottom of her totem pole. At these times Dan, loving her there, goes to the top of his totem pole, to his forty-one-year-old fatherly self. He then takes care of Chris for a while in the ways that any kind fatherly being would take care of his frightened baby girl. And when Dan is in *his* youngest self, his wounded and very sad self—when he's down at the bottom of his totem pole—Chris, loving him there, goes to the top of her totem pole to her forty-two-year-old motherly self. Then she can take care of Dan in the ways that any kind motherly being would take care of her very sad little boy. When both partners are in their ten-year-old selves, they can hold hands and skip down the sidewalk together, trying not to step on any cracks. When both are in their teenage selves, they can put on their high-heeled sneakers, go to the hop, and dance the night away.

There is no need for judgment, correction, or even commentary in all this movement up and down the totem poles; there is just the moving to the appropriate self at the appropriate time.

And in those moments when they are both in their youngest and most wounded and frightened selves—as they often are when fighting—the best thing they can do for each other and for themselves is to keep the talking to a minimum, go lie down together in bed, pull the covers over their heads, and hold on tight to each other until one or both of them can get up and try to deal with life again.

ONE SAFE PLACE

Careful of my heart,
Careful of this heart of mine.

> —Tracy Chapman,
> "Be Careful of My Heart"

Many of us grew up unsafe, subject at any moment to emotional and/or physical hurt in our families of origin. And all of us are still unsafe, subject to emotional and/or physical hurt in the world we have to go out into every day. Life isn't *safe*.

But while life isn't safe, marriage is supposed to be. It's supposed to be the one consistently safe place in the world, the shelter from the big storm that seems to always be blowing out there, the *hortus conclusus*—enclosed garden[3]—where the sun is warm and the shade cool and the breezes are gentle.

In an ideal marriage, the marriage vows are really a lifetime pledge of absolute safety made by one human being to another human being: "I will keep you safe. I will *be* safe. In a world where just about everything and everybody else is unsafe, *I* will be a haven for you. Whatever wounds you received in your childhood, and continue to receive in the world, I will not touch them except with the healing balm of kindness and gentleness.[4] You might have to be afraid that everything and everyone else in the world will hurt you, but you don't have to be afraid that *I* will hurt you because you are safe with me."

In the marriages that most of us are in, we haven't achieved that level of safety yet. We must do the work of becoming more and more of a haven for our partner, behaving in a kinder and kinder, softer and softer, more and more loving manner. If at any time you feel like doing or saying something to your partner that would cause her fear or hurt, remember that your partner has already had enough fear and hurt in her lifetime to last a lifetime and doesn't need one more ounce of it from you. If there's any idea floating around in your head that makes you think it's okay to scare or hurt your partner, treat it as a form of temporary insanity and drop it. If anything remains in you that is still capable of scaring or hurting your partner, work on it in you until you work it out of you. That's the work of marriage.

The Keys to Hell

The likelihood is that we will find ourselves forced to deal in our marriage with the core themes and struggles of our early life.
— Augustus Y. Napier,
The Fragile Bond

Samuel and Pamela, both in their late thirties, had been married for twelve years and had two young children. They had been in therapy for a year and a half, and, while working through some difficult and long-standing issues between them had uncovered some important truths about their childhoods. They had developed some understanding of each other's personal hells. Samuel's hell was that ever since he'd been a child, he'd had "a bottomless black hole of badness" inside him that he was always standing at the edge of, trying to keep his footing by trying to be perfect at everything he did—*especially* for Pamela. Pamela's hell was that, having come from a family "that put on a good show of being a family, but was really four people sitting around a dining room table with nothing to say to each other, *ever,*" she desperately wanted connection with Samuel. When that connection wasn't there—as when Samuel went on one of his frequent long business trips, or when, at home, he was so mentally and emotionally preoccupied with business that he barely spoke to anyone—Pamela, feeling utterly alone, would sink rapidly into a suicidal depression.

Walking into the office, they both looked like hell—dark, closed, sad, silent, stricken. I asked them what was going on. Samuel, stealing a glance at Pamela, who was staring blank-eyed at the chair arm, told me the story.

"I made a big mistake last week," he said. "Half inadvertently, half because I was afraid she'd disagree, I made a pretty important career decision without consulting her. I kind of sprang it on her over the weekend."

"You *totally* sprang it on me," Pamela said angrily.

"Okay," said Samuel, his voice rising a little. "I totally sprang it on you. I made a mistake. I'm sorry. It was wrong."

"It feels like we've wasted a year and half of therapy," she said, still too upset to look at him.

"Oh, come on, Pam!" Samuel said. "We went through all this Saturday night. I apologized a hundred times. You make me feel like I've committed the crime of the century."

"I don't understand," Pamela said, looking at him for the first time. Her eyes were sunken and dull. "Why? Why did you do that?"

"I told you!" he said sharply. "I was afraid. I was unconscious. I fell into an old pattern. What do you want me to say?"

Pamela fell silent. Samuel sank back into his chair and shook his head. A long time passed.

"You make me feel like shit," Samuel said finally.

Pamela started to cry. "We haven't gotten anywhere," she said. "I'm as alone in this marriage as I've always been."

"Jesus!" Samuel said.

They both sat there, eyes open, staring at nothing.

"Welcome to hell," I said.

☽ ☽ ☽

As marriage partners and soul mates, each of us holds the key to hell for the other. When we said "I do" on that altar, at that very instant each of us exchanged keys that, if turned, opened the door to our deepest emotional pain. It's an invisible part of every wedding ceremony, the secret exchanging of the keys to hell.

Many of us spend years of our married life unconscious that we hold this key, and in our ignorance we turn it again and again, sending our partner into emotional hell on a fairly regular basis. Then comes therapy—or some other tool of insight into these matters—and we learn a few things. We learn, first of all, that our partner *has* a private hell, and we view its terrain. We learn why—what happened to him in the past that dug such a place in him. We learn what in the present causes her plunge into that place. From experience we learn that, more than anyone or anything else on this earth, *we* cause our partner's plunge into that place—*we* have that power, *we* hold that key. Then by some means the message gets through to us that *we're never supposed to turn that key*. It's at this point, I think, that everything changes in our relationship.

Because now we *know*. Now we're conscious—which means that now we're responsible. Now we're aware that it's our duty to not put our partner into their private emotional hell. Once we know we can put them there, we can't put them there anymore.

It seems to me that once Samuel realized that Pamela goes into emotional hell whenever he abandons or ignores her, he had to accept that he couldn't abandon or ignore her anymore. Once Pamela realized that Samuel goes into emotional hell when he's made to feel bad about himself for making a mistake, she no longer had the right to make him feel bad about himself for making a mistake.

But both of them did so anyway. We all turn the keys and put our partners into hell. Like St. Paul said, "The evil that I would not do, that I do." Despite our best intentions, despite our knowledge that we hold in our hands the key to our partner's hell, we forget, we lapse, we relapse, we're careless and imperfect or just too damn angry. In short, we blow it. We turn the key again. And our partner returns to hell again. And so on, turning and returning, in a long process of learning to not hurt each other anymore. Marriage is that long process of learning to not hurt each other anymore.

We do the best we can. It takes time. Marriage *is* time.

Until finally one day we fulfill the trust invisibly conferred on us at our wedding ceremony. We refrain from turning the key to our partner's emotional hell. We become the keepers of each other's keys, and we keep them instead of turning them.

THE KNOTS IN THE BOARDS

Endure rough surfaces that smooth you.
> —Jalaluddin Rumi,
> "The Lost Camel"

Close relationships between family members, friends, roommates, colleagues, coworkers, and especially romantic partners are like two boards put side by side on a machine. They slowly rub back and forth, back and forth, creating a friction that, in time, wears down the rough places on each board until they fit together. It's a kind of cosmic carpentry.

Hitting the knots is the hard part. The knots are those hard spots in our personalities where we're scared, angry, defended, disrespectful, judgmental, self-centered, and ignorant. The constant friction of the machine of the relationship wears them down. The knots are often hidden in the boards, so we come upon them suddenly. And because the cosmic Carpenter is also a bit of a Jokester, we often hit two knots simultaneously, one in each board. Then the two knots rub against each other with such intense friction that both people start to burn up.

One of these knots is jealousy. But a deeper and a kinder name for jealousy is fear—fear of losing your partner to someone else. Most of us have it. Another knot is misunderstanding. Rose and Valerie had hit these very knots.

A lesbian couple in their late thirties, Rose and Valerie had come into therapy because, after three peaceful and happy years of marriage, they suddenly found themselves arguing with each other, sometimes loudly and abusively, almost every day. This had been precipitated four months before by the arrival in town of one of Rose's old lovers, Joan. Rose and Valerie's discussions about Joan would inevitably turn into arguments and then fights, and now, four months later, separation loomed.

"We used to love each other," Valerie explained. "We've been as happy as clams for three solid years. Now it feels like the relationship from hell. This is getting scary. What's happening?"

☽ ☽ ☽

The problem, I explained, was knots in the boards. Valerie's board had the knot of jealousy, while Rose's had that of misunderstanding.

Jealousy, which is a disguised form of feeling badly about ourselves, is a deep dishonoring of ourselves, a form, actually, of self-hatred. Like all forms of self-hatred on our journey of self knowledge, jealousy must eventually go and be replaced with feeling so good about ourselves that the idea that our partner could find someone better than us is preposterous. On the other hand, thinking that you can maintain *any* kind of relationship with a former lover while your marriage partner is burning with jealousy and fear is misunderstanding the dharma—the duty—of marriage. It is a violation of the *hortus conclusus,* the walled garden, that a marriage should be. It is an attenuated form of infidelity. As a form of infidelity, it is a form of cruelty.

We must all get to know our own knots as well as those in the boards of the people we love. And remember: As the knots rub, both of you burn. Sometimes in relationships there's nothing else to do but burn. The burning hurts, but it hurts a little less if, while you're burning, you remember that the knots are burning too. Over time, the surface of your board gets smoother and smoother against that of your partner.[5]

EVERYBODY'S A DAMN HERO!

Hero: (hê'rō), n. a person of distinguished valor or fortitude, sometimes honored . . .

—Merriam Webster's Collegiate Dictionary

Kevin, forty-two, a regional administrator of a hotel chain, and Charlotte, thirty-eight, a homemaker and the caretaker of their four children, had been married for eighteen years. Both had had very difficult, traumatic childhoods: Kevin had grown up with two alcoholic parents, Charlotte with an untreated manic-depressive mother and a philandering father. Both had lives with tremendous stress and very little rest. Kevin was working eleven hours a day and often traveling up and down the eastern seaboard overseeing his hotels, and Charlotte tirelessly cared for their children and their house. And both of them were very angry with the other for eighteen years of conflicts and unresolved hurts, and for the other's inability to be sympathetic and supportive.

This particular session was turning out like so many of their sessions. Both of them were glaring at each other, arguing about an incident that had happened during the week, and the argument kept getting bigger, more intense, and so convoluted it was getting hard to follow.

When I realized I had totally lost control of the session, as I frequently did with them, I made the only intervention I know how to make at such times. I yelled, "STOP!" They both looked at me in the sudden silence.

"There is absolutely no way out of your marital problems by doing and saying the things you're doing and saying," I told them. "You can't get out if you see each other as villains, adversaries, or enemies. You can only get out if you see each other as heroes."

"Look at her, Kevin," I said. "Really *see* her. See the little girl who was never allowed to be little because her emotionally disturbed mother could not take care of her. Picture a little girl sitting silently on the couch, hiding a seething rage because her mother is talking a blue streak of megalomania at her and not even caring about or even *noticing* Charlotte's silent anger. See *that* scene over and over and you'll start to see Charlotte. Picture her father in her bedroom tucking her in and telling her confidentially and proudly of his latest sexual exploits with his secretary. Replay that scene a hundred times, as it was replayed in Charlotte's life. See Charlotte in the backseat of a Ford Falcon, trying unsuccessfully to fend off the attack from her high school boyfriend. See the terror and fury on her face. See her manage to get through all of that and arrive emotionally intact enough at the age of twenty to marry you. And now see her for the past eighteen years chasing four kids around a house, being cook, waitress, maid, nurse, chauffeur, teacher, doctor, adviser, policewoman, psychologist, and referee to them all, sacrificing her time, energy, youth, and life to the raising of your children. Visualize all of that, and then look at the woman sitting across from you, the tension in her jaw, the frown in her mouth, the blear of fatigue in her eyes. Do you see her, Kevin? Do you *see* her? Do you see the hero in her?"

Then I turned to Charlotte.

"And do you see Kevin, Charlotte? Look. See the bags under his eyes, the tic in his cheek. See the slump in his frame, the pallor of his skin. That's exhaustion from getting up at five o'clock every morning for the past eighteen years to go to work to make enough money to support the six of you. That's not easy. Picture him in his office dealing with all he has to deal with every day, problems he doesn't even want to be dealing with because he doesn't want to be doing the work that he's doing anymore but he has to because he has to provide for his family. See him coming home exhausted from work at seven or eight in the evening, saying good night to the kids, and then sitting alone at the dining room table eating, often falling asleep with his head on his chest, his fork in his hand. *See* him there. And now see him as a boy coming home from school and trying to tiptoe past his mother passed out on the couch to get to his bedroom to do his homework, because if she wakes up while he's still in the living room, she'll scream at him and throw beer cans at him. Replay that scene in your mind a few thousand times and you'll start to see Kevin. And now see his father come home, not after work but after the bars, coming home long past when Kevin was asleep for the night, and then leaving the next morning for work before Kevin woke up. Peer inside Kevin now and see what it took for that man to get through all that and somehow manage to get to college and then to business school to get to where he is today. Do you see him, Charlotte? Do you *see* him?"

They were both silent.

"He's a hero, Charlotte. He's a damn hero. And so are you. With everything you've both had to deal with in your lives, you're both heroes, and the only way you two will solve your marital problems is to see each other as heroes and begin treating each other with the respect due heroes."

☽ ☽ ☽

It's so easy for us to forget the past and present hurts that cause suffering in those we love, and the strength and courage they've needed to deal with it all. What we have to remember every day, every time we look into our loved ones' eyes, is that they are heroes—and so are we.

Everybody's a damn hero! If we only knew everything everybody has been through in their lives, our judgment of anybody, even the most bizarre person muttering curses to us as we pass him on the sidewalk, would come to a screeching halt. We're all heroes. And heroes don't judge and bicker and fight with each other. Instead, they recognize each other's heroism, and look for greater and greater ways to honor each other.

A QUESTION OF BOUNDARIES

Let me tell you what the boundaries are.
> —Chuang-Tzu

Back off!
> —Yosemite Sam

It's hard for many of us, especially those whose healthy boundaries have been violated time and again since childhood, to make a stand and insist that our boundaries—our right to choose the level of physical closeness and emotional intimacy *we* want in a relationship—be respected by other people. That was the issue Anita wanted to address in our session.

Anita was a twenty-one-year-old hairdresser who, since early adolescence, had had a series of romantic relationships with boys in which they had been sexually coercive with her, including the time her high school boyfriend tried to rape her one night on a golf course. She had been dating Kenny for about a month. She told me that she really liked him because "deep down inside he had a heart of gold" and that they were both beginning to get serious about the relationship, but that Kenny sometimes did and said things that made her feel uncomfortable. I asked her to describe some of those things. Without hesitation, she launched into a list of his behaviors that were troubling her.

"He talks about his old girlfriends all the time, which I wouldn't mind so much, except he keeps comparing me to them, especially with his last girlfriend, Chrissie, who I hate. He's always looking at other women. He's always trying to go farther sexually than I want to go, like touching my thigh or breast. He keeps saying he can see himself married to me, which pisses me off. He's always making little sexual jokes, the way guys do, which also pisses me off. Last Friday he tried to get me drunk so I'd have sex with him. And he keeps wanting to know more about what those other guys did to me, and then, after I tell him, he asks me did that *really* happen or am I exaggerating it, which makes me furious. Things like that."

"This is a question of boundaries," I said. "Survivors of any kind of abuse, but particularly sexual abuse, have had their boundaries severely violated and sometimes almost totally destroyed when they were young, like fences with most of the sections removed. In their adult lives they have to take on the project of rebuilding their fences, reconstructing and maintaining their boundaries in all their relationships."

"I have lousy boundaries," she said.

"No, you have *good* boundaries," I said, "because you at least know what pisses you off. That's a way of knowing when your boundaries have been violated: when you get pissed off. What you're not yet good at is telling other people what your boundaries are, and insisting that they respect them."

Anita needed to learn that it was okay to state her boundaries, without apologies or long explanations. I could hear her saying something like this to Kenny:

"I like you, Kenny, and I really am interested in pursuing this relationship with you, and if you want to pursue this relationship with me, you need to know what's not okay for you to do and say in my company—what my boundaries are.

"My boundaries are important to me because, as I've told you, I've had to deal with a lot of crap from guys. For me to recover from all that abuse, I have to reestablish my boundaries in my adult relationships, particularly with men. I'm sure you can understand that.

"Here are some of my boundaries, Kenny.

"At this point in our relationship, it is okay for you to talk about your past girlfriends in my presence, but it is not okay to compare me to them. It is not okay to talk about Chrissie in my presence, except extremely negatively. It's not okay to ogle other women when you're with me, and I call 'ogling' any double take you do on any woman for any reason. It is okay to stroke my hair whenever you want, but it's not okay to put your hand on my thigh or to try to touch my breast without my permission. It is okay to kiss me whenever you want, including on the lips, but it's not okay to stick your tongue in my mouth. It is okay to call me your girlfriend, but it's not okay to say you could see yourself married to me—that's too much too fast. It's not okay to make those stupid male sexual jokes and innuendoes in my presence. It is okay to ask me if I want to talk about my history with guys, but it's not okay for you to start talking about it. It's okay to say, 'What happened?,' but it's not okay to say, 'Did it really happen?' It's okay to offer me a drink, but it's not okay to try to get me drunk—like you were doing last Friday night—so that I'll relax these boundaries. And finally, it's perfectly okay to hold my hand, to put your arm around me, to say that you like me a lot, to say that I'm pretty, and to say that you like me for a lot of reasons having nothing to do with my prettiness.

"Those are the boundaries that come to my mind right now, but there may be more that I think of later. I'll keep you posted. I'll also keep you posted if my boundaries change over time, as I set and reset my fences according to the state of our relationship, the state of my recovery, and my general mental state on a particular day. I know this may drive you crazy and it will certainly keep you on your toes, but that's the way it is with me. If you choose to be in a relationship with me, you have to choose to respect these boundaries, because I don't stay in relationships where they're not respected.

"You have the right to set and reset your boundaries with me also. If there's ever anything I say or do to you that's not okay with you, tell me. I know that underneath you're really a good guy, and I am seriously interested in having a good relationship with you, maybe even a long relationship with you. That's why I want our boundaries to be clear."

It is our right, always, to open or close the gates to our beings. To whatever degree we think it's not our right, or not possible, or not enforceable to set and reset our boundaries in our relationships, we still have some work to do on our boundaries. Remember: Good and long relationships happen across clear boundaries.

There's No Such Thing as Oversensitive

> *You sometimes have feelings within your marriage that seem alarmingly out of proportion to the events that triggered them.*
> —Harville Hendrix,
> *Getting the Love You Want*

Ray and Anthony were a gay couple in their late forties who had been together for six years and were on the verge of splitting up. Ray was very angry with Anthony for six years of judging and criticizing him, "making me feel that everything I do is wrong." Anthony didn't understand, and was angry.

"I just give my opinion. What? I can't have an opinion?"

"Your opinion is always critical," said Ray.

"It's just my *opinion*. I have a right to my *opinion*. You're so oversensitive!"

Ray looked defeated. He turned to me.

"Am I oversensitive?" he asked. "He's always calling me 'oversensitive.' I never know what to say back to that."

"Say this," I said. "*There's no such thing as oversensitive.*"

☽ ☽ ☽

The expressions "too sensitive," "hypersensitive," and "oversensitive" are used by people who hurt other people and don't want the other people to say, feel, or even notice that they're being hurt. The hidden message of these terms is that there's something wrong with you for feeling hurt when I hurt you.

Ray is not oversensitive. He's as sensitive as he is, and if he's more sensitive than he has seemed to be in the past, it's because he has more self-respect now. He has grown, and now he can recognize when he's feeling hurt.

We all have a right to our opinion, but Anthony needed to understand that while what comes out of his mouth may seem like mere opinion to him, it may seem to Ray a massive castigation and condemnation of him even if it's just a little critical. A little criticism from Anthony is like a small gear that drives a huge gear inside Ray. That big gear was installed many years ago—in Ray's case by his father's relentless verbal attacks on him. We all have such gears inside us, gears that are easily set in motion by another's words. It's just that some people, like Ray, have more of these gears—or bigger ones—than other people do.

We human beings don't always accurately reflect what's happening outside us, we sometimes refract it through the denser-than-air medium of our own past pain. That's why a seemingly little thing can look like a really big thing to us. This happens in Ray with almost anything that's said to him that falls short of "You're totally perfect, Ray!" That's dear old dad's doing. How easy it is to forget the power of the past, to overlook the way our partner is set up internally, which causes him to react so strongly to our criticism.

This is what they call PTSD—post-traumatic stress disorder. Combat veterans often have it. Because of the severity of the trauma they have lived through in combat, their reactions to certain experiences can sometimes seem like "overreactions." They can react to a cap pistol going off behind them with the same intensity of emotion and responsive action as they reacted to the trauma of incoming shells exploding around them. No one scolds or ridicules them for their "oversensitivity" because we understand that they are not overreacting. Coming from an abusive background makes Ray, like so many people, a combat veteran experiencing his own form of PTSD. On some level, we all have PTSD.

In couples therapy I try to help couples help each other come out of their own private PTSD into the present relationship, where, for many couples, there is significantly less pain and danger than there was in the past. The quickest way I know to get the reactions from the past cleared out of a relationship is for each partner in the relationship to stop judging and stigmatizing the other as "oversensitive" or "overreactive."

As soon as the thought "He or she is being oversensitive" enters our brain, we need to stop. We need to flip that thought upside down and think of ourselves as needing to be more sensitive—more sensitive to how our partner will experience our opinion. Remember the source of her sensitivity. We can also go on an "opinion fast." For a set length of time—say, two weeks—we can choose not to share any of our opinions with our partner. This is a good time to work on the compulsion to be always having and sharing opinions. Then again, if at any moment it's your opinion that your partner is totally perfect and surpassingly wonderful, break the silence and share *that* opinion with him, but keep all your other opinions to yourself. In this way, the wounds in the soul of our partner can begin to heal at the same time we are increasing our own sensitivity. It is our sensitivity to our partner's sensitivities that helps to eventually remove the inner gears that were installed in them so long ago.

THE MIDDLE WAY

*In a successful marriage, there is no such thing as one's way. There is
only the way of both, only the bumpy, dusty, difficult, but always mutual
path!*

—Phyllis McGinley

According to legend, Gautama Siddhartha, the Buddha, was meditating
one day under the bodhi tree, trying to find the way to supreme inner
happiness and peace. A group of musicians came walking along tuning
their stringed instruments. When they tuned the strings too tightly, the
Buddha heard that the notes were sharp. When the musicians tuned the
strings too loosely, the Buddha heard that the notes were flat. It was only
when the musicians tuned the strings neither too tightly nor too loosely
but right in the middle that the notes sounded right. According to legend, that was the moment the Buddha saw that the way to attain
supreme inner happiness and peace was the "middle way."

The middle way is the place of balance between two ways that are off
balance. Some of us are off balance in one direction, others of us are off
balance in the opposite direction, and our job in every aspect of our life,
including in our primary relationships, is to come to balance from the
direction we're off in.

There is no single prescription for all of us. The direction we must
travel depends upon where we are. Some people, for example, are off in
the direction of not having enough discipline, which usually makes
them lazy and torpid, while others are off in the direction of having too
much discipline, which usually makes them self-righteous and rigid.
Some people talk too much, some people talk too little. There are many
ways to be off.

Nelson, the owner of a small publishing house, and Tim, a waiter,
had been living together for four years. A major issue between them,
and the primary reason they had come into therapy, was that Nelson
lived by the work ethic and Tim did not. Nelson worked ten to twelve
hours a day, including some Saturdays, leaving little or no time for
relaxation and recreation with Tim. Tim didn't like his work, and did as
little of it as he could, preferring to sun himself in the backyard or

"party." They pathologized each other, Tim calling Nelson "an anal-retentive workaholic," and Nelson calling Tim "the good-for-nothing playboy of the western world." They endlessly argued back and forth about this conflict in lifestyles.

During one of their arguments, I told them they were wasting their breath by talking in this polarized, emotional way. If they wanted to talk intelligently about their differences, they would have to realize that both of them were "off" in opposite directions. Nelson, filled with anxiety and not knowing what else to do with himself, worked compulsively, and needed to learn to work less and play more. Tim, never having found any work he truly wanted to do in life, avoided work as much as possible, had built up a whole specious philosophy against it, and played too much.

The way out of their impasse was for both of them to think of their relationship as a teaching that each was bringing the other: Nelson was teaching Tim the importance of responsibility and moderation, and Tim was teaching Nelson the importance of relaxation and moderation. Their connection was no accident. They had come into a relationship with each other because they each had a great gift for the other.

All they had to do was find the middle way—work and play in moderation for both. The middle way is the way of moderation in all things. When you are a couple, the middle way is found by listening respectfully to your partner's teachings to you—when those teachings are offered respectfully—and then changing according to those teachings.

HELP WANTED

I know some good marriages—marriages where both people are just trying to get through their days by helping each other, being good to each other.

—Erica Jong

Leslie had been sick all week with the flu, spending most of her time in bed. She was angry with her husband, Dov, for not attending to her enough.

Dov was defensive and angry. "Every time you asked me for something, I was there with it. You name it: medicine, food, tea, massage, magazines, I was *there*, and I resent you for saying I wasn't."

"I'm not saying you weren't there, Dov. You *were* there, with everything I asked for. I'm just saying"—she paused for a long moment, thinking—"I don't know what I'm saying."

She sat in silence pondering, and then shrugged her shoulders. "I don't know what I'm saying. Forget it."

"Can I try to say what I think you're saying?" I asked her.

"Go ahead," she said.

⊃ ⊃ ⊂

Marriage is primarily a place to give help to each other. Far too many of us did not have our childhood needs for nurturing adequately met, and so our ability to feel we deserve help and to ask for it has been damaged. How can we heal the hurts that are so deeply embedded in our hearts? Our partners can help us—on three different levels.

The first level is when you know you need help from your spouse in the forms of tending, caretaking, assistance, or support, and you ask for it, and your spouse provides it. Leslie is lying in bed, weak with the flu, feeling hot and dry and thirsty, and asks Dov to bring her some juice, which he does willingly. At the same time that he's helping her by bringing her juice, he's assisting her in another way as well: He is helping to repair her damaged ability to feel she truly deserves help. This is good, but there is a deeper hurt that this level of loving behavior cannot reach. We all have a part of us that thinks, "I'm a bother and a pest and my provider of help is just grudgingly giving it and really hates me for imposing my needy, disgusting self on him." This part of us is not touched by this first level of help. This is why Leslie, even after a whole week of being nurtured and cared for by Dov on this level, ends up, in some part of her being, still feeling unhelped.

The second level of help is when the provider, voluntarily and without being asked, comes to the one who needs help and asks, "What can I do for you?" When we hear a voluntary offering of help from a person who seems to care about us, something spontaneously relaxes deep inside us, and in that relaxation deep inner repair happens. We begin to believe we're not annoying and disgusting for wanting and needing help, and that this person must therefore really care about us.

The third level of help is when the provider of help, without being asked, voluntarily comes to the one who needs help, but this time doesn't ask, "What can I do for you?" because he already knows what she needs. He simply brings it to her: He shows up in the bedroom in the early morning with tea and toast and a newspaper. He comes back later in the morning, sits on the edge of the bed, and says, "Hi, honey! I'm here to keep you company." Later he comes into her room, unasked and unannounced, and gives her a back massage as she drifts off to sleep. Each time what he gives her is exactly what she needs at the time, and he knows all that because he knows her completely, loves her truly, and took the time to tune in to her accurately. This unannounced, voluntary help is the deepest level of help. It repairs even her deepest emotional damage because it brings her the message we all wanted to hear from our parents: "I care about you, and I am here, in this world, to care *for* you. I know you, and I know that sometimes you need help. I even know, sometimes without your saying a word, the precise help that you need and I am here with that help right now!"

When we deliver that message to our spouse, we become what all marriage partners are supposed to be—true helpmates. And always, underneath whatever level of help we're providing for our partners, we're helping them move along their journey toward feeling the one thing that so many of us have such a hard time feeling—that we're deserving of care and worthy of love.

The Seeing of the Seventy Faces

*I take thee to my wedded spouse, to have and to hold, from this day
forward, for better for worse, for richer for poorer, in sickness and in
health, to love and to cherish, till death do us part.*
—"Solemnization of Matrimony,"
Book of Common Prayer

In the Jewish wedding ritual called The Seeing of the Seventy Faces, a
couple experiences what it is like to recognize all the many faces—or
facets—of their partner and to love them all, something we all need to
do in our relationships. It's easy to love our partner's favorite faces, but
often we look away when another face is presented to us, one that we
fear, or find fault with, or resent, or scorn. But if we are to spend our
lives together, we must see all seventy (in Jewish mysticism, seventy
means "many" or "infinite") faces of our partner, and love them all.

In this ritual, the rabbi asks the prospective bride and groom to sit
gazing at each other in front of the congregation, and to silently look at
each other's face and see the seventy faces there. They see the face of
happiness and the face of sadness in the other; the face of faith and the
face of fear; the young and the old face; the warm and the cold face; the
worried, wounded, withdrawn, angry, jealous, joyful, peaceful, crying,
laughing, ailing, aging, and dying face—and for each face they see, they
silently, in their heart, vow to marry it. While they are seeing the seventy
faces, they are saying something like this in their heart:

> "There is nothing hidden that is not revealed, nothing in you I
> do not see, nothing of you I do not wed. I see all of who you are
> and may be during our lives together, and I marry it all. I see you
> in sickness and in health, for better or for worse. I see the light in
> you and the darkness in you and the love in your heart and the
> hurt in your heart, and I install it all in the temple of my heart.
>
> "Looking at you at this moment, I see the face of your beautiful
> heart and the face of your broken heart, and I commit myself to
> realize and remember that your broken heart is your beautiful
> heart, and I marry that heart.

"I see you, all of you. And I marry all of you. As God and this gathering of our family and friends are my witnesses, I see every single face of every single you who dwells inside you and I choose to marry you."

Their families and friends witness, and bless them. Often the married couples in the congregation, and those planning or considering marriage, are asked to turn to each other during this time and participate in this ritual as well. Those who are single are asked to close their eyes and see inside themselves the seventy faces they have, and for each face seen to welcome and embrace it, loving all the different selves within their self.

Look inside your partner. See everything there is to be seen. Then love it all, and marry it all.

The Meditation of Marriage

There is no more lovely, friendly, and charming relationship, communion,
or company than a good marriage.
—Martin Luther

In meditation you direct the flow of your awareness toward a chosen object such as your breath. You *watch* your breath. That peaceful watching is meditation.

Marriage too is a kind of meditation. In marriage your awareness flows toward a chosen object—in this case, your spouse. In the meditation of marriage, you watch your spouse being who he or she is. You watch the never-ending stream of events that happen to her in her life, and you watch her reactions and responses to those events. You watch the lifelong succession of feelings in your spouse. You watch the slow-motion film of changes in his body as it matures, ages, and decays. You listen to her words as she tries daily to describe and share the blessings and burdens of her life. You are privy to, as no one else is privy to, all the fluctuations of mind and mood constantly taking place within him, and you watch those too. You watch everything. You watch her as the wheel of thoughts and feelings revolves slowly around her weeks and years, and you watch him periodically go crazy in the ways that he is so gifted at going crazy. You watch the outer life and the inner life of your spouse and the constant interplay between the two. You watch it all. It is your labor of love to watch it.

What else can either of you do but sit and watch and listen as the other lives his life and has his feelings about his life? What else *is* there to do? What else is a marriage but the willingness and the ability to sit in compassionate, peaceful meditation on another human being as that person lives out her life before your eyes?

What else is love?

SEXUAL WRECKAGE

We do not go to bed in single pairs; even if we choose not to refer to them, we still drag there with us . . . our social class, our parents' lives . . . our sexual and emotional expectations, our whole biographies.
 —Angela Carter, *The Sadeian Woman*

Most couples who have come to see me in the past twenty-two years have had sexual problems. Usually the man thinks there's something wrong with the woman's sexuality, and the woman thinks there's something wrong with the man's sexuality. Usually they're both right. Whatever they think of each other's sexuality, in most cases the couple ends up having little or no, or just plain *bad*, sex.

"We haven't had sex in a month," they say.

"We haven't had sex in three months," they say.

"We haven't had sex in a year," they say.

"Our sex is so mechanical and boring, it's hardly worth it," they say.

"What's wrong with us?" they ask.

"More than you probably want to know about," I say.

To understand the sexual problems faced by every couple in our culture, we must first understand that every one of us, by being a member of this culture and having floated across the sea of its sexuality for so many years, is a piece of sexual wreckage. Men are one kind of sexual wreckage and women are another, but we're all sexually wrecked. We're all victims and only partial survivors of a culture that is saturated with the sexual distress of all the generations before us.

The essential sexual distress of our culture is the fact that it is totally, maniacally obsessed with sex, and terrified and ashamed of it at the same time. Trying to stay afloat in the cross-pummeling of those waves has driven most of us pretty insane about sex. I have never met anyone who wasn't, in one way or another, pretty insane about sex. I have never met anyone who made it across those seas unwrecked.

Sometimes two sexually wrecked beings accidentally bump into each other on a wave in those seas, and they wash up on the shore of marriage together. They try their best to make their sexuality work in the marriage, and sometimes it does, even very well, for a while, like maybe for the honeymoon. But after a while it doesn't work and stops being exciting and fun, and for some couples, it just stops, period. There is a lot of pain on the way to its stopping, and there is more pain, a different pain, after it stops. If the two people in the marriage are lazy, they'll let the sexual pain go on for so long that they'll settle dejectedly into a dreary sex life or none at all; or they'll bring their sexuality outside the marriage into extramarital affairs, which wreaks havoc in the marriage, the children, and everywhere else in the universe; or they'll end the marriage. If the two people are smart and have some gumption, they'll seek help with their sexual problems.

To overcome their pain, the first thing a couple must do is admit that they are both pieces of sexual wreckage. Then they must learn about their own and their partner's sexual damage, and then fix it, using the marriage relationship as it should be used—for patient and loving repair of all forms of human wreckage, including sexual wreckage.

To that end, when the two of you close the bedroom door and slip into bed for sex, stay in more than physical touch with each other. Stay in emotional and verbal touch, from time to time talking about what's going on for you during sex: How does that feel? . . . Do you like to be touched here? . . . What are you experiencing? . . . Are you scared, or sad, or shy right now? . . . Should we stop for a while? . . . I'd like you to do this now, but gently, and very, very slowly. . . . May I share my fantasy with you? . . . Is this okay? . . . Say something sexy. . . . Are you okay? . . . Hold me now, just hold me tight. . . . Say something sweet. . . . Can we rest now? Let's just lie here and rest now. . . . And so on . . .

When the two of you close the bedroom door and slip into bed for sex, have the time of your lives with each other, if you can, but when you can't, remember that both of you are bringing into that bed everything that ever happened to you in your lives, and not only your bodies but your hearts and souls are naked too.

THE ESSENCE OF MALE SEXUALITY

Then with a quiver of exquisite pleasure he touched the warm soft body. . . .
And he had to come into her at once, to enter the peace on earth of her soft-
quiescent body. It was the moment of pure peace for him, the entry into the
body of a woman.

—D. H. Lawrence,
Lady Chatterley's Lover

Dolph, a handsome, virile-looking thirty-nine-year-old lawyer, had slept with many women. He wanted to settle down with one woman in marriage and start a family, but he couldn't imagine "letting go of all the great sex" he had always gotten as a bachelor, or being faithful to one woman for the rest of his life.

"You don't have to let go of anything," I said. "You just have to understand the essence of your sexual drive—what you're trying to *get* through sexuality—and then get *that* with one woman in a marriage for the rest of your life."

"What I'm trying to get through my sexuality is *laid,* Robert."

"Getting laid is *how* you're trying to get this other thing that you're trying to get."

"And what would that be?"

"That would be softness. That would be stillness. That would be an experience of your own inner Self."

☾ ☾ ☾

Males search sexually for females because they're searching for softness. Think for a second about the physical characteristics of women that men typically find sexual: lips, thighs, breasts—they are all soft, curved, pliable.

Behind all the sexual attraction, flirtation, manipulation, seduction, and intrigue, behind the immense amount of time, energy, thought, and money that goes into the whole megillah[6] of male sexual pursuit and pleasure, men are primarily looking for the soft parts of a woman's body. To a man's eye, a woman's body is an exquisitely arranged collage of soft parts. To experience all that softness is the essence of male heterosexuality.

That's the softness that you knew, or should have known, in your mother's womb and at your mother's breast. That's the archetypal softness that you knew, or should have known, when you felt most welcomed and nurtured and loved by her, therefore most quiet and calm and restful inside yourself. That's the archetype of softness you feel—and are—in your own deepest nature. The softness that men are looking for in women is actually an aspect of their own deepest nature. Unfortunately, men have been pressured to forsake and even forget their own softness, replacing it with physical and emotional hardness in the service of power, competition, conflict, conquest, and domination. So here we men are, deprived of the connection to our own deepest, softest selves, and projecting it like crazy on women, running all over the planet doing manipulative and sometimes unconscionable things to women—all because we are missing a major part of ourselves.

The essence of male sexuality is not sexual or physical but emotional and spiritual. His sexuality is his desire for an experience of his spiritual Self, and his awed entry into the enfolding and nestlike softness of a woman's body leads down into the quietude and stillness of his own inner Self. It is far easier to experience this with one woman in a monogamous marriage over the course of a lifetime than with a series of many women over the course of a weekend, because the woman in the marriage, if it's a wonderful marriage with a good and faithful man, will grace that man with all her many favors, including all the softness and stillness and solace of her vast sexuality.

For men who are trying to stop their sexual nonsense and settle down into monogamous sexuality, it is good to know that your essential sexuality is really a search for a lost aspect of your own being, for your deepest being. You can most successfully conduct that search in the company of, and in the sexual embrace of, one woman for the rest of your life.

EIGHT DAYS A WEEK:
TOWARD GREAT SEX IN MARRIAGE

He has sprouted; he has burgeoned;
He is lettuce planted by the water.
He is the one my womb loves best. . . .
My eager impetuous caresser of the navel,
My caresser of the soft thighs.
He is the one my womb loves best.

—Inanna,
Inanna: Queen of Heaven and Earth

I am athirst for thy beauty; I am hungry for thy body; and neither wine
nor grapes can appease my desire.

—Oscar Wilde, *Salomé*

Many marriages suffer because the partners are not having good sex in them, especially after a few years. It's often dull, predictable, and unfulfilling sex, leaving both partners less and less interested in sex—at least with each other—and in some marriages the sex has dwindled to a peck on the cheek at night before they both pick up their books. The partners' decreased interest in sex, and the ever-decreasing frequency of sex, are widely thought to be inherent in marriage, and our culture is rife with not-tonight-I-have-a-headache jokes about that. But the decay and eventual demise of sex is *not* inherent in marriage. It happens because the partners don't understand and therefore don't practice good sex. What is good sex? I think that good sex is eight energies. It is procreation; it is play; it is gift; it is sanctuary; it is connection, it is lust; it is love; and it is worship.

SEX AS PROCREATION

And God blessed them, and God said unto them, Be fruitful, and multiply.
—Genesis 1:28

God loves life, and wants His luxuriant earthly garden teeming with life, including human life. So God gave us sex, and the exquisite ecstatic pleasures of sex, to get us all into our bedrooms busily and blissfully having sex and producing more and more life. If procreation is your purpose, God has made it your pleasure, so enjoy!

SEX AS PLAY

We are seas mingling, we are two of those cheerful waves rolling over each other . . .

—Walt Whitman, "We Two, How
Long We Were Fool'd"

Let's face it, sex is *fun*. Two people close their bedroom door and start talking and joking and hugging and kissing, and spend the next couple of hours having the time of their lives with each other. They fool around. They play. They take off all their clothes and roll around the room doing spontaneous, impulsive, frolicsome, and frisky things with each other. Like play, it feels good. Good sex is two people who really like each other playing with each other.

SEX AS GIFT

When I get that feeling, I want sexual healing.
Oh baby, makes me feel so fine,
Helps to relieve my mind.

—Marvin Gaye, "Sexual Healing"

Two people kiss good-bye in the morning and go out into the world and then later come home from that world, bringing with them some or all of the things they met up with out there, like agitation, anxiety, anger, sadness, and sexual yearning. There's a build-up of energy inside them that feels uncomfortable and needs to be released. Within a marriage, good sex allows each partner to help the other let loose the energies that have built up inside. The hugging and holding, the sounds we bring forth from deep within, and our body movements are all powerful releases of energy, as, of course, is the orgasm. If it's been really good sex, the energy continues being released after the experience, in the restful afterglow of sex, in the flushed cheeks and the tingling of the nerves, and in the continuing affection between the couple. This kind of sex can be long or short, one way or two, depending on the time, the need, and the kids. It is something the partners like doing for each other; it's a gift they give each other.

Sex as Sanctuary

Sexual experience provides a deep immersion in body contact. This body-to-body meeting . . . leaves both partners feeling literally swaddled in physical warmth. For a few moments at least, we are able to return to some of the primitive sense of nurturance which we experienced as infants.
—Augustus Y. Napier,
The Fragile Bond

Sex returns us to the time of care, comfort, and safety, when we were infants lying next to our mother's body. . . . The room is dark and warm. The other body is dark and warm. You turn your body to that other body. The flesh smells sweet, like musk, and faintly burning. You flow out toward it, all your limbs relaxing. You settle deeply in, folding fetal and eyeless into the flesh of the other body, your body becoming smaller and smaller, your mind calmer. Like an infant, you have found peace and quiet in the closeness with another body, and you settle in deeper. . . . You breathe in deeply . . . a small shudder on your out-breath. . . . Sanctuary. . . . Soon, you sleep.

Sex as Connection

Sex? What is sex, you say?
My dear, what isn't?
—Lady Stafford

In a true marriage where there is true connection between the partners, the sexual relationship is connected to all the other parts of the relationship. The hug in the morning, the phone call or E-mail in the afternoon, the conversation at dinner, the walk in the evening—the warm smiles, looks, words, touches, and kindnesses—the warm hearts that radiate between you during the day ignite the hot sex that burns between you at night. In a true marriage, the whole relationship is a long rolling wave of human connection that frequently rises into spectacular erotic connection. In such a marriage, everything you do with each other, everything you say to each other, on one level, is a form of foreplay.

SEX AS LUST

I'm so excited!
And I just can't hide it!
I'm about to lose control
And I think I like it!

—The Pointer Sisters,
"I'm So Excited"

There's a certain raw and primitive energy in us that is totally of the body and drives us to have sex with another body. There's a carnal appetite in us, a dark, focused, fixed hunger, something ancient and primal and animal and deep. You can see it in the rapt face and the lit and febrile eyes that stare out at you from the darkness, desiring knowledge of you. Being engulfed in that energy can be a little frightening. All the controls come off and out pour looks and words and doings and imaginings and a Möbius strip of two bodies gliding and sliding over each other that is a wonder to behold. The power of it makes it a little embarrassing to speak of afterward as you're eating cookies in the kitchen, thinking, "What the hell was *THAT*?!" It was lust, a kind of confession partners make to each other in the dark cave of their desire, in the smolder in their eyes, in their bedrooms. In a good marriage where there's good sex, there's a lot of lust.

SEX AS LOVE

The warm bodies
shine together
in the darkness,
the hand moves
to the center
of the flesh,
the skin trembles
in happiness
and the soul comes
joyful to the eye.

—Allen Ginsberg, "Song"

There are many forms of love and connection on this earth. Married love is one of those forms—when you love somebody so much that you want to be with them for the rest of your life, with their minds, with their hearts, with their spirits, with their bodies. In good married sex, the two bodies who very much want to be with each other *are* with each other, giving and receiving sweet pleasure with each other, for a whole lifetime, exclusively, in the most intimate way that human bodies can be with each other on this earth. If the marriage is good, and the love and the connection deep, then the intimacy deepens over the lifetime of the marriage, the desire to give pleasure grows and grows, and the sex keeps getting lovelier and lovelier.

SEX AS WORSHIP

With this Ring I thee wed,
With my body I thee worship . . .

—"Solemnization of Matrimony,"
Book of Common Prayer

Good sex in marriage is Woman worshiping Man and Man worshiping Woman, simultaneously and eternally. It is the mutual appreciation and interpenetration and adoration of the two primal energies in the universe. When a married man and woman enter their bedroom for sex, they are entering a sacred place, a temple, and what happens there is the ceremony of worship. The man worships the woman of circles and spheres and curves and coils and the woman worships the man of hard muscle and pulse and sinuous and straight lines. There is movement, but it is slow, and, as with all ceremony, there is stillness underneath the movement. It is worship, and adoration, and awe, one energy in the universe genuflecting in a kind of stunned ecstatic silence at the revealed vision of the other energy in the universe. On this level, good sex in marriage is mutual and simultaneous rapture.

☾ ☾ ☾

In a good marriage, on a good night, many of these kinds of sex, and more, happen, and the two of you move from one to the other and back again in this sweet, infinite circling dance of bodies and hearts. It takes commitment and work and patience and love to get to them all, but you can get to them all.

Companions of Consciousness

Milagros, thirty-six, and George, thirty-four, had been married for eleven years. Milagros had brought George into therapy because they were having "communication problems," and she was feeling increasingly isolated and bored with their marriage. As their story came out, I learned that Milagros had been attending workshops about women's issues, and had read some books on meditation, and was beginning to think more deeply about her life journey. George wasn't particularly interested in any of that. When Milagros talked in therapy about her childhood, her womanhood, or her longing to experience God in her life, he looked bewildered and blank.

☽ ☽ ☽

We are living in a time when human consciousness is expanding all over the planet. We are living in the midst of a revolution of human consciousness that is blowing in the wind and blowing into many marriages. It brings change with it, radical and irreversible change in the way people think, feel, and live their lives. If the married couple is fortunate, the expansion of consciousness blows into both of them simultaneously and they start changing and growing together. Their consciousness expands downward into their own personal psychology, finding much darkness down there, ghosts and monsters from the past, and a child with scars on its heart. Each partner greets and befriends that child and introduces him or her to the spouse, who becomes a lifelong companion and healer for it.

During this revolution of consciousness, not only do we expand downward into a knowledge of our personal psychological self, we also expand upward into the realm of our spiritual Self. There are dizzying heights and dazzling lights up there, mystical experiences and epiphanies, and a transcendence of our personal self that is both thrilling to our hearts and threatening to every concept we've ever had about who we are. Up there we are letting go and leaving behind our old self, the bound and burdened one we've been completely identified with since birth, and discovering our identity with *the* Self, with God. If the couple is fortunate, this upward expansion of consciousness also happens in both of them at the same time and they become companions and consorts in the ethereal regions too.

It can be very challenging for a couple when this revolutionary expansion of consciousness happens in one of them and not the other.[7] When that's the case, the partner whose consciousness is expanding into both the lowest and the loftiest places in her being does not have a partner who is there with her in those places and who can talk to her about them or can even understand them. That can lead to a profound loneliness—in *both* partners—that can destabilize or destroy their marriage.

A great marriage is when both partners are taking that upward and downward journey of consciousness *together*, each one understanding and accompanying the other into the depths and heights of the inner world. If you know from personal experience the general lay of the land inside the whole territory of your own being, it is easier to know the territory inside your partner's being, and you can therefore walk with them as they travel through it. That is a great marriage because it is a marriage without loneliness.

If we're already taking the same psychological and spiritual journey as our partner is taking, let's just keep going, side by side. If we're not, if our partner is becoming conscious of herself at levels that we've never been to inside ourselves, let's fix that. Let's get on the bus. Let's begin the inner journey. Let's start to become conscious of what's going on inside ourselves. Let's all start asking questions about what's going on inside our partner. Let's listen attentively, ask more questions, show lots of interest. Let's show serious interest by asking to read some of the books our partner is reading—and then actually *read* them—and maybe even accompany her to workshops and retreats. If need be, let's get into therapy together for the huge mutual expansion of consciousness that's possible in therapy. The journey of consciousness is a long pilgrimage inside ourselves that goes to the peaks of the tallest mountains and into the valleys of the shadow of death, and it's *much* more fun when we have our partner walking right alongside us.

The Divorce

Associations formed on this earth are not necessarily for the duration of the lifespan. Separation takes place constantly, and as long as it takes place lovingly, not only is there no spiritual injury, but spiritual progress may actually be helped.

—Peace Pilgrim,
Peace Pilgrim: Her Life and
Work in Her Own Words

Marion, a fifty-four-year-old bank executive, and her husband, Harvey, fifty-eight, an executive in a large computer company, had been married for thirty-two years. Their three children were grown up with families of their own. Marion and Harvey had come into therapy a year before because for years Marion had been feeling a growing distance and deepening silence between them. Over the past few years Marion had gotten into "alternative" kinds of things like yoga, meditation, and natural foods, while Harvey's interests were business, golf, retirement, and sex (their sexual relationship had been mechanical and uninteresting for years, they both agreed). In our therapy sessions, Marion would talk about her latest meditation experiences while Harvey looked at the pictures on the walls, and Harvey would talk about his business problems or their sexual problems while Marion looked at me for help.

"We've done a year of therapy now, Robert," Marion said, "and nothing seems to be changing. We've just grown apart to the point where I don't think the relationship is viable anymore. We're both so *lonely* in the relationship."

"What do you think, Harvey?" I asked.

"I don't know who she is anymore," he said. "I don't feel I've had a wife for years now. And she's right, the therapy isn't working. We're as far apart as we've ever been, and in some ways, farther. The therapy has seemed to highlight, not reconcile, our differences."

Tears were welling up in Marion's eyes. Harvey looked at her, then looked away. He seemed very sad, stricken. A long silence ensued.

"Do you think it's time for the two of you to move on?" I said.

☽ ☽ ☽

Once the children are grown and gone—and for a thousand other reasons—many couples find themselves in Marion and Harvey's situation: grown apart, disconnected, and thinking about separation. In Marion and Harvey's case, Marion had undergone a certain transformation in herself and in many ways was a new person, not the woman Harvey married. She and Harvey scarcely had anything in common anymore. After a year in therapy trying to find commonality between them, they came to the realization that it wasn't working, and it was probably never going to work. It's sad and scary, but sometimes this parting just happens. Sometimes there's an event, or a series of events, or a betrayal, or an inner transformation in one or both partners, or just the mysterious ending of the cycle of a particular relationship, and the winds of change blow so strong into the marriage that they blow the partners in separate directions and there's no getting back to each other. It becomes clear that they have new and separate paths to travel, and that parting is best for them both.

Of course, I encourage married couples to try as hard as they can not to let this happen. Whenever possible, we should try to preserve a marriage, for it is a sacred relationship that helps hold everything else in the universe in relationship and order.[8] But when it cannot be preserved, sometimes it is best to say good-bye and move on—without rancor or resentment.

Sometimes separation is just meant to happen. It's always sad when it happens, and I think the whole universe winces a little each time it happens—but it happens. When, after a long time of trying to reconnect, we come to the realization that we need to let go, we must let go and let our partner walk down a different path, the wind at her back, the sun on his face. We say "farewell," and we mean it. We mean it as a blessing: "Fare thee well."

CAN WE TALK?
THE ART OF MARITAL CONVERSATION

Then we talk'd—oh, how we talk'd!

> —Elizabeth Barrett Browning,
> "Lady Geraldine's Courtship"

In an ideal marriage, there are no major communication problems. Talking and sharing feelings and ideas and dreams is pleasant, relaxed, frequent, and looked forward to. But in the real world, most couples have communication problems—big time. At first they may ignore them, or dismiss them, but such problems usually persist and worsen over time until the couple gets inured to the unpleasant communication patterns and they mutter, yell, or snap at each other for the rest of their lives, or they stop communicating altogether and slip into that dense and downcast silence that you see in so many marriages. When this happens, all the other forms of marital communication and "conversation"— spending time with each other, having fun with each other, making love with each other, making a life with each other—tend to gradually disappear. Slowly, the marriage begins to dry up, and many times it withers away.

How do we rescue ourselves from this slow death of communication? Start with the assumption that the talking doesn't work in your marriage—that it's broken. In some marriages, the talking is so broken that—in the same way that a cast must be temporarily put around a broken limb to hold the bone in place while it heals—a *form*, or format, like a script, must be temporarily put around the marital conversation to hold it in place while it heals.

The best form I've ever come across to repair broken marital conversation is Harville Hendrix's "couples dialogue." In this exercise, both partners voluntarily agree to follow a script in which they truly listen to what the other is saying while suppressing all their negative reactions to it, and they understand, validate, respect, and empathize with the thoughts, concerns, and feelings of the other. During the winter that Jane and I were doing the major repair work on our talking, we used Hendrix's couples dialogue, as needed, until over time the emotional and behavioral disciplines and the empathic spirit of the couples dialogue seeped into our everyday conversations and we didn't need the scripts anymore except for emergencies.[9]

It is always good to remember that most of us adult human beings have lived through childhood experiences that have seriously damaged our ability to speak. As a result, there is, in many of us, a reticence, bordering on an incapacity, to clearly and concisely speak our minds and offer our ideas, honestly and vulnerably share our feelings, relate our outer and inner experiences in life, and ask for what we need and want. Marriage is a place to repair all that. When both partners feel safe to speak to each other, the childhood damage done to their speaking gets repaired, and the marriage turns into one continuous lifelong conversation you're having with your very best friend—interrupted from time to time by having to go to the office or the bathroom.

As partners, we need to make our marriage a safe place in which to talk. To do that, there are certain rules of conversation:

- Give your undivided attention to your partner when she's talking. Without wavering or wandering, turn to her with your body and face, look at her with your eyes, and listen to her with your ears—as if the thing she's saying at that moment is the most interesting and important thing happening in the universe at that moment. What she's saying at that moment *is* the most interesting and important thing happening in the universe at that moment—for *you*. Be still and pay very close attention to it.

- Listen! Learn to truly and interestedly listen. The Chinese verb "to listen" contains the characters signifying "ears," "eyes," "heart," "undivided attention," and "you." *That's* listening. When my wife was growing up and came home from her day out in the world, her father, with great and genuine interest in her life, would ask her to tell him everything she had done that day—"So you left the house? Then what happened? . . . " Then he would sit there, rapt, while she told him every detail. *That's* listening. Interested listening is an action, an energetic force, that reaches deep into your partner like a powerful magnet and draws forth the words that he's never said to anybody. True listening is one of the greatest gifts we can give our partner. On some level, we've all been searching throughout our lives for someone to truly listen to us. In the kind of marriage I'm talking about, that someone turns out to be the person we're living with for the rest of our lives!

- There are certain ways of speaking that are actually part of the act of listening. The greatest one is asking questions of your partner. I don't mean rhetorical or hostile or leading or trick questions, I mean ones that show genuine interest in your partner's feelings and experiences in life; questions that acknowledge that she's a unique human being having her own feelings and experiences in life; questions that sincerely inquire into the meaning of what he's saying; questions that open him up and draw him out; questions with proper question marks at the end of them. Those question marks are hooks that pull your partner's words to you and the two of you closer together.

- Speak in a gentle, relaxed tone of voice with your partner. This will put your partner at ease, and, in turn, he will speak in a gentle, relaxed tone to you. Our tones of voice are sound vibrations that travel to our partner and are returned to us, like echoes, in the tones our partners speak to us in. Do not be impatient, aggressive, argumentative, accusatory, or defensive unless you want to hear your partner talking to you in the same way. Remember: After the first two or three months of marriage, your partner doesn't even hear your words anymore, he's just hearing your tones, reacting to them, and responding in the same tones—so watch those tones.

- When you're trying to make an important point to your partner—to really get her attention so she'll be sure to get your point—do not go on and on. Everybody goes on and on. Most people speak three to ten times the amount of words they need to make their point—usually they've made it about two miles back. When trying to make a point to your partner, look for the first possible stopping place—look for the *period*!—and stop there.

- Stops and pauses are good in marital conversation. They're open spaces that welcome your partner into the conversation. Many of us are very shy and won't come in if we can't easily find a way in. Stops and pauses open a door and lay out a welcome mat for the words of a partner who is reticent or who, for whatever reason, is finding it difficult to speak in that moment. Open that door.

- When your partner is sharing a feeling, hear it, accept it, believe it, remember it, and respond to it. Do not reject, correct, deflect, or neglect his feeling, or in any way deny it; do not try to guide her into feeling a different emotion (for example, the one *you* think she should be feeling!); do not judge him; and do not try to solve her problem when she's trying to express her feelings. Simply tell your partner, "I'm glad you're telling me how you feel."

- When your partner is sharing her experiences with you, you can share experiences of your own that match and mirror hers in order to express your understanding and support of her. Be brief; return to listening to your partner's experiences quickly. If you see or sense that your partner feels interrupted by you sharing your experience— a good clue is if she's glaring at you with folded arms and rapidly tapping her foot while you're talking!—immediately and deftly stop telling her about your own experience and go back to listening to hers.

- A good marital conversation is a conversation in which both partners feel good, so say a lot of things that make your partner feel good. If your partner is not being compassionate toward or forgiving of himself, say compassionate and forgiving things to him. If your partner feels that she's abnormal, weird, aberrant, and uniquely screwed up, tell her that she's just normally screwed up and that it's normal to be screwed up. If your partner lacks confidence in himself, tell him that *you* have confidence in him. If she's discouraged, encourage her. If she isn't liking, loving, respecting, or appreciating herself, say liking, loving, respectful, and appreciative things to her. If he puts himself down in any way, pull him back up with your high regard for him. Sometimes you'll need to pull him a long way up: "You're such a great person, Mike. You're a great husband and a great father and a great seeker of the truth." If you're ever at a loss as to how to make your partner feel good in a conversation, think of something to thank or admire him for and thank and admire him. Use all of these techniques, and any others you can think of, to make your partner feel good in the conversation even when the conversation has friction, discord, and the sharing of painful feelings in it; use them *especially* then because that's when you'll really need them.

- Remember that all forms of bickering, dispute, altercation, and argument—all squabbles, tiffs, spats, and fights—are lower life-forms of human conversation and should be avoided, ended, and transcended at all costs. "Argument is the *worst* sort of conversation," said Jonathan Swift—so leave it behind as a way of speaking to each other. If you should, by some monumental manifestation of human stupidity, find yourself arguing with your partner, stop it immediately and start over again. Where there is genuine and sincere disagreement between you, reconceive the conversation as a vehicle to come to agreement (often, compromise), and then come to agreement. If you can't, amicably agree to disagree. But don't argue. And whatever you do, never argue in front of your children! Teach them and model for them that people can disagree about things and feel anger toward each other—children understand that—but don't accuse, blame, insult, intimidate, swear, yell, angrily gesture, threaten violence, do violence, or otherwise try to overpower and scare your partner— you'll be scaring and depressing your children. I once worked with a couple who did nothing *but* accuse and blame and yell and fight with each other in front of their four-year-old son. The horrible energy in their conversations was afflicting their son, who was already having physical, emotional, and behavioral problems. After a year of therapy, the couple had a breakthrough. During a family dinner, they started speaking gently and softly to each other, and actually kissed at the end of the conversation. At that point, the little boy stood up, walked into the living room, and literally started dancing!

- If at any time you need to use anger to correct and critique your partner, make sure you use the anger as a temporary tool you pick up to do a specific piece of transformative work on your partner, and then put the tool down when the work is done. Whenever possible, eschew anger as a means of communication with your partner because most of us are so frightened by anger that the moment it starts coming at us, especially from our partners, we completely dissociate from our bodies and are up somewhere in the ionosphere, not hearing a single word of it until it blows over. Except in times of dire necessity—when your partner's behavior is completely off the wall and he's so stubborn that nothing *but* anger will get through to him—anger usually doesn't work to help a person change.

- If you need to correct or critique your partner for the purpose of changing his wrong behaviors or ideas, be very careful. Most of us feel pretty bad about ourselves inside, and get very defensive when we feel we're being told we're bad, especially if it's by our partners criticizing us. So if you're trying to tell your partner to change or shape up in some way, you'd better say it in a way that does not deploy his defenses. Good luck. Whenever you feel the impulse to correct your partner, before you actually *say* anything, send it through the filter of "Do I *really* need to say this? Is it something about *her* that needs to be corrected, or about *me*? My negativity? My judgmentalness? My addiction to faultfinding? My arrogance?" If it makes it through that filter, run it through again just in case you were fooling yourself the first time. When something must be said, say it right. Say it as positively and nicely as you can. Say it with the intention to help, not hurt. Do not castigate and vilify your partner for past crimes and errors, but, based on those past errors, suggest and request changes "for future reference." If your partner has some work to do on herself, the best way to tell her is to say that you have some work to do on yourself too, and tell her what your work is, and do it. Conceive all correction and critique of your partner to be a benevolent offering to him of how to make the relationship and/or life in general work better, and then, taking a deep breath, give it a shot.

- The guiding principle behind all marital conversation can be found in the roots of the word "conversation" itself. The syllable "vers" means "turn" (as in "reverse," "to turn back") and the prefix "con" means "with." Therefore, a "con-vers-ation" is "a turning with" another person: The thoughts and sentiments and feelings of one person are turned over in words to the other person, who then returns her thoughts and sentiments and feelings in words, and so on, back and forth, each one taking his or her turn. The relationship lifts higher and higher on the currents of this sweet, circling gyre of words until it rises to the empyrean of true marital intimacy. To this end, use every technique you can think of to keep turning the conversation over to your partner, to keep the conversation turning.

- Think of conversation between you and your partner as a deep and diligent inquiry into truth conducted over the course of a lifetime by two people who are devoted to the truth and who like looking for it and finding it together through talking. The truth might be pragmatic, practical truth—like where to shop for the new carpeting Saturday—or it might be psychological, intellectual, political, or moral truth—like what is the right thing to say or do in this situation—or it might be philosophical, spiritual truth—like what is going on in the universe and what exactly are we supposed to be doing in it besides shopping for carpeting? Whatever the level of truth you're inquiring into, in an ideal marriage the conversation is a lifelong "conversation of discovery" of that truth.[10] Where two are gathered together in such a marriage, the spirit of truth is in the midst of them and turning round and round between them as the couple takes sweet counsel together—talking about the events and adventures of their lives, solving their problems, sharing their feelings about everything they have feelings about, confiding in each other about their hopes and dreams, and discovering the magical mystery of reality together.

So can we talk? To our partners? Safely? About anything? Can we enjoy talking to them and become better and wiser people by talking to them till death do us part?

Absolutely.

DISMISSING WOMEN

It is well within the order of things
That man should listen when his mate sings;
But the true male never yet walked
Who liked to listen when his mate talked.

—Anna Wickham, "The Affinity"

"It's like he doesn't hear me," said Jeanne-Louise, a thirty-one-year-old elementary school teacher, referring to her husband, Norm. "I tell him I want things done a certain way—I ask him to do something for me, I tell him not to drive so fast, I tell him I don't want sex right now, I suggest that we go somewhere together, or talk about a problem we're having, or *anything* I suggest—I feel like I'm talking to a *wall*. It's really like he doesn't even *hear* it."

⌣ ⌣ ⌣

Of course, Norm does hear it, but he dismisses it, and her, so quickly that he might as well have not heard it; whether he hears it or not, what she says has no effect on him. Men are very good at dismissing women. We took a course in it in junior high school. While the girls were baking cupcakes in Home Ec, we boys were in a back room near the gym learning the ten thousand ways to dismiss women, with or without them knowing it. It's part of our curriculum. And all those years you thought we were taking Shop!

Part of the training that goes on for men in this culture, and in most cultures around the world, is to instantly and totally dismiss a woman's voice. It doesn't much matter if a woman asks, requests, pleads, suggests, explains, complains, insists, demands, or simply states, we men have been taught to dismiss it if it comes from a woman. We don't do it with malicious or abusive intent most of the time, and we don't even do it consciously most of the time, we just do it. If we think you're being too weak and whiny, we'll dismiss you as immature little things unworthy of our attention and respect, basically pests; and if we think you're being too strong and bossy, we'll dismiss you as nags, bitches, and ball busters. And everything in between—no matter what tone of voice you use—we'll dismiss that too.

We have been taught well to want you subservient, obedient, nurturing, friendly, and sexy. We want you competent in minor things like cleaning, sewing, and color-coordinating the bathroom. We want you independent in small ways so that you have enough of a life to leave us alone in our life, and we want you dependent on us in big ways so that you're economically and emotionally attached to us so you won't leave us. That's the secret about men: We don't want you to leave us, we just want you to leave us alone. So we have little or no interest in what you say to us, and we're dismissing you even as you're opening your mouths to say it. Males are trained from birth to dismiss females' wishes, and the voices that express those wishes, as trivial and not worth our attention. We dismiss women by ignoring them, by belittling them, by intimidating them, and by maligning them if they try to assert themselves.

Sometimes men's dismissal of women can be hard and heartless; it also pervades lighter levels of our lives, in our common everyday interactions with women.

One morning a few years ago, while shaving in the bathroom, I heard my wife's voice from the kitchen tell me to remember to wipe up around the sink when I was done. This was hardly the first time she had told me to do this in the twenty-five years of our living together, but I had never done it. This time I didn't do it either. Instead, the *moment* I heard her voice there appeared on my face—which I was looking at in the mirror—a little wrinkled sneer of disdain, as if I were saying, "Don't *bother* me, lady!" and I immediately and automatically dismissed her reminder. I dismissed it so fast I completely forgot about it by the time I walked out of the bathroom thirty seconds later.

It's downright frightening, isn't it—the disrespect with which we men sometimes treat women? The way I'm working with this disrespect in myself is: First, identify it when it comes up in me; second, not judge myself when it does come up because this disrespect for women is not really *me*, it's been taught to me by the society I grew up in; and third, I make the effort to put respect for women in the place where disrespect and dismissal has always lived in me, and act accordingly. I'm retraining myself to act differently with my wife, my cotrainer who points out to me when I'm disrespecting or dismissing her yet again and doesn't let me get away with it—in other words, she stays on my case. I like the fact that Jane stays on my case, because sometimes I can be kind of a hard case, and I don't want to be a case anymore.

MALE STANDARD TIME

What time is it?
Macho time!

—Hector "Macho Man" Camacho

Adriana and Parke had been married for fourteen years. Parke was the chief financial officer of a large corporation, and Adriana took care of the house and their three children. One of the reasons they were in therapy was that Adriana was angry with Parke for not devoting enough time to her, the marriage, or the family.

"He's out of the house by seven, and not home till late evening, and even then he's so stressed from his day that all he can do is sit there at the dinner table looking preoccupied. And then he sits in front of the TV for the rest of the night, completely unapproachable. The kids have learned to not even get near him, and I'm afraid to also. I can't live like this. I want—"

"Wait a second!" Parke interrupted. "How many times do we have to have this discussion? I have to *work*, Adriana. To do my work, I *have* to be out of the house at seven, and I *can't* come home earlier than I do. There are huge demands on my time and energy at work, and I can't change that, and neither of us should forget for a second that if I didn't work as long and as hard as I do we wouldn't have all that we have in the world. I have no choice in all this, Adriana, and I resent your attacking me as if I do. *You* try doing what I do all day. *You* try dealing with the level of responsibility I have at work and see if *you're* not stressed out in the evening. What the hell do you want from me?"

Adriana stared at him for a few seconds, exasperated, then turned to me.

"I never know what to say at this point," she said. "We've had this discussion a thousand times, and he argues me down every time. Then I just get depressed. All I know is that he's never home, and even when he is, he's not really there. I feel completely stuck. He can't seem to hear me. I don't even know what the problem is anymore."

"The problem is the time zone you two live in," I said. "Male Standard Time."

In Male Standard Time, all the time there is in a relationship gets appropriated to serve the interests and needs of men. It is very hard to understand our society, our relationships, and ourselves unless we understand that the dominant, governing group of the whole system is men. The supremacy of men in our culture goes by different names: male chauvinism, sexism, patriarchy. The patriarchal system is the secret sociopolitical structure underneath our culture that values traditionally masculine behaviors and ways of being and perceiving above traditionally feminine ways. It is insidious and pervasive and so deeply systemic that no one, not women, not men, is fully conscious of it, either in the culture or in themselves. We're all in this together, both genders trying to uproot sexism from the depths of our beings and the patterns of our behavior. It's easier for men to overlook it because they benefit from it in so many ways: It gives them preeminence and power over women; it gives them the freedom to do pretty much what they want to do; and it makes it easy for them to live their lives without ever looking at their lives or themselves. Introspection is not valued in this system, because if men and women were ever to see, in the clear light of consciousness, how the system affects them, they would see how destructive it is for both of them, and would tear it down in a second.

Since the rules of the system say that the main purpose of life is the fear-driven endless accumulation of money through work, men do whatever they can to get as much time as they can for this purpose. All these men, frantically laboring and accumulating and developing serious heart conditions, have created a socioeconomic system—corporate capitalism—in which using time in this way is imperative. So in a relationship between a man and a woman, the man ends up dictating how all, or most, of the time in the relationship is to be used, and it usually gets used for his work.

In Male Standard Time, if time is not claimed *directly* for the man's work ("I'm going to work, honey. See you this evening"), it is claimed indirectly. Even when the man is home from work with his wife and children, he is either preparing for work ("I need to be alone this evening; I have to have this report out by Wednesday"); doing extra work ("I'll just be a few moments, I have a couple of business calls to make"); destressing from work ("I didn't have a moment to myself today, and I need to veg out in front of the TV for a while"); or relaxing recreation-ally in between times of work ("I'm going to play golf, honey! See you for dinner!"). In this system, time, like everything else on the earth, is a commodity for men's interests and purposes.

That means that the woman and the children in the relationship with the man never get to do what *they* want to do with time, which is to use it to have something that looks like a real *relationship* with the man. Until women *and* men recognize, scrutinize, and begin to reshape the under-lying order that makes men's priorities the ultimate priorities, mar-riages and families and women and men will continue to suffer.

In other words, it's time to change the time.

THE GREAT CONTINENTAL DRIFT

Over and over again, like the ballast of a ship, the attention tips to what's going on with the men.

> —Janet Surrey and Stephen J. Bergman,
> *The Woman-Man Relationship:*
> *Impasses and Possibilities*

It is hard to fight an enemy who has outposts in your head.

> —Sally Kempton, "Cutting Loose"

For the past month Shepp had been working many overtime hours at his editor's job at the community newspaper, often getting home at ten or eleven at night. His wife, Clare, a financial adviser, would usually be asleep by that time, and would be gone the next morning before Shepp woke up. In therapy, Clare reported that for the past two weeks she had been very lonely for Shepp and had been sobbing uncontrollably in the evenings.

I asked Clare to continue talking to Shepp about her loneliness, relating it also to her childhood. With Shepp listening attentively, she began doing that. At a certain point, Shepp, looking at Clare sympathetically, said that he felt guilty that he hadn't been able to spend more time with her. Clare returned Shepp's sympathetic look.

"I know—you feel guilty *a lot*," she said softly.

Shepp then started talking about his tendency to feel guilt not only in his relationship with Clare but in all aspects of his life, including his relationship with his parents and also in his job, where he felt guilty if he didn't put in overtime to help a writer finish a story. Then Shepp talked more about his guilt, his acute sense of responsibility, and his perfectionism, and the pain they caused him.

Clare and I listened attentively as Shepp spoke insightfully and interestingly about his inner conflicts. Clare asked questions and offered suggestions, all the while looking at Shepp sympathetically.

It was a very sweet scene. I sat there mesmerized in a mist of sympathy. Then, suddenly, the mist lifted, I saw what had just happened, and, clearing my throat, I said, "I have to stop this. This is not the solution. This is the problem."

We had started the session talking about Clare's loneliness. When a person is sobbing uncontrollably in her kitchen every evening for two weeks, that's loneliness. Clare talked about that for about ten minutes, with Shepp paying attention to her. Then something happened. Gradually, and then suddenly, we weren't talking about Clare's loneliness anymore, we were talking about Shepp's guilt, Shepp's sense of responsibility, and Shepp's perfectionism, and for the last twenty minutes Clare had been paying attention to Shepp. In other words, the focus of attention shifted from the woman's pain to the man's pain, with full complicity, if not prompting, on the part of the woman, not to mention the therapist. Of the three people in this room, none of us was conscious that that had happened, that the woman was, in effect, again being left alone in her pain by the man.

The shift of attention from woman to man doesn't happen all the time in couples—in fact, in some couples, it goes the other way—and not all couples engineer the shift in the way Shepp and Clare did; but it happens a lot of the time. Like the continental drift that separated South America from Africa 225 million years ago, the shift of attention from woman to man may be imperceptible, but it is sure and steady and enormous. I call it the "Great Continental Drift of Attention to Men." Without any of us clearly seeing it, the man somehow becomes the center of attention: *his* conflicts, *his* problems, *his* feelings become the focus.

Men have been deeply trained to want, deserve, expect, take, and enjoy this attention, while women have been deeply trained *not* to want, deserve, expect, take, or enjoy it, but to give it. To the man. Interminably. And both have been deeply trained not to notice when it happens. A woman's deeply conditioned pattern of subordination to a man makes the woman exquisitely sensitive to the man's will and strategically, ingeniously, and invisibly deferring to it at every turn.

When a woman and a man are talking together, or doing anything together, both of us need to check and see who's the focus of attention; if it's the man, if we've allowed the culturally conditioned forces in us to pull our attention away from the woman and toward the man once again, we should turn back to the woman.

So . . . Clare . . . You were saying? . . .

Ten Good Things About Men

Masculinity is not in its essence abusive. We have within us the innate potential to use our masculine power for blessing, stewardship, and servant leadership.

—Robert Moore and Douglas Gillette,
The King Within

I sensed each one of my steps. They resonated on the ground; their echo produced the indescribable euphoria of being a man.

—Carlos Castaneda,
The Teachings of Don Juan

In many relationships, the woman is often angry with the man, who is angry back at her for being so mad at him. That anger is an obstacle in a relationship and has to be eliminated if the couple wants to have a great relationship. The first steps in eliminating the anger are to acknowledge it, to talk about it—and to understand that just about all of it is appropriate. I think that anyone's anger at men is appropriate given what men have done in and to the world in the last five thousand years. I know that my anger at men is, in part, my personal anger at my own male elders, and the delusions and the lies of sexism in them. I also know that my anger is my anger at myself for having every one of those delusions and lies in myself, and having acted them out in my past. I also know that some of my anger is sheer moral outrage at a social, economic, and political system that has resulted in so much fear, greed, violence, cruelty, ignorance, and arrogance on this earth.

There is nothing I say about men that I'm not also saying about myself. Chekhov said, "When people ask me how I know so much about men, they get a simple answer: everything I know about men, I have learned from me." "It is myself that I portray," said Montaigne.

For all my anger with men, and with myself, I still find it easy to praise men, to say good things about them. Pure male energy is beautiful, and I love the male energy I see in myself. Women also have beautiful energy. I think men and women are supposed to learn to love each other's pure energy and work with each other's energy and not be mad at each other anymore.

Ten good things to say about men come to mind right away. To the degree that we men are becoming the embodiment of all these things, the women can start to let go of their anger at us.

☽ ☽ ☽

- Even at our worst, we're not evil, we're just hurt and we act out our hurt by hurting others. Even when we do evil and cruel things, our cruelty is not intrinsic, but is a consequence of being traumatized by the teachings of our culture, which tell us to control and dominate, to be hard and unfeeling, to put ourselves first, to not respect women. It's not that our behavior is excusable—in fact, it's sometimes unconscionable—but it is explainable. When men behave badly, that behavior has been caused by trauma. That means we can overcome it—because trauma is healable.

- Many men, and more and more men, are trying to heal. To do the work they need to do on themselves to stop being so hurt, they are reading books, listening to tapes, attending meetings and men's groups and lectures and workshops and retreats, going to churches and temples and meditation centers, laughing at the silliness of macho behavior as it's pointed out by comedians and sitcoms and movies, coming to therapy with their wives, and coming to therapy alone. More and more men are looking at themselves. More and more of us are doing the work of healing.

- Underneath the damage wrought in us by the delusions and lies of our elders, we find kindness, generosity, and the desire to be supportive and helpful. We love to use our muscular strength, our resourcefulness, and our intelligence to help whoever comes to us seeking our help. We love to solve problems. We love to serve. At our best, we understand the duty and purpose of our lives to be a covenant of service to those whom we love.

- At our best, we are protectors and providers, struggling on behalf of the whole human race to make the sometimes unfriendly physical environment here on earth safe and secure. This is rooted very deep within us. We are instinctually and often self-sacrificially compelled to protect our families, our communities, our nations, and our species from want or harm, by providing, to the best of our ability and the limits of our strength and ingenuity, the food, shelter, clothing, fuel, and tools we all need in order to feel safe and secure in our environment. We are not afraid of hard work, and are capable of vast amounts of it. We take on our protector and provider responsibilities with the fervor of a knight and the endurance of a mule.

- Even though feeling our feelings is not our strong suit, and we get kind of agitated when anyone is feeling their feelings anywhere in our vicinity, we're working hard on it and we're starting to get more comfortable with feelings. That's a big one for us. Therapist though I am, it's certainly still a big one for me.

Once, my wife and I were out skating on a pond when she fell and hurt her knee. She lay curled up on the ice, holding her knee, loudly moaning "OW!," and crying. I stood over her, leaning on my hockey stick, feeling an interesting mixture of embarrassment, compassion, contempt, admiration, and panic. *How can she be* crying, *for god's sakes?! She* just *fell on the ice! No one cries when they fall on the ice! Rusty and Marty Swartz didn't cry when* they *fell on the ice! Bobby Hare didn't cry when* he *fell on the ice! They just got up and* skate it off*! That's what you're supposed to do when you fall on the ice—get up and* skate it off*!—not lie there crying. Am I supposed to comfort her? Am I supposed to kneel down and actually* do *something? What* am *I supposed to do? I guess I'll just stand here leaning jauntily on my hockey stick until it blows over.*

This is pretty much what it sounds like inside a man when someone's feeling their feelings near him; but I think we're finally realizing that feelings are not going to blow over, and that we've got to welcome feelings in others and feel them in ourselves.

- Our hearts are filled with the joy and exuberance of life itself. We are full of energy, and all we really want to do with that energy is play and have fun in life. There is a part of us that was, is, and will always be a boy playing football with his friends on a late Saturday afternoon in October and having a semiecstatic experience every time he gets tackled in the leaves. The part of us that is not Russell but Rusty and not Martin but Marty and not Robert but Bobby, the part of us that is not and will never be grown up, is a beautiful part of us, and will always be young and will always be playing.

- Some of us are really funny, clowns and comedians at heart, with quick wits and antic ways. We love to make people laugh, and we *really* love to make the women we love laugh.

- We are strong. Some of us have physical strength, our bodies hard and tight, with big bulging muscles that carry human beings out of burning houses. In some of us, the strength is inside—strength of intellect, of purpose, of generosity, of love and loyalty and devotion, the strength of the aspiring spiritual heart. Look at the strength of us! Look for the strength *in* us!

- We are Buddha. Socrates. Jesus. Moses. Mahatma Gandhi. Muhammed. Muhammed Ali. Nelson Mandela. César Chávez. Abraham Lincoln. Shakespeare. Schweitzer. Einstein. Martin Luther King. B. B. King. Black Elk. Omar Bradley. Michael Jordan. Larry Bird. Wayne Gretzky. Christopher Reeve. And so on. We are every great and gifted man who has ever lived in the history of the human species. We are every decent and upright and hard-working man who has ever lived and loved and looked after or fought to protect his family or his society. We are many; and we are worthy of the world's respect, gratitude, admiration, and love.

- We are spiritual warriors, searching within our own beings for the Divine Consciousness that lies at the core of our beings. We seek the Holy of Holies in our own hearts. Just as it is for women, our life is a quest for the Truth of our own nature, and we are warriors staunch and steady on that quest.

Those are ten good things about men. And they're *big* things. Thank God that the women have hung in there with us, putting up with some not-so-good things about us, for a long time, and have given us time to pull ourselves together. Maybe that's the best thing about us men these days: We're pulling ourselves together.

Saintmaker, Saintmaker, Make Me a Saint

We will be together
even when old age comes.
And the days in between
will be food set before us,
dates and honey, bread and wine.

—ancient Egyptian song

Like two swimmers who love the water, their souls knit
together without being sewn, no seam.

—Jalaluddin Rumi, "The King and
the Handmaiden and the Doctor"

Caddy and Mark, both in their mid-twenties, had entered therapy with me a year and a half before, in preparation for their marriage. They had overcome their tendency to compete with each other, learned the importance of kindness and respect for one another, and now the preparation was over. They had set a date for the wedding, and were terminating therapy tonight. With a few minutes left in the session, they asked me if I had some final words for them.

I thought about it for a moment, and said that I did.

• Remember that marriage is a sacrament—*holy* matrimony—entered into with solemn vows spoken before God. Marriage is a holy vessel consecrated by God for the purification of the human heart and the spiritual upliftment of the world. You should therefore treat your marriage and your marriage partner with great reverence. Your relationship with your marriage partner is your relationship with the sacred.

• At its deepest level, marriage is for sainthood. I don't mean that we must be totally perfect human beings to start with, but we should all be striving in our marriages to make our partner's welfare as important as our own. Marriages are designed to push, pull, prod, drive, drag, goad, and generally force each partner to stop identifying with, and acting from, the separate, contracted, self-centered place inside and start identifying with, and acting from, the highest, most selfless, most loving place within—the place of sainthood.

Once, during a particularly challenging time in our marriage, Jane and I went before our meditation teacher, and, briefly describing the difficulties we were having, asked for her blessing. Sitting cross-legged in her chair, leaning forward, her eyes bright with interest, our meditation teacher listened to us, then smiled at us very lovingly, and said, "Ah! . . . Which one of you is going to make the other a saint *first*?" and she laughed delightedly, as did we.

If you understand that your marriage is for sainthood, marriage is easy. At any time of the night or day, in any situation with your partner, you can just think, "My highest purpose in this marriage is to selflessly love that self over there. What would selfless love do here?" And then do that.

- Over the course of your life together, write tens of thousands of little notes to each other expressing love, appreciation, friendship, compassion, and passion to each other. Leave these notes all over the place. A sample note might read, *"Hi, honey. Welcome home. I'm napping in the bedroom. Thanks for holding me last night when I was sad, and for every other way you've ever shown love to me. I appreciate everything you do, and are. Come nap with me. If upon seeing me napping, you are suddenly filled with an overwhelming desire to make wild, passionate love to me, you may wake me up for that purpose. Otherwise, forget it. I love you."*

  Or something like that.

- Last summer at a hotel swimming pool, Jane and I watched with rapt interest as an elderly couple got up from their chairs to go into the pool. They captured our interest because they were both infirm, and neither could get out of their chairs alone. To get up, they both sat on the edges of their chairs, facing each other, their knees almost touching, and gripped each other's forearms. Then they pushed and pulled each other back and forth, rocking back and forth, gradually gathering speed and momentum until finally they had enough lift to get them both in the air at the same time, standing up suddenly and together, steadying themselves. Then they gingerly walked to the pool, holding each other's arms like skating partners. They performed the entire procedure as a matter of course, without saying a word to each other.

I laughed. "That's us in thirty years."

Jane was quiet for a few moments, watching the couple easing into the pool together, still holding on to each other.

"Looks good to me," she said.

8
THE JOURNEY

Journeys bring power and love
back into you.

>—Jalaluddin Rumi,
>"If a Tree Could Fly Off"

Everything is laid out for you.
Your path is straight ahead of you.
Sometimes it's invisible, but it's there.
You may not know where it's going,
But you have to follow that path.
It's the path to the Creator.
It's the only path there is.

>—Chief Leon Shenandoah

Sages say the path is narrow and difficult to tread, narrow as the edge of
a razor.

>—*Katha Upanishad*

What is the journey we are taking, this "getting the soul right"? I've heard it called, among other things, the journey of awakening, the journey of consciousness, the journey of self-awareness, the journey to the truth, and the journey to God. John Bunyan called it the "Pilgrim's Progress." In Sanskrit, the journey is called *sadhana*. Since this journey takes you through the back alleys and catacombs of your psychological nature at the same time that it lifts you into the blue empyrean of your spiritual nature, I have also heard it called, perhaps most accurately, "the psycho-spiritual journey," but that's a mouthful, so in my therapy practice I just call it "the journey" and let it go at that.

There are ways of conceptualizing and understanding the course of this journey that make it easier to take; there are things to do, say, and remember on the journey that make it easier as well. And there are things to bring along that you will find helpful. Everything in this chapter is to help make it easier for you to take this journey—which we all ought to take, and are taking, whether we know it or not.

THE SCHOOL FOR SOULS
or
WHAT IT'S ALL ABOUT, ALFIE

We have all come to the right place.
We all sit in God's classroom.

—Hafiz, "For a While"

We're all living basically the same life. The details of your life are different from the details of my life, but the general idea is the same:
Basically, life goes up and down, with good and bad and sometimes wonderful and sometimes horrible things happening to us in an unbroken
string of different things happening to us, birth to death. That's pretty
much it.

The important thing is the way you look at it.

I believe life is a school. All the universe is a university in which all
our souls must take all the courses in the curriculum. The name of the
curriculum is Love, and we keep taking courses in Love until we know
everything there is to know about it, including that we, in our essential
nature, *are* love. Some of the courses are: Introduction to Happiness;
Niceness 101; Intermediate Patience; Advanced Surrender; The
Theory and Practice of Humility; and The Principles of Purification.
There are other courses in Respect and Reverence for All; Compassion
and Contentment; Sucking It Up: Discipline, Perseverance, and Sacrifice;
Forgiveness; Personal Power; Overcoming Self-Hatred (a seventy-nine-
year seminar); and Service to Humanity. And there are other courses that
don't look or sound at all like Love—like Behaving Yourself; Get Over
It: An Honors Practicum; and Pain and Suffering: A Comprehensive
Survey—but they're part of the curriculum of Love too. We keep taking and retaking a course, and intermediate and advanced and gradu-
ate levels of that course, until we've learned the material, and then we
can move on to the next course. We are always taking several classes
simultaneously, and some of us are carrying a very heavy course load.
When we at last learn to love everything there is—our neighbor as
ourself, ourself, our earth, life, and God—we've completed the curriculum.

Everything that happens in your life—every event, experience, encounter, and relationship; every accident (there are no accidents); every coincidence (there are no coincidences); every mistake (there are no mistakes); every piece of good or bad luck; every up or down; every coming, every going; every gain, every loss; every second of every minute of every hour of every day happens *for a reason,* and the reason is that it's part of a course you're taking at the time. The courses you'll be taking at a particular time will be different from everybody else's courses because you're a different person with different things to learn about Love.

As a matter of fact, if you want to know why something is happening in your life, don't waste too much time looking at the thing that's happening. Instead, look at the learning you will need to do in order to deal with the thing that's happening. *That's* where the action is. *That's* why it happened. The learning on the inside is the main show, and the thing that's happening in your life is the sideshow.

And the entire curriculum is leading us to a degree in Love. Always— for the sake of Love—the perfect experience and the perfect person is sent for the perfect amount of time to force us to learn just what we need to learn at that time. The whole thing is a huge long learning process that we're all going through together—independently, interdependently, and simultaneously. How God set this whole school up, with its interrelated and intersecting courses, is way beyond what my meager mind can handle, but interesting to think about. *Why* God set it up is more clear—the answer is, *for Love!*

DE-VELCRO YOURSELF

When an inner situation is not made conscious, it happens outside as fate.
—Carl Jung, *Aion*

As we go through life, despite our intention to look for the best in people and to not let anyone "get to" us, we will always find that while some of those we meet inspire or delight or comfort us, some people drive us absolutely nuts. Sometimes it's hard to pinpoint exactly what it is that makes another person's presence feel like fingernails raking across a blackboard. What's going on here? Why are we so *affected* by other people?

Velcro.

If we have anything inside us that can be disturbed or perturbed by the traits of another human being—something deep within that is "hookable"—depend on it, somebody with those traits will show up in our lives and stick to us just like a matching piece of Velcro. Sometimes we will be so hooked, so stuck on that person's behavior that we think, "I can't stand him! I feel like strangling him!" These hookable traits will show up in our acquaintances, in our friends and neighbors, in our colleagues and coworkers, in our parents and children, and of course—*big time!*—in our partners. The closer the relationship, the bigger our pieces of Velcro will be. That's why we can feel driven almost completely crazy by the very people we spend the most time with in our lives.

I once saw a David Letterman show where Dave, wearing a bodysuit made entirely of Velcro, jumps off a springboard onto a wall made entirely of Velcro, and hangs there, spread-eagled and helplessly hooked from head to toe. That's how it is when we still have Velcro inside: The matching pieces always show up, and we get hooked like hell. In fact, it's uncanny how they always show up. And it's the Velcro we carry inside that causes them to show up.

There's a purpose to all this misery. How can we know what is hookable in us—the places inside where we still have negative, aversive, and uncomfortable reactions to people—unless people come into our lives custom-designed to bring out those reactions in us? The people who disturb, perturb, and hook the hell out of us reveal the inner work we still need to do.

Once we understand how this system works, relationships, even uncomfortable ones, get a lot more interesting, even fun, because then we can use them to find our own patches of Velcro. In this way, we no longer spend so much of our time frustrated and accusing the other person of driving us crazy. Instead, we're too busy looking at all the fascinating ways that we ourselves are going crazy, too busy looking for all our patches of Velcro and de-Velcroing ourselves.

De-Velcro yourself. This isn't about your obnoxious new coworker, or your busybody neighbor, or your endlessly procrastinating spouse. This is about *you* and your powerful negative reaction to the other person's behavior. Don't mind her; de-Velcro yourself of your powerful negative reaction to her. We're all here to de-Velcro ourselves.

It's difficult to do this, and it takes perseverance. But when you have worked through your issues inside, they will stop showing up so much outside, and even when they do show up, you won't care anymore. If you have a negative reaction to a particular behavior, I personally guarantee you that a whole swarm of people who act that way will keep coming into your life until you rid yourself of your hooks, until you are no longer perturbed by them. Then you won't need the other half of your Velcro to show up and remind you that you need to work on getting rid of all those hooks inside. Lo and behold: By transforming your inner life, you transform your outer life.

CATCH-22
or
THE CLEANER YOU GET,
THE CLEANER YOU HAVE TO GET

The game of life is a game of boomerangs. Our thoughts, deeds, and
words return to us sooner or later, with astounding accuracy.
    —Florence Scovel Shin

One of the little-known facts about the healing journey is that the more
we clean up our act, the cleaner our act has to get. The closer we get to
physical, emotional, and spiritual purity, the lower our tolerance for
impurity gets. It's like a mirror: Only when it's almost totally clean does
every speck of dust on it show.

Our bodies operate on this principle. The six-pack of beer we could
drink ten years ago to blithe intoxication makes us bloated and nau-
seous today. The cigarette we could smoke with pleasure last year sends
us into paroxysms of coughing this year. The two hamburgers, fries, and
a Coke we could eat without blinking an eye as a teenager put us on the
toilet for a day and a half now. On one level, it's very good, because it
impels our journey toward total purity of body, mind, and heart; on
another level, it's a colossal drag. "Better not to begin," says Chogyam
Rinpoche, because once we begin, "we are in for it." Or, as a client of
mine once jokingly put it, "What I have done to try and find truth in my
life has completely screwed up my entire life!"

Our minds and hearts operate on the same principle. Thoughts, feelings, and actions that you once could get away with now come bouncing
back to you correctively and quickly.

I was in the drugstore the other day waiting to copy something on the
copy machine. As usual, I was in a hurry. An elderly woman ahead of me
was copying page after page out of a book, *very* slowly, totally oblivious
of me. After ten minutes of waiting, I was furious with her and silently
seething.

A little voice inside me was saying, *Robert, cut it out. You're more evolved
than this! You've done enough work on yourself by now to be standing here patiently,
sending respect and love, not rage, into that elderly woman. Just cut it out.*

But I ignored the voice and stood there in a rage. When she was finished, I sent a sidelong contemptuous glance to her stooped, retreating back, and angrily stepped up to the machine and did my copying.

Walking home from the drugstore, I saw an elderly man standing on the corner with a cocker spaniel on a leash. I stopped and stretched out my hand to pet the dog, but it barked and snapped at me. Then the man yelled—at *me*!—for bothering his dog! I walked home shaken by the anger that had just come at me from the man and his dog.

I can't prove this, but I am *sure* that their anger was the quick corrective return of the anger I had felt with the old woman at the copying machine. It was, as John Lennon warned us, "instant karma." I am sure that I was supposed to learn something there, once and for all, and I did. I learned that for where I am on this journey, I have to watch not only my outer actions and words but my inner feelings and thoughts as well.

The cleaner we get, the cleaner we have to get—in our bodies, behaviors, minds, and hearts. It's the price we pay for cleaning up our act. It's the way God makes sure that we *keep* cleaning up our act. It's a catch-22 all the way.

STOP EATING SUGAR

Example is not the main thing in influencing others. It is the only thing.
—Albert Schweitzer

Dorothy, a single mother of two unruly teenage girls, was having a difficult time disciplining them and wanted help. I started asking her about her own disciplines in life. Did she herself practice self-control? Did she think of herself as a disciplined person?

She got annoyed with me. "I feel like I'm being interrogated," she said. "We're talking about my daughters, not me."

One of the great secrets of life is that, no matter what or whom we're talking about, we're always talking about "me." Even if we seem to be talking about our children, or any other people, things, circumstances, or events that are supposedly not "me," we're really talking about "me." If we're not, we should be.

In order for us to help our children develop self-discipline, we ourselves must develop self-discipline, because we can't give someone something we don't have.

We must practice what we preach. The authority we need to tell other people—especially teenagers—to get their act together, and have it stick, derives from our having gotten our own act together. There are no exceptions to this principle. Pedagogical, ethical, and spiritual teaching carries no weight and has no authority unless it's filled with the authority of your own attainment.

Once a woman came to Mahatma Gandhi with her ten-year-old son in tow.

"O great-souled one," she said, "please help us! We have walked all day from our village to ask for your help! You are our last hope."

"How can I help you?" asked Gandhi.

"My son, Sanjay, all he does is eat sugar. He eats nothing else, and he won't listen to me when I tell him it's not good for him. But he respects you, sir. So maybe if you tell him to stop eating sugar, he will stop eating sugar. Please help us!"

Gandhi looked at the distraught woman, then at the boy. "Come back in a week," he said to them.

The woman looked puzzled, but obeyed. She bowed her head in respect and left with her son, walking all day back to their village.

In a week's time, she came back to Gandhi and once again said, "Help us, please, Mr. Gandhi. He still eats nothing but sugar."

Gandhi stared at the boy for a long time, and then said softly and firmly, "Stop eating sugar, Sanjay." Then Gandhi became silent, as if that was all he was going to say.

The woman looked surprised, confused. "Mr. Gandhi, I don't understand. It is such a simple instruction you have given to my son, why could you not have told Sanjay last week to stop eating sugar, to save us the long walk to and from our village?"

"A week ago I hadn't stopped eating sugar," said Gandhi.

The Oaks of the Forest:
In Praise of Discipline

The sun became full of light when it got hold of itself.
Angels only began shining when they achieved discipline.
>   —Jalaluddin Rumi,
>   "Praising Manners"

Freedom is feeling good in harness.
>   —Robert Frost

Discipline is a word that many people resist. Often, it brings to our mind's eye images of overly strict teachers or parents who believed there were two ways to do things: their way, and the wrong way. No wonder so many of us think of discipline as a cruel restriction, a clipping of our wings.

But discipline does not mean a Spartan denial of the things we enjoy in life, it means we enjoy them in moderation. We don't say an absolute "No!" to our bodies, our senses, and our pleasures, we say "To a point." The *fun* of discipline is finding that point. I, for example, *love* ice cream and could probably spend my life eating nothing *but* ice cream, except for the fact that it makes me sick as a dog. But there is, thank God, a certain amount of ice cream I can eat and not get sick, and my ice cream discipline is finding that certain amount (which happens to be a kiddie-size scoop two or three times a week) and eating no more than that. Having found that point, I can now truly enjoy ice cream without apprehension or guilt. Discipline, then—the practice of moderation— doesn't forbid us from doing something, it actually *allows* us to do it. It doesn't take away our freedom, it grants us freedom.

Discipline is not *being* controlled, it is being *in* control. It is taking control (and power!) back from our senses, our cravings, our addictions, and our wandering minds. No longer are we at the mercy of these forces because *we're* in charge now.

The spiritual disciplines I practice in my daily life, like inspirational reading and meditation and contemplation, don't make me feel like I'm being controlled, constrained, restrained, or denied anything.

They make me feel like I'm being supported, cushioned, buoyed up and along, transported from one peaceful place to another. By making the effort to be disciplined in my life, I live my life more effortlessly— transferring my load to the disciplined practices—like in the Greyhound ads: "Leave the driving to us."

Discipline *is* like driving—in a lane, between the lines. When you're out on the highway, for your peace of mind and for everybody's safety, you drive between the lines. Same thing with discipline. For peace of mind, for safety, for comfortable traveling on this journey of consciousness, we travel between the lines of our disciplined daily practices. There's a structure and an elegance and a tranquillity to it that John Greenleaf Whittier calls "the calm beauty of an ordered life," and that feels better than any undisciplined behavior feels.

The energy you will need to travel on this journey of consciousness comes from discipline. If you spill ten gallons of gasoline on the ground and ignite it, all you'll get is a violent explosion; but if you take the same ten gallons of gasoline and run it through the carburetor and cylinders of an automobile engine, you'll get a series of controlled—that is, *disciplined*—explosions that will take you along the highway to where you want to go. Discipline is the harnessing and focusing of our life energy. Instead of dissipating that energy through our endless pursuit of sensory pleasures, we run that same energy through our spiritual disciplines and it becomes clarity of mind, purity of heart, and physical well-being. These qualities enhance our ability to take the journey of psychological and spiritual growth, and to serve the world with love.

Etymologically, the word "discipline" is related to the word "disciple," and both words are related to the Latin word "*docere,*" meaning "to teach." In other words, if you are here on this earth to be *taught,* if you conceive of yourself as a student studying the teachings of truth and wisdom, you practice discipline. In this sense, our disciplined daily practices are the tuition we voluntarily, even joyfully, pay for receiving the teachings.

Explaining why there is discipline, or "rule," in the religious life, St. Thérèse of Lisieux, who was a cloistered nun from age fifteen to her death at twenty-four, said:

> Consider the oaks of the countryside, how crooked they are;
> they thrust their branches to right and left, nothing checks them

so they never reach a great height. On the other hand, consider the oaks of the forest, which are hemmed in on all sides, they see light only up above, so their trunk is free of all those shapeless branches which rob it of the sap needed to lift it aloft. It sees only heaven, so all its strength is turned in that direction, and soon it attains a prodigious height. In the religious life, the soul like the young oak is hemmed in on all sides by its rule.[1]

On any journey you take what you need in order to get where you want to go. On the journey of consciousness, which is a journey to happiness, we take discipline. Discipline will not only bring us to happiness, it is a sweet support that is, in itself, happiness.

The Glimpse

*Like a saint's vision of beatitude. Like the veil of things as they seem
drawn back by an unseen hand. For a second you see—and seeing the
secret, are the secret. For a second there is meaning! Then the hand lets the
veil fall . . .*

—Eugene O'Neill,
Long Day's Journey into Night

*Every saint who has penetrated to the core of Reality has testified that a
divine universal plan exists and that it is beautiful and full of joy.*
—Paramahansa Yogananda,
Autobiography of a Yogi

After our three-minute meditation at the beginning of the session,
Peter, a twenty-year-old college student suffering from depression,
reported that during the meditation he had experienced a moment of
"complete peace—like everything *stopped,* and I somehow knew that
everything everywhere in the whole world was okay.

"It was like the time when I was eight, riding in the backseat of my
parents' car," he continued. "It was fall and the leaves were these brilliant reds and oranges and yellows in the bright sunlight, and there was
this one moment looking at the trees going by when something happened inside me, like something *opened,* and I saw that everything was
beautiful and I knew that everything was fine. Everything was *right.*
Everything was happening perfectly. It was a feeling of complete peace.
It's hard to put into words. But it was really cool. Then my father or
mother said something, and it's like I snapped out of it and it was gone."

"In the brief space of twenty years, you've already had two glimpses of
it, Peter."

"Of what?"

"Of the truth."

The truth is exactly as Peter says: Everything *is* fine, everything *is* right,
everything *is* beautiful, everything *is* perfect. The saints and sages and
mystics and masters of the world throughout the ages keep trying to tell

us this truth, but we have a hard time believing them because the veils of illusion that cover the truth and the film of ignorance that covers our eyes are so thick that until we've done a lot of work on ourselves—cleansing our "doors of perception," as William Blake puts it—we can't see it. In India this illusion is called *maya,* and is part of the game that God is playing in the universe. All psychological and spiritual effort—including psychotherapy—is to penetrate the veil of maya so that we can see the truth and live in the experience of the truth. The experience of living in the truth is one of complete contentment, unshakable strength, total wisdom, unconditional love, and absolute peace. St. Paul, finding this peace hard to put into words, called it, "the peace of God, which passeth understanding." The ancient Hindu sages put it into one word—*Shanti.*

To keep us going toward this experience of the truth on the rather long journey there, from time to time God graciously gives us glimpses of it. Sometimes God pulls back the veils of illusion and clears the film off our eyes and we *see.* We see what Peter saw in the foliage twelve years ago—the truth of the way things really are in the universe. Things in the universe are *fine.*

We never know when these glimpses are coming. When they do come, a camera shutter opens for a split second and the brilliant light of the truth pours through and into our dazzled eyes. On this journey, we're very fortunate to be given these momentary glimpses into perfection and joy, and it's good to try to remember these moments at other times, when the camera shutter snaps shut again, and we trek more darkly on toward the light we have glimpsed.

THE ILLUSION OF STUCKNESS

Dottie Hinson: It just got too hard.
Jimmy Dugan: It's supposed to be hard. If it wasn't hard, everybody would do it. The hard is what makes it great.

—from the movie
A League of Their Own

There are times when we find that the going is slow on the journey, when we are discouraged and frustrated by our lack of progress. We feel stuck, and we wonder if we will ever get unstuck.

It is important to remember that as we take the journey toward Self-realization there is no such thing as *stuck*. It's an optical illusion. There is no more *stuck* on this journey than there is *stuck* in the growth of a tree, which one can never see growing all the time that it is growing. There is no more *stuck* on this journey than there is *stuck* in the frozen mud of a meadow in winter, from which a lush carpet of grass and wildflowers will be growing in the spring. Nothing is *stuck* in nature. It is all motion, though sometimes very slow motion.

But when you *feel* stuck on your journey, and you feel like giving up and making no more effort on it, know that that's just one of the feelings that sometimes comes up on the journey, and then remember the story of the two frogs in a pail of cream:

Once there were two frogs, a big frog and a little frog, who were hopping across a field on their way to a pond. In the middle of the field, they came to a big pail and, being curious frogs, they jumped in to see what was in it. There was cream in it! These two particular frogs happened to love cream, so they stayed in the pail and drank their fill. When they were done, they tried to jump out of the pail, but couldn't because there was nothing solid in the pail for their back legs to jump off from.

The big frog was kind of a negative, depressed type, and immediately said, "Forget it! We'll never get out of here! This is hopeless! We're stuck!" But the little frog was more of an upbeat, positive type, with a sanguine nature, and he said, "Well, it certainly *looks* like we're stuck, but while we're trying to think of something to do, why don't we just swim around? After all, we're frogs! What else can we do but swim around?"

So they started swimming around and around the pail of cream, trying to think of what to do, all the while the big frog complaining that they'd never get out of there and that they might as well quit. "I'm so tired," he said every minute or so. "I can't go on."

"No, no, let's keep swimming around," said the little frog, who, though a little tired himself, was not discouraged. "I mean, what else is there to do?"

So they kept swimming around. They swam around and around for many hours, the big frog moaning and groaning about their plight every kick of the way. Eventually he got so discouraged that he stopped kicking, took one last breath, and sank wearily to the bottom of the pail and died. The little frog glanced down, felt sad about his friend, but just kept swimming around, and swam around for many more hours, all through the night, just keeping going, until around dawn he noticed that something was happening . . . it was getting harder to swim around through the cream . . . it was getting . . . thicker . . . and thicker! . . . *and thicker!* All that swimming had churned the cream into butter! After another few moments, the little frog was able to get his back legs on top of the butter, and with a great leap sprang out and was free!

So when you think you're stuck, you're really not; some important, though invisible, process is happening within you, so just keep on swimming.

CROSSING A CRISIS

Crisis is an attempt of nature, of the natural, cosmic lawfulness of the universe, to effect change. . . . It tears down and breaks up, which is momentarily painful, but transformation is unthinkable without it.
—Eva Pierrakos,
"The Spiritual Meaning of Crisis"

[A]s soon as suffering becomes acute enough, one goes forward.
—Hermann Hesse,
The Journey to the East

On this journey we move from being wounded to being healed of our wounds. For a long time we behave in the ways our wounds tell us to behave, and since our wounds have messed us all up inside, we create one mess after another in our lives.

For a time we're allowed to get away with our wounded behavior. We either experience minor consequences from it or we ignore the serious consequences. The familiarity of our behavior is comforting in its own way; we feel right at home in our patterns, juggling two lovers, manipulating others in order to get what we want, overworking, overeating. Then a time comes when it becomes hard or impossible to continue in that behavior. That time is usually signaled by a big mess we make in our lives, a chaotic disaster, a crisis. But the crisis is really God's way of saying it's time to move on from our wounded patterns. The consequences of our behavior become so serious that we finally feel impelled to change. Now the universe is saying to you, "Look, pal, you can continue to do things the old way, if you want, but if you do, you're going to pay the price."

Visualize in your mind the two words "crisis" and "crossing." They look alike, and are alike, because a crisis is really a crossing from an old way of being to a new way of being. To make a crossing, one needs a bridge. The crisis is the bridge you walk across to get over to the new way of operating. It might be a health crisis, or a relationship crisis, or a financial, moral, or spiritual crisis. If seen clearly and used correctly, these *crises* are all bridges, all *crossings* to the new way. Once you've crossed over, you don't need crises anymore, so you will stop creating them in your life.

THE MESSENGERS

Behold, I will send my messenger . . .
> —Malachi 3:1

Darren's business deal had not worked out, and he was called on the carpet by his vice-president, Mortie. Mortie told him that he wasn't surprised that the deal had fallen through because Darren was "antagonistic, argumentative, and almost impossible to work with." After reporting this to me, Darren went on to rail at Mortie and pretty much everybody else in the company for misunderstanding and misrepresenting him because, in his opinion, they all envied him. I sat nodding supportively for a few minutes, then stopped him.

"But have you thought about what Mortie said to you, Darren? Is there any *truth* in it? Is Mortie giving you a message?"

Darren's eyes blazed at me. "Message? Mortie? Mortie's a two-faced little prick with the heart of a lizard and the backbone of an amoeba, and he's had it in for me since the day I walked in there."

"I am *sure* you're right about Mortie," I said, "but sometimes it's the two-faced little pricks who have the most important messages for us."

☽ ☽ ☽

As we go along in our lives trying to change and grow, we get helped. One of the ways we get helped is that at certain moments we get messages about ourselves that we need to hear. These messages are sent to us by God through any messenger He can get His hands on at the moment. The messenger might be a spouse, a friend, a child, a billboard, a bumper sticker, a song on the car radio, chance words you hear spoken by people passing on the sidewalk, or a two-faced little prick. When it's a two-faced little prick who's delivering God's message, our job is not to get stuck in his two-faced little prickiness, but to *get the message*.

How do you do that?

It's sometimes hard, but the way I do it is to "delete" the tone, or "attitude," from the speaker's words so that I hear the words without letting the static of the speaker's personality interfere with them, and simply *hear the message*, neutral and edifying, as if it were being written by God in clear, bold type on a piece of paper: **You are antagonistic, argumentative, and almost impossible to work with.** Period. Just hear the words.

The journey we're on is so difficult and so tricky that we don't want to miss too many of God's messages, so we need to be able to *sense* that moment when a messenger is speaking to us. When a messenger is speaking to me, it feels like the entire rest of the universe quiets down for a second, and in that silence I'm suddenly hearing pristine words of wisdom being uttered to me. If we can develop that sense, if we can recognize the messengers, we start picking up messages as we talk and walk and look around our lives, changing and growing as we hear and obey them,[2] meanwhile developing a deep appreciation for God, who seems to be spending most of eternity up there devising ingenious and timely ways to deliver messages to us.

When God doesn't want us to ignore or forget a message, He will often send it through two or three messengers in a relatively short period of time. For example, if I, your therapist, sit here right now and echo what the two-faced little prick Mortie said to you—that you are, indeed, "antagonistic, argumentative, and almost impossible to work with"—that may be God *really* trying to get that message to you.

"And are you doing that? Are you giving me the same message as Mortie?" asked Darren.

"I am," I said.

Darren stared back at me, thinking. His barrel chest relaxed a bit. "My sister said pretty much the same thing to me two nights ago on the phone," he said. "That's three in a week."

There's a Yiddish proverb about messages:

If one person calls you a horse's ass, you can disregard it.

If two people call you a horse's ass, you might want to think about it.

If three people call you a horse's ass, get a saddle.

Welcome to Boston:
A Dharma Talk

Words do not matter, what matters is Dharma. What matters is action rightly performed.

—Buddha, the *Dhammapada*

I will put my laws into their hearts, and in their minds will I write them.

—Hebrews 10:16

"How should we treat my old friends Tess and Bob when they come to town next week?" asked Martha, her husband, Stan, sitting next to her. "When they hurt me so badly last year, I cut off all communication with them, but I've done some healing on that, and some forgiving, so I'm back in phone communication with them, and now they're coming to Boston and Stan and I were wondering how we should relate to them."

"It's easier to think about questions like that if you ask them in the form of 'What is the dharma of this situation?' *Dharma* is a Sanskrit word that means the right thing to do—one's righteous duty, the accurate and appropriate action in a particular situation—the *law*, as it were, for that situation."

"So how do you know what the dharma of a situation is?" she asked.

☽ ☽ ☽

It's written in the scriptures of the world, which are the divinely inspired utterances of the Self-realized beings of the world,[3] and it's written in your own heart. I told Martha that if she and Stan wanted to know how to relate to their friends, they should just go into their hearts, ask their question there, and wait for an answer. The instruction that comes from the heart is dharma.

Except when it's not.

It's not dharma when the voice you're hearing from within is not the voice of your heart, but the voice of the fears, hurts, resentments, revenges, and other negative reactions of your wounded self. Your dharmic self is your real Self, a sonorous voice of truth that will always tell you the right thing to do and always feels like some form of love. In a situation where you don't know what to do, ask within, "*What would love do here?*" Then wait for the answer. Remember, however, that love takes many forms. In one situation, it might take the form of a warm welcome. In another situation, it might take the form of a cold shoulder. There's sweet love and tough love and everything in between. Love is tricky that way. You have to listen within to your own wisdom for the particular form of love—for the dharma—that is appropriate to that situation.

"I've been hearing inside me something that sounds like wisdom," Stan said. "As you've been talking, I've been hearing a voice inside me that keeps telling me we're supposed to warmly welcome them when they come to Boston."

"And you, Martha?"

"For me, it's the same," said Martha. "The same words even."

"I hear the same thing in my heart," I said. "'*Welcome them to Boston with respect and love.*' That's three out of the three of us—we are all getting the same message about the dharma."

"That was easy," Martha said.

Knowing the dharma of a particular situation is often easy—when you listen to your heart. What great beings we are, each one of us knowing somewhere within ourselves the totally right and perfectly appropriate thing to do in every situation, each one of us, in our hearts, *the* dharma! And what a great world it will be when all of us live from our hearts, listening to the voice of dharma there, always doing our duty, always doing the right thing.

Life is really quite simple. Just follow dharma.

IN THE TIME OF HIS DYING

May God grant that my father's memory ever inspire me, and may his soul be bound up in the bond of eternal life, together with the souls of all the righteous that are in Thy keeping.
                    —Jewish prayer

Beverly's father was dying. He was eighty-nine and had prostate cancer that had metastasized to his liver, and the doctors were giving him another two or three months to live. While Beverly told herself that her father was old and had led a good, long life, she still wasn't ready to let him go. She wanted to find something to do, some way to come to peace with his impending death.

"I want to use this time of his dying the best way I can," she told me, her voice cracking. "But I don't know how. What's the best way I can use this time?"

"I don't know if I know the best way," I told her gently, "but I know that on our journeys we all have to face the dying and death of loved ones sometimes; and I know that we can use even such difficult times to grow and to share our love. Here are a few ways you might use these last few months with your father."

꜀ ꜀ ꜀

Use the time of your father's dying for service. Whatever your father's needs are in this time of his dying—his physical, emotional, and spiritual needs—serve them to the best of your ability and with a full heart. Be there for him.

Use the time of your father's dying for saying good-bye to him, and for feeling the emotions involved in saying good-bye forever to someone you love. If your father was a good and a loving father to you, those feelings will be primarily sadness and grief, and when they come up in you, it is good to experience them, and to cry about them. Talk about them with any comforting person in your life. Talk to your father about your emotions, if it feels right, and cry with him, especially if by expressing your sadness and grief you can help your father feel his own sadness and grief.

Use the time of your father's dying for love. If there are blocks to the full expression of your love—unresolved anger, or resentment from the past—try to remove the blocks so that you can fully express your love to him. It is one of the sweetest of human experiences to fully express your love to someone. If, for any reason, you can't remove the blocks and heal the relationship, realize that something in *you*, not in the relationship, needs healing. So find the thing that needs healing in you—find the *unforgiveness* in you, and do your best to heal it—*then* fully express your love. Whether or not you heal it, express as much love as you can to your father before he dies.

Use the time of your father's dying for honor. In your heart; in conversation with other family members; in conversation with anybody; in prayer; in meditation; in a eulogy you write and then, with your father's permission, send or read to your father before he dies—honor your father's life. Good people who have led good lives should be greatly honored, and what greater honor is there than the honor of a child? With your honor, engrave the greatness of his life on everybody's heart, including his, so he can take it with him when he goes. If there's still too much pain in you about the relationship and you can't honor your father before he goes, so be it, but keep working on yourself so you can do it before *you* go.

Use the time of your father's dying for greeting your own life with gladness and love. Go out into your life with senses sharpened under the shadow of death, and love your life. Love the early morning. Love the cottony white moon setting over the gray river and the sun rising like a huge orange wafer through the trees. Love the ripples of light spreading in the wake of the ducks gliding on the river. Love the clarion song of the cardinal sounding in the woods. Love the crows. Love the roots, and the rocks, and the lichen on the rocks. Love the clouds. Love the sound of passing cars on the street, and the pungent smell of their exhaust, and the warm puff of wind on your face as they pass. Love the faces you see in those cars, bravely driving out into their day. Love the day. Love the night. *Fiercely* love it all, and be glad for it. Each phenomenon. Each face. It is all the face of God. This is God's earth—this garden, this heaven. Use the time of your father's dying to experience the ecstasy of being here for the achingly short time that we are here.

Use the time of your father's dying for wisdom, awe, humility, surrender, and faith in God. During the time of your father's dying, read what the saints and sages and enlightened beings of the world have said about death, for they are the ones who understand a universe that includes death as part of life. The understanding of death will lead you into spiritual understanding, because there is no way to understand death except spiritually. At the very heart of spiritual understanding is the humbling realization that there are forces on this earth and in this universe that are far more powerful than you or your father or any human being, and that one of these forces is death. No matter how it happens or to whom or when, death is in the plan of God. To be wise is to surrender to the awesome sovereignty of God's will, even when He wills death. In the end, use the time of your father's dying to surrender your father to God, to give him back to God, and to have faith in that God who has willed that your father leave his body now and continue his journey elsewhere.

Two Parrots and a Cockatoo

One who has finally learned that it is in the nature of objects to come and go without ceasing, she rests in detachment and is no longer subject to suffering.

—Ashtavakra, *Ashtavakra Gita*

Lena, twenty-eight, was despondent and tearful. Earlier today she had received in the mail yet another publisher's rejection of a book she had written. She had been crying, off and on, most of the day.

"I don't think I can send it out again," she said. "It's too hard. This is the fifth time. Everything I've worked for for the last three years—a total failure. What am I going to do?"

"Two things," I said. "One, keep sending it out; it's a good book, and certainly there are more than five publishers in the world. Two, keep looking for the *source* of your suffering whenever the book gets sent back to you. Do you know what that source is?"

"Not really," she said. "Maybe the rejections from the world are keying into the constant rejection from my parents when I was young."

"Psychologically speaking, that *contributes* to your suffering, but our psychology is never the *source* of our suffering. The source of our suffering is always deeper, and always has something to do with attachment."

"Attachment? To what?"

"In your case, to your book . . . your talent . . . success . . . achievement . . . the pleasures and treasures of the world."

"What's wrong with attachment?"

"Nothing—except that it's the source of *all* our suffering."

☽ ☽ ☽

Attachment is when you desire to acquire, attain, achieve, possess, or keep something. Attachment is when you desire that one thing happen instead of another. In a culture like ours, which is totally based on fulfilling as many desires as possible before you die, the proposition that desire and attachment are the source of all our suffering appears preposterous. This message actually makes us furious because it contradicts the fundamental beliefs upon which we've been conditioned to build our whole lives, so we often end up banishing, imprisoning, torturing, murdering, or crucifying the great beings who bring us this message.

That desire and attachment are the source of all our suffering is common sense, however. Attachment to anything that is of this world *must* cause suffering because all the things that are of this world come and go. Experiences, relationships, material things—all things come and go. Thieves break through and steal and moths destroy our treasures. We get sick. We get old. We die. There's nothing permanent or certain out there. To try to derive our happiness, peace of mind, well-being, and self-worth from anything impermanent is ridiculous. To get attached to any of it is just plain silly. It's like putting your most valuable possession—your own happiness!—on a boat that you *know* is going to drift away and sink. Where does that leave you? It leaves you right where Lena was—crying because she used the writing skill she was attached to, to produce a book she was attached to, which has not yet achieved the publisher's acceptance she was attached to, to get her the recognition, the fame, and the fortune she was attached to.

That's a lot of attachment. No wonder Lena was having a rough day.

I understood only too well the suffering Lena was experiencing because of her attachments. Eighteen years ago I wrote a book about addictions and compulsions and, ironically, the breaking of attachments. It was a kind of how-to book, and a good book—pithy, funny, readable, practical. Before I sent it out into the world, I tried to make it as perfect a book on the breaking of attachments as I could. The only thing I forgot to do before I sent it into the world was to break my attachment to it.

Although it was a first book by a totally unknown author, a prominent New York literary agent accepted it within a week of my sending it to her, and, within another two weeks, had sold it to a major New York publisher who gave me a big advance and the prediction that the book, which would be published in hardcover, would be "the *Jonathan Livingston Seagull* of self-help books." I was *psyched*! This was going to be the fulfillment of my lifelong dream—fame and fortune as a writer! I started watching all the talk shows on television—at that time, Johnny Carson, Mike Douglas, Dick Cavett, and the *Today Show*—to prepare myself for my nationwide promotional tour. That was going to be the best part: going on the *Tonight Show* after Paul Newman and Joanne Woodward, and then sitting there talking to Johnny in front of a packed studio audience and millions of viewers who all found me charming and wise. I was *totally* attached to it all.

But an interesting thing happened on the way to fame and fortune: None of it happened to me. It didn't even come close to happening. A month after the book was published, it was dead on the shelves.

I got depressed for about a year. During that year, I would spend most of my days in bed watching TV and feeling sorry for myself, getting up only to go out in the evening to teach a course on "The Literature of Inner Peace"—if you can believe that—at the local community college.

I actually *did* appear on a television talk show that first year, although it wasn't quite the *Tonight Show*. It was a local talk show here in Boston called *Five All Night Live*. I came on at 2:38 A.M., sat down on a chair, and was asked stupid, superficial questions for about seven minutes by a guy who didn't have a clue as to what my book was about and probably hadn't even read the flap copy, much less the book. There was one person in the studio audience that night. I think he was the custodian taking a break. And the guests who preceded me on the show that night were not Paul Newman and Joanne Woodward, they were—I swear to God this is true!—two parrots and a cockatoo.

It is not easy to break our attachments, but two parrots and a cockatoo help a lot to bring things back into perspective. Still, the breaking of our attachments is the work of a lifetime. It takes that long to begin to understand that whatever our destiny may bring us, good fortune or bad, attainment of our desires or not, we have to go inside ourselves for the happiness, peace of mind, well-being, and self-worth that we want.

FOUR WAYS OF GOING TO EL SALVADOR

I see all of Southeast Asia
I can see El Salvador
I hear the cries of children
And the other songs of war
It's like a mighty melody
That rings down from the sky
Standing here upon the moon
I watch it all roll by . . .

> —The Grateful Dead,
> "Standing on the Moon"

Change yourself and you have done your part in changing the world.
Every individual must change his own life if he wants to live in a
peaceful world.

> —Paramahansa Yogananda,
> *Autobiography of a Yogi*

Carolyn, fifty-nine, an independently wealthy woman, was going to El Salvador in four months to live in a peasant village and help the villagers with a building project. This would be her third trip there. She was troubled.

"I think if I let myself, I could stay there the rest of my life," she said. "And I *know* I could just give them all of my money. The poverty there is unbelievable, Robert. It breaks your heart. I feel I could give and give and give, and I'd hardly make a dent in it all. I *so* want to make a difference for those people, for this *world*, but there's *so* much to do. Then I get overwhelmed by it all, and depressed, and I end up immobilized, just sitting in my house all day staring out the window at the woods. How can I find peace with all the suffering in the world?"

I thought for a moment. "I can think of four ways to respond to the suffering in the world. They seem to contradict each other, but if you can somehow meld them together in your mind, they might bring you some peace."

The Bodhisattva of Compassion

Sentient beings are numberless; I vow to save them all.
     —The Bodhisattva

We should all devote everything we have in our lives—our time, energy, talents, and resources—to alleviating the suffering in the world. We should all be bodhisattvas of compassion, enlightened beings who take on the responsibility of ending the suffering. We should all just finally *get* it that we're all in this together, and not one of us can be personally and individually happy as long as there is a single one of us who isn't. It doesn't matter if it's the suffering of a poor person in El Salvador or a homeless person in Boston or an abused child in a loveless home or an animal being cruelly treated. Suffering is suffering and all of it is *our* suffering. When we understand that, when our hearts expand with infinite compassion into that, we can all get our personal act together in order to go out there and finally put an end to it.

A Change of Heart

You must be the change you wish to see in the world.
     —Mohandas K. Gandhi

The best thing you can do for the world, and the only way to truly change the world, is to change yourself. Everything that's wrong out there is wrong in here. Because the world is a hologram of myself, I must heal myself, purifying myself of everything that is not love. This sad world of ours, full of human beings trying so hard to love while so full of hurt and fear, needs millions of people whose hearts have become love, and who bring that love wherever they go. I must work on myself, therefore, until my heart is pure. *That's* my responsibility to the world. Whenever I am doing anything that purifies my heart—sitting alone in a room meditating or praying; reading the words of the saints and sages; walking in the woods in the tranquillity of nature; eating and exercising to maintain and enhance my physical, emotional, and spiritual health; coming to therapy to heal my wounds—I am doing something helpful for the world.

The Arm in the Bucket

God wants the fire on the altar to burn with a small flame.
—a Jewish sage

This universe of time and space, infinite and eternal in all directions and dimensions, is beyond anything you can conceive of, and you and your efforts to improve it don't make an iota of difference in it. Everything you do or might ever do is irrelevant. There is a level of reality on which we are totally insignificant, and only when we get to the truth of our own insignificance will we understand that trying to do anything important in the world always ends up being some form of hubris. Someone once said that if you want to know how important you are in the world, you should put your arm in a bucket of water and then take it out, and the impression left by your arm in the water after you take it out is how important you are in the world.

A Perfect World

That is perfect.
This is perfect.
From the perfect springs the perfect.
If the perfect is taken from the perfect, only the perfect remains.
—*Brihadaranyaka Upanishad*

The world does not need improvement. It is only your limited understanding that makes you think that it needs improvement. Everything in the world is perfect—afloat, governed, and embraced by the love and law of God—and when your understanding improves and your vision clears, you will know that. You will know that suffering is only an outer appearance and that in reality everything is held in God's love and everything is already perfect.

☽ ☽ ☽

So when you go to El Salvador, go with these four understandings. They're all true, even though they sound contradictory. And God bless you for going.

The Greatest Moment in Boston Sports

We know how rough the road will be,
how heavy here the load will be,
we know about the barricades
that wait along the track;
but we have set our soul ahead
upon a certain goal ahead,
and nothing left from hell to sky
shall ever turn us back.

—Vince Lombardi

I once asked a very wise friend, a woman who's been on the journey of transformation for three decades, what she thought was most needed for this great endeavor. "Perseverance!" she shouted. "Perseverance and grit!" I think she's right, and I find inspiration and strength for my journey when I see or hear of a human being who exhibits these qualities.

Ever since I was a kid, I've enjoyed standing on Commonwealth Avenue in Newton on Patriots Day to watch the Boston marathon, and every year I walk over to watch it where it comes through my neighborhood. I especially like to watch the men and women in wheelchairs, and cheer them on. Four years ago I saw something that *totally* inspired me, and I wrote a piece about it that was published in my local newspaper.[4] It's called "The Greatest Moment in Boston Sports."

☽ ☽ ☽

I have lived in the Boston area all my fifty years, and have seen the greatest moments—either live, on television, or on video—in the last five decades of Boston sports history.

I saw Havlicek steal the ball. I saw Larry Bird steal the ball and pass it to DJ for the layup. I saw Cousy dribble and Russell block and Sharman shoot. I saw Ted Williams hit. I saw Lonborg and Luis pitch in a dream that sort of came true. I saw Fisk hit one down the left-field line and keep it fair with the sheer willpower of his waving arms as he jumped sideways down the first base line. I saw Yaz run his farewell lap around Fenway. I saw Clemens strike out twenty. I saw Marciano knock out everybody. I saw Derek Sanderson from behind the net pass the puck out to Bobby Orr cutting in front and shooting and scoring and then sailing through the air with his arms flung high in Stanley Cup ecstasy. I saw Borque take off his number seven jersey to reveal his new number seventy-seven while the real and true and only number seven, Phil Esposito, watched his number rising to the rafters. I saw Flutie hit Phelan in the end zone in Miami, and I saw the Patriots, after eighteen trips to the Orange Bowl, finally beat Miami in the AFC championship game in '86. I sat glued to the television for every moment of "Larry Bird Night" at the Garden, especially the moment when Larry and Magic hugged and an era ended.

I saw all those great moments in Boston sports, and thousands more, and I loved each one. I get chills sometimes just thinking about them.

But none of those moments was the greatest moment I've ever seen in Boston sports. The greatest moment I ever saw was a moment in the Boston marathon last year. I was standing on Commonwealth Avenue in Newton on the long, steep hill that rises from the fire station to the Brae Burn Country Club. A man in a wheelchair was pushing himself up the hill slowly . . . very slowly . . . inch by inch . . . his helmeted head bent down on his thin, drawn-up knees, his muscular arms, glistening with sweat, hanging wearily to the pavement after each push, beads of sweat dripping off his face, his wheelchair going slower and slower and slower up the hill . . . until finally it couldn't go anymore . . . and he stopped, exhausted, about halfway up.

All of us watching stared in anxious silence. The man lifted his head and looked up the hill, expressionless. Then, gripping his wheels once again, he turned his wheelchair sideways, toward us, as if to get off Commonwealth Avenue and leave the race. But he didn't do that. He kept turning his wheelchair until now it was pointing back down the hill he had just struggled up, as if he was going to coast back down to the fire station for rest and care. But he didn't do that either.

He took a deep breath and carefully placed his head back down on his knees. His hands tightened on the wheels and he started pushing himself up the hill again—backward!—using a different set of muscles that still had some strength in them. We watched him as he slowly, methodically, steadily backed up the hill, his huge arms pumping like slow pistons. We all rose to our feet, applauding quietly, knowing it was too great a moment for cheering.

I lost sight of him at the top of the hill. I don't know what happened to him. I don't know if he finished the race. I don't know his name. I didn't stay for the runners.

But I have never really lost sight of him. He is still pushing that wheelchair backward up that hill—in my mind—whenever I have long, steep hills to climb in my life; and—no offense to Larry or Bobby or Bill or Ted—it is the greatest moment I ever saw in Boston sports.

FATHERS AND MOTHERS:
THE LOVING PATH OF PARENTING

Welcome to the world, dear child,
Welcome to the earth,
All our love surrounds you at your birth.
Though our paths will someday part,
Right now you're too small to be alone,
So the Lord has placed you in our home.

—Robbie Gass,
"Welcome to the World"

For some of us, the journey of self-knowledge takes us to parenting. Parenting is the part of the journey when we're called upon to guide newly arrived human souls on their journey through life. The nature and degree of the guidance changes over time, but I don't think it ever stops. Parenting is also the part of the journey when we have to travel very deeply into ourselves, looking for everything unconscious and unkind we can find in there that, if it comes out at our children, might hinder or encumber them on their journeys. As loving parents, we want our children to have fruitful journeys and clear sailing, so we try to offer clear parenting to them.

☽ ☽ ☽

Whenever I am asked about my role as a father, I realize I don't think about my role very much. I feel I'm just doing what needs to be done. I help my daughter. I am here on earth to help her. My role as a father is to remember, as often as I can, to help her, in whatever way I can.

When my daughter Greta was a child in elementary school, I would wake her up in the mornings and help her find her clothes. Then I would go downstairs and make breakfast for her and sit down and chat with her while she ate. Then I brushed her hair and bundled her up, handed her her lunch box, and walked her up the path to the road and kissed her good-bye as she climbed into Katie's car and went off to school at eight A.M.

At two P.M. I picked her up from school and chatted with her on the ride home. I listened to her. I played with her. I played catch, tag, marbles, and gin rummy with her. I fixed her toys, washed her face, scratched her back, and laughed at her jokes. I drove her to her friends' houses, and drove her friends to our house. I held her a lot and I told her that she was wonderful a lot. I told her the truth about life, if I knew it, and if I didn't, I told her that. I told her about God. I listened to her when she was upset about things, and I held her when she cried. I made her dinner and I washed the dishes and then we went upstairs and I helped her get ready for bed. I tucked her in and read her a story. We chatted about the day. I kissed her good night. Sometimes I lay down next to her as she fell asleep, her hand rubbing my forearm.

Jane did all of this too. Mostly we loved it, and we really didn't talk about our roles as mother and father. I don't think Greta saw much difference between us, except once she said that Jane's forearm was softer than mine.

I've always tried to be a good father to Greta, but sometimes I've had to work at it. Somewhere underneath all my images, ideas, models, and memories of a father, somewhere underneath Jack Alter, Ozzie Nelson, *Father Knows Best,* and the Marlboro man there is the father that I truly am, and my fathering is a journey to him.

As a father, I have always tried to be a safe, gentle man in the presence of my daughter because I represent men and manhood to her. I tried not to scare her or overpower her. If I saw fear of me in her eyes, I was admonished. When she fought back with me, I was glad. The world needs women of power who are unafraid of men, and I was doing what I could to help send it one.

I tried to become a happy and healthy human being for my daughter, because, in the final analysis, the real gift I give her, and the truest teaching I teach her, is *me.* In the act of my becoming myself, I am being a father. So there is really nothing to do, and no role to be in, but just Robert becoming Robert while Greta watched and became Greta.

☽ ☽ ☽

So, what is the difference between a mother's and a father's love for a child? I would say that a mother's love is not a father's love because a woman is not a man, and a woman's body is not a man's body, and we carry different energies inside us. I would say that love, however, is love. I would say that Jane's forearm *is* softer than mine. And then I would say: The role of the mother and that of the father are different *and* the same. That's the yin and yang of it. That's the koan. On one level, fathering passes down certain energies to a child, and mothering passes down different ones. On a deeper level, fathering is the same as mothering. At our centers, we are not fathers or mothers, but beings of love, pure consciousness.

When she was seven, I asked Greta if she thought there was any difference between fathers and mothers.

"I don't know," she said.

"Think about it," I said.

She thought about it.

"Fathers drive more."

☽ ☽ ☽

So what is parenting?

Whether as a father or a mother, parenting is love. And every other feeling it is possible for a human being to feel.

Parenting is also attachment. I'm hopelessly attached to my daughter. The Buddha named his son Rahula, which means "obstacle."

Parenting is whatever we are doing in the moment we are in with our children.

Parenting is all the forms of love between Jane and me that Greta saw every day as she grew up. She saw us supporting and helping each other, talking sweetly to each other, smiling and joking and laughing, sympathizing and commiserating, and being physically affectionate with each other. She saw us holding hands, hugging, cuddling, and dancing with each other.[5] As Greta's eyes filled with all these forms of her parents' love for each other, her heart filled with security and happiness.

One morning in the winter when Greta was six, she sat bundled up behind me in her red sled, singing, as I was pulling her over the snow up the path. I felt the rope taut in my glove. I felt the strength in my legs. Without looking back, I saw her watching me, her tall father in his boots and winter hat, striding through the snow and pulling her smoothly across it. Her eyes were at peace, her face loved me. Without looking back, I saw that picture enter her consciousness and settle in as a memory, a memory that would never die even though she would sometimes forget it. It would be an image that would come to her when she needed it, when life got hard for her. It was the secret truth of the way things were for Greta, her father with her, his strength hers, the path smooth and her safe. *Remember, my little one. Hold me like a jewel in your heart. I am always with you.*[6]

KARMA AND REINCARNATION
AND ALL THAT EASTERN STUFF

Be not deceived; God is not mocked: for whatsoever a man soweth, that
shall he also reap.

—Galatians 6:7

"Whatever a man sows, that shall he reap." The law of Karma is
inexorable and impossible of evasion. There is thus hardly any need for
God to interfere. He laid down the law and, as it were, retired.

—Mohandas K. Gandhi,

An Autobiography

For the last twenty-five years of my life, almost everything I've read has
been the writings of the enlightened and awakened seers from all the
world's great spiritual traditions. Basically, I've found they all say the
exact same things about the universe, and one of the truths of the universe is that karma and reincarnation exist.

Karma is the universal law of cause and effect. It says that for every
action (the root of the Sanskrit word *karma* means "action"), there's a
reaction. If it's a good action that comes out of you, good will return to
you. If it's a bad action that comes out of you, bad will return to you. In
other words, everything that happens to you is returning to you.

The law of karma means that, ethically speaking, every single pigeon
comes home to roost, that all our actions have consequences and there
are no loopholes. The Hindu sage Vasishtha says, "There is no place in
the universe, no mountain, no sky, no ocean, no heaven, where one
does not undergo the consequences of actions performed by oneself."
The law of karma is the mechanism by which God administers justice in
the universe and ensures that each soul will be guided toward the good.
The absolute and self-operating law of karma holds each soul in its ethical grip until that soul evolves to knowing that its highest ethic and its
essential nature is love.

This process of spiritual evolution, often likened to a journey, takes a
very long time to reach completion, longer than the body of any one
particular life form, which is where reincarnation comes in. The soul

must come back to inhabit body after body in different life forms in order to learn all it must learn on its journey toward its own purity and perfection. It starts off in each body where it left off at the death of the previous body, and keeps traveling through bodies, each time learning more until there's no more to learn. At this point the soul no longer needs bodies and goes to other planes of existence, and does not return. "Him that overcometh will I make a pillar in the temple of my God, and he shall go no more out," as it says in Revelations.

You may ask, why are we all taking these journeys toward purity and perfection? And if the goal is purity and perfection, why is there so much horror in the world?

I see the horror too. I see more forms of injustice and cruelty and seemingly random suffering on this earth than my mind can conceive of or contain. I see cancer strike my friends and ravage their bodies. I see people mutilated and murdered in wars all over the earth. I see refugees carrying their children and aged parents over mountain ranges to escape those wars. I see people killing their neighbors, relatives, schoolmates, and random strangers. I see starving children in Africa. I'm Jewish, so I always see the Holocaust. I see fires and floods. I see airplanes falling out of the sky, strewing bodies and parts of bodies over cornfields in Indiana. What in God's name is happening here?

The enlightened ones, the Great Beings, the knowers of the Truth, say that what happens to a person in a particular lifetime is the karmic consequence of his actions in past lifetimes. All suffering is the payment of karmic debt, and all events, good and bad, are the self-organizing and self-adjusting movements of the universe as it balances all karmic accounts. Every action we've ever committed in past lifetimes is bread cast upon the waters, which finds us, as the Bible says, "after many days." Sometimes those days are so many that they span lifetimes. This is the self-operating law of action and reaction in the universe—the law of karma.

I believe in karma and reincarnation and all that Eastern stuff because these concepts bring some peace to my mind when I look around at the world. With them, and only with them, can I understand what I'm seeing. As a friend of mine once said, "Reincarnation is a way of understanding things that are otherwise inexplicable. From the point of view of one lifetime, let's face it, most of us are getting screwed." In this universe, actions really *do* have consequences. These consequences follow us around from lifetime to lifetime, and what we call accident and what we call coincidence, and what we call fortune and what we call misfortune are the consequences of our past actions finally catching up to us according to some unbelievably complicated cosmic plan that nobody but God's mind could concoct, so don't even try to think about it.

And the purpose of it all is that all the souls in the universe attain purity and perfection—which is to say, *love*—so all our actions—and our words, and our thoughts—will be love. And when only love is coming out of us, by karmic law only love will be returning to us, so there's only love turning and returning around the whole universe. That's paradise, and that's the purpose of it all.

Make a Joyful Noise!

Make a joyful noise unto the Lord, all the earth: make a loud noise, and rejoice, and sing praise.
—Psalm 98:4

Chanting is a supreme therapy. Singing and chanting have the power to uproot the pain in the heart and reveal the fountain of bliss below.
—Maharani, "Sounding the Heart"

In therapy sessions, I will sometimes play tapes and CDs for clients: the spoken words of sages and healers, classical music, popular songs that have wisdom in them, spiritual songs, and chants. Since singing and chanting play such an important role in my own spiritual journey, I sometimes suggest that clients make them part of their journey too. This is usually a new and surprising idea for many people ("Chanting?" said a client once. "What am I? Some Gregorian monk or Hare Krishna nut?"), yet spiritual singing and chanting can be an important part of therapy and part of our journey to Self-realization.

Modern physicists tell us that the whole universe is really energy in constant vibrational motion. Energy in vibrational motion produces sound—*is* sound—which means that the whole universe is essentially a form of sound.[7] This truth is supported not only by physics but by all the world's scriptures, including the Judaeo-Christian Bible. In Genesis, God creates the universe by speaking it: "And God said, Let there be light: and there was light." And in the Gospel of John, it is written, "In the beginning was the Word, and the Word was with God, and the Word was God."[8] In other words, words have immense spiritual power! In all religions, the singing of spiritual words—hymns, gospels, mantras, chants, etc.—is a major spiritual practice that, over time, attunes and harmonizes the instrument of our individual being with the universal divine Being until we finally realize our oneness with that Being. No wonder there's so much singing and chanting and the lifting up of human voices wafting out the windows of all those temples and mosques and synagogues and churches all over the world. Those are human beings singing their hearts out as they sing their way into the Divine Heart.

Singing and chanting are powerful spiritual practices that can sometimes give us a direct and immediate experience of our heart. They release a special energy in us that leaves both our minds and our bodies behind and takes us straight to the joy in our hearts. I know from many personal experiences that when I'm in one of my really dark moods, a total funk, and *nothing*, not meditation, not my wife, not even my dish of chocolate ice cream, can get me out of it, singing and chanting can. They have tremendous power to lift my spirits, to change my negative feelings into positive feelings, to completely transform my inner state. Sometimes when I chant, especially in groups, I am lifted like a rocket to a height of happiness and well-being that I didn't even know I had in me. Once, while chanting with my meditation teacher in a large hall with thousands of other people, as the chant got faster and faster over the course of an hour, suddenly something that felt like pure joy rose in my heart, a rush of energy that sent chills rippling up and up my spine, and spilled and flowed and flooded through my being like the beatitude that the mystics and saints speak of. "*What is this?!*" I remember thinking. "*This is you!*" came the answer back.

Singing and chanting have the power to send a laser beam of pure luminous energy down to the very depths of our old and frozen psychological pain—pain that no amount of time or therapy or self-help reading is able to reach to—and melt it down to the nectar of letting go and love. A friend of mine's wife had been unfaithful to him twelve years before, and his heart was still suffering with hurt and anger and unforgiveness. He was pretty stuck there, he said. One day, after another failed attempt to get her to truly empathize with the pain he had gone through, he was chanting when tears suddenly started flowing out of his eyes, welling up and spilling down his cheeks profusely, with no words and for no apparent reason. After a moment, he had the vague sense that his tears were about his wife's unfaithfulness. Chanting as best he could through his tears, after some time an amazing thing happened. Rising up over the hurt of his wife's infidelity, transcending his twelve-year need for the perfect apology from her, came a feeling of opening, like the drawing of a deep breath, and then, to his surprise, came the words, forming and reforming in his mind, again and again—"*I forgive you . . . I forgive you . . . I forgive you . . .*" Gradually, as he continued chanting and the pain melted, he felt a soft, loving glow expanding in his heart and radiating out through his whole being. He felt clear, cleansed, as if a big piece of the pain that had constricted his heart for twelve years had been dislodged. The power of the chant—the power of sound—had penetrated to that pain and had released the tears that washed his heart clean of this sorrow, finally allowing him to forgive her.

WIND AND WEATHER PERMITTING
or
WHY THERAPY?

The greatest challenge of the day is how to bring about a revolution of the heart, a revolution which has to start with each one of us.
—Dorothy Day

If enough people think of a thing and work hard enough at it, I guess it's pretty nearly bound to happen, wind and weather permitting.
—Laura Ingalls Wilder,
By the Shores of Silver Lake

Many of you are in therapy, many are not. Those who are not may wonder, What's the point of therapy? I'm a little neurotic, but I get along pretty well, don't I? My marriage may not be great, but at least we're still together. And so on.

But there's another reason why we might want to do therapy.

I believe that while therapy helps us to grow as people, and better equips us to deal with our lives, it can have a larger purpose as well. When we heal ourselves, we heal the world itself, a world that desperately needs healing. There's so much suffering on our planet! Human beings are suffering, animals are suffering, the skies and the oceans and the rain forests are suffering—the whole earth is suffering. If you listen very carefully on a very quiet night, you can hear cries out there.

I would say that the reason for most of the suffering on the earth is the misunderstanding in the human mind—the confused and misguided thinking, the ignorance, arrogance, anger, and fear in the human mind, which causes human beings to act irrationally, dishonestly, selfishly, and cruelly. The cause of the misunderstanding in the human mind is the wound in the human heart, and the core wound in the human heart is *hurt*. Deep inside we are all hurt.[9]

There are a lot of human beings on the planet today—many in positions of power and influence—whose actions are rooted in their hurt, and they inflict physical and mental and spiritual suffering on other human beings, on other sentient creatures, on the whole planet. I believe the only way this is going to stop is if a significant number of people heal the pain in their minds and hearts, because once human minds and hearts are healed, we will act in the world with intelligence, kindness, respect, and love, for that is our essential nature.

Anything human beings do to heal their wounds is a good thing to do. To the extent that therapy helps a person heal his or her wounds, thus helping a person act with intelligence, kindness, respect, and love, therapy is a good thing to do, and everybody who feels they need to do it, and who has the means to do it, and who finds someone good to do it with, should do it.

There are cries out there. We have to do *something*.

The Words of Wise Beings

Let your conduct be marked by right action, including study and teaching of the scriptures. . . . If at any time there is any doubt with regard to right conduct, follow the practice of great souls, who are guileless, of good judgment, and devoted to Truth.

—Taittiriya Upanishad

The journey to the Self is a long and winding road through all that is limited and contracted and fearful and painful inside ourselves to our core of joy and love and peace. That journey is long, and it's hard.

The main thing we need as we travel is information about the journey, and inspiration and comfort to help keep us going when the going gets tough. I find all of these in the words of wise beings—the people who have finished this journey to their innermost Self. These are the saints and sages and siddhas, the tzaddiks and sachems, the meditation masters and Self-realized beings of all the world's spiritual traditions.

The wise beings give us information about the journey. Many of them compare it to climbing a mountain. It's high; it's steep; it's slippery; it's storm swept; there are narrow ledges and sheer cliffs, difficult handholds, no shortcuts. Sometimes you have to go down to go up; the days are short, the dark nights of the soul long. The wise beings are our guides, our sherpas. They've climbed the mountain, and they know every crevice and crag, every single pebble and rock. They reach down to us with their words and their love, and help us move inch by inch up the mountain toward the azure peak where they dwell.

They give us inspiration too. In order to keep going, I need to know not only that it is possible to get to the top, but that great, courageous, determined beings have actually done it. They are my models, and their words are my inspiration. Frankly, there is so much darkness and pain one has to go through on this journey that if I hadn't been reading the inspiring words of wise beings all my adult life, I'm pretty sure I would have given up long ago, sat down in front of the TV, and spent the rest of my life watching reruns of *Bonanza*.

The wise beings also give us comfort. Sometimes I think I have more darkness and pain to go through than anybody else in the world, but then I read about what they've had to go through in themselves. Their problems sound a lot like my problems—the same doubts and fears and flaws and frailties—and reading their words reminds me that these difficulties are just the human experience and that we're all going through it together. It's a comfort when I think of Jesus' fear in the garden of Gethsemane, or Moses' self-doubt in the desert of Midian when God told him to go down to Egypt. It's a comfort to remember that Martin Luther King and Mahatma Gandhi, heroes of mine, were not supernatural saints but flawed human beings working on themselves just like you and me. When I feel that I'm having a hard time on the spiritual path, it's a comfort to read the words of the fourteenth-century Indian woman poet-saint Lalleshwari:

> You must bear the lightning and thunder along the path.
> You have to endure the difficulties in the dark midnight of sadhana.
> Be calm; do not turn back.
> It will be like being crushed to powder between grinding stones.

Oh! I think. Lalleshwari has been there, done that, made it through that. I'm not crazy or bad or spineless for feeling this way. I can make it through that too.

> But if you can endure it, O Lalli,
> God will come looking for you,
> and happiness and contentment
> will welcome you home.[10]

Ah! I think. I can make it home too.

The wise beings are my teachers. They are my spiritual teachers because the journey I'm talking about and taking is a spiritual journey, and they are my psychology teachers because, make no mistake, *the spiritual journey is a journey through all our psychology*. The spiritual masters of the world are the master psychologists of the world, with an understanding of the human psyche so deep and complete that they and only they can show us the way completely through it.

Read the words of wise beings; feel their truths resonating in your own heart; imbibe the truths contained in those words; conduct yourself according to the teachings taught in those words; and live the rest of your life guided, inspired, and comforted by those words.

Many people take their journey of self-knowledge by using the words and living examples of friends, parents, loved ones, mentors, even strangers observed in a caring moment for their spiritual inspiration and guidance. It is our good fortune that we have these people in our lives. And if, on your journey, you ever have the *great* good fortune to meet a fully Self-realized being[11]—a living master, a contemporary saint—spend as much time as you can with her or him. "If I knew so wise a man as could teach me purity, I would go to seek him forthwith," says Thoreau in *Walden*.[12] And if you ever find a pure one, fill your heart with her words, her love, her happiness, her state of being. It is a lot easier to go on a journey, especially a long and arduous journey, if we know where we're going—and the saint's state of being is where we're going. It is a state of perfect compassion, lightheartedness, repose, and wisdom. It is as strong as a mountain, and as tender as a flower. It just wants to *give*, and the only thing it gives—because the only thing it *is*—is love. It's the model for everything we are trying to become on this journey (and actually already *are)*, right there before our eyes, as if the transcendent, formless God, difficult to be known but wanting to be known, manifests in human form in order to be known. If, on your journey, you ever have the great good fortune to be in the company of a Self-realized being, go to her and look at a living model of the deepest and purest part of yourself looking back at you like a mirror and, with great respect and with great love, beckoning you forward to your Self.

Good-bye

This love you now have of the Truth
Will never forsake you.

—Hafiz, "They Call You to Sing"

Good-bye. You are finished here, and it is time for you to move on now. But you are not finished out there, in your life. There is always farther to go out there. I don't say this to discourage you, but to encourage and inspire you.

It's an interesting word, "good-bye." It's a contraction of the four Middle English words "God be with ye." It's a blessing and a benediction.

God be with you.

God *is* with you.

God is *in* you, *as* you.

Keep looking.

Good-bye.

ACKNOWLEDGMENTS

O Lord! that lends me life,
Lend me a heart replete with thankfulness.
          —William Shakespeare,
          Henry VI, Part II

This book could not have been written without the support, the friend-ship, the instruction, the inspiration, the help, and the love of many, many people, and I want to thank some of them here. Those people whose names are written in italics have died, and I write this book in memory of them.

All my relatives and ancestors, especially my grandparents, *Anna and Willie Alter* and *Florence and Eddie Simons,* for their spirituality, their tra-ditions, their labors, and their love.

My parents-in-law, Yvette and *Irving* Lebow, and my brother-in-law, River Lebow, for warmly welcoming me into their family in 1970, and for being cornucopias of acceptance, support, encouragement, and love ever since. And Al Colombo, for continuing in that tradition of love.

My sister and brother-in-law, Gail and Milton Jacobson, and their children, Steven, Lynne, and Jon (and of course Wiley and Jake!), for many forms of assistance and generosity over the years.

Ruth and Jon Berenson, Lana Bessey, Marilyn Bornstein, Bobby Copeland, Diane d'Almeida, *Roger* and Dinny Drury, Lyra Engel, Nick and Julianne Etcheverry, Mary and Michael Faber, Robbie and Judith Gass, Richard Gillett, Jeff Hicks, *John Ingersoll, Keith Kitchener,* Gitte Kushner, Fay Larkin and Miguel Gómez-Ibáñez, Pamela Lerman, Dick Lockwood, Luke, John and Cathy McCabe, Joe Michael, Vince Morello, Harry Newell, *Karen Paine-Gerneé,* Sandra Pell, Jim Poffley, Laury

Rappaport, Patrick Rice, Mike Rotkin, *Mike Shaffer*, Carol Stevenson, Swami Anantananda, Rusty and Marty Swartz, Rebecca Wilson, Shomer Zwelling—and especially Gita and David Haddad and Lora and Stephen Maurer—for being my friends over many years.

All my other friends who have ever hung out with me, tried to figure out with me how life works, and played sports with me—on Westchester Road—at Camp Day—at Newton High—in Ithaca, Sheffield, Ashby, Greenville, Auburndale, South Fallsburg—and everywhere else on earth I've ever been.

Bob Henderson and Jack, Claire and Peter, Ginny and Joyce—for neighborliness.

All my clients and all my students for the past thirty-two years—for inspiring me by their efforts and for helping me, by their belief in me, to believe in myself.

Henry David Thoreau, Mahatma Gandhi, Martin Luther King, Mother Teresa, Ernest Hemingway, Sylvia Plath, Lenny Bruce, Bob Cousy, Bobby Orr, and Muhammad Ali—for modeling greatness to me and for being my heroes.

Jalaladdin Rumi, Sufi poet-saint of the thirteenth century—I have strung a bright necklace of Rumi's words through this book, to adorn it with the gems of his great mystical heart. And to Rumi's poet-translators—Coleman Barks, John Moyne, Camille and Kabir Helminski, Robert Bly, and Jonathan Star—and to Daniel Ladinsky, poet-translator of Hafiz—thank you for giving these great beings to the English-speaking world, and for so generously lending them to this book.

Bob Dylan, whose songs have been accompanying me on my journey of consciousness since 1963, when, as a freshman in college, I bought *The Times They Are A'Changing*. The times started changing for me, in my consciousness, the first time I played that album. When I first heard "When the Ship Comes In," I got on that ship right then and there, and I'm still on it, and it's still comin' in. It's been good sailing with you all these years, Bob. I have used some of your lyrics in this book, as my way of thanking and honoring you. I think the things I want to thank you for the most are your wondrous songs, your truth-filled heart, your outlaw voice that rasps and pierces the heart, and just how unbelievably cool you are.

Ned Leavitt, our extraordinary agent, for faithfulness and steadfastness, and for always seeing the way to go and then getting us there in a perfect and ongoing act of literary representation. Libby Stephens, for *total* helpfulness, niceness, and competence over the phone. Priscilla Stuckey, for expertly cutting the diamond out of the rough in a six-month act of editorial magic. Uma Hayes and Harriet Odlum, for the friendship, the time, the care, and the *seva*. Swami Kripananda and Joel Fowler, for gracious reference support. Ralph Berliner and Valerie Eads, for indefatigable work and expertise in the rights and permissions trenches, and Valerie, for translating Thomas à Kempis for us. Matt Jacobson-Carroll, for the patience of a saint while teaching me the computer. James Fox, Zick Rubin, and Barry Finkel, for wise legal counsel. Harville Hendrix, for uncovering the key that unlocks the psychological and spiritual mysteries of marriage, and for generously and graciously supporting this book with his time and enthusiasm. Dana Isaacson, for the open heart that welcomed this book to the publishing world. Vanessa Stich, our fine editor and fine-tuner at ReganBooks, for skillfully and respectfully shepherding it through that world. Doug Corcoran and Carl Mark Raymond at ReganBooks, for their commitment to getting the book right. Judith Regan, our publisher, for holding the high vision that brought this book to the reading world.

Matthew West Fruhan—many dreams have come true in our family; you are one of them. With great respect and with great love we welcome you into our family with all our hearts.

Greta, my daughter, my laughter, my gentle adviser, my pride, my pal, the light of my life. There's a level on which this book, like everything else I've done for the past twenty-eight years of our lives, is for you, kiddo, and I hope it is worthy of you. . . .

> *She openeth her mouth with wisdom, and in her tongue is the law of*
> *kindness. . . .*
> *Many daughters have done virtuously, but thou excellest them all.*
> —Proverbs 31:26, 29

Jane, my wife, my beauty, my editor, my teacher, my best friend, my comedienne, my inspiration. I love you on infinite levels of love, and here are the main three:

I loved her, and sought her out from my youth, I desired to make her my
spouse, and I was a lover of her beauty.

> King Solomon, the *Apocrypha*

I came in from the wilderness
A creature void of form.
"Come in," she said, "I'll give you
Shelter from the storm."

> —Bob Dylan,
>   "Shelter from the Storm"

A perfect woman, nobly planned,
To warn, to comfort, and command.
And yet a Spirit still, and bright
With something of angelic light . . .

> —William Wordsworth,
>   "She Was a Phantom of Delight"

All the saints and sages and *siddhas* and meditation masters and other great beings who have appeared in the world since the beginning of the world—for the *darshan*,[1] the awakening, the teachings, and the path. In very partial return, this book is an offering.

---

1. *Darshan* (literally, sight, vision) means, in Sanskrit, "seeing or being in the physical presence of an enlightened spiritual master." *Siddhas* are perfected beings, Self-realized ones.

NOTES

PREFACE

1. Richard Grossinger, *Planet Medicine,* quoted in Ron Kurtz, *Body-Centered Psychotherapy: The Hakomi Method* (Mendocino, Calif.: LifeRhythm, 1990), p. 40.

2. *Night and Sleep: Versions of Rumi,* translated by Coleman Barks and Robert Bly (Cambridge, Mass.: Yellow Moon Press, 1981).

CHAPTER 1

1. Nicolina Fedele and Elizabeth Harrington, *Women's Groups: How Connections Heal,* Stone Center paper. Used by kind permission of Jean Baker Miller and the Stone Center, Wellesley College, Wellesley, Massachusetts.

2. Alice Miller, *For Your Own Good: Hidden Cruelty in Child-Rearing and the Roots of Violence* (New York: Farrar, Straus & Giroux, 1983), p. 106. Dr. Miller's other books include *The Drama of the Gifted Child, Thou Shalt Not Be Aware, The Untouched Key, Banished Knowledge.* I am indebted to Steven Maurer, who encouraged me to read her. I am also indebted to Jon Berenson, David Breakstone, Marc Cloutier, Billie Jo Joy, David Ratta, Naomi Raiselle, and Phil Sardella for introducing me to other authors whose ideas have influenced me.

3. In the north Indian philosophical tradition known as Kashmir Shaivism, the individual human soul *(jiva)* is created by God *(Shiva)* with three innate impurities, or limited and false perceptions of itself. These impurities are the *anava mala,* the *mayiya mala,* and the *karma mala,* which we will all eventually overcome on the path to Self-realization. The *anava mala* is the root impurity that makes us all feel imperfect and incomplete and not good enough. For more information on the *malas,* see J. C. Chatterji, *Kashmir Shaivism* (Albany: State University of New York Press, 1986) and *The Doctrine of Recognition: A Translation of Pratyabhijnahrdayam with an Introduction and Notes by Jaideva Singh* (Albany: State University of New York Press, 1990).

CHAPTER 2

1. Those who believe in reincarnation would say that many of these thought-channels, especially the deeper ones, were cut before our childhood, in previous lives, and we come into life with them. See chapter 5, note 1, for more on this subject.

2. Firesign Theatre, *Waiting for the Electrician or Someone Like Him,* Columbia Records/CBS, Inc., New York, 1968.

3. Sir Walter Scott, *Marmion,* canto 6, stanza xvii.

CHAPTER 3

1. On one level God is nameless. On another level, God has many names. The sound of our breath is one of those names.

2. For scriptural mention of the four states, see "Brihadaranyaka Upanishad" in *The Upanishads,* translated by Swami Prabhavananda and Frederick Manchester (New York: New American Library, 1957), pp. 105–106. See also "Mandukya Upanishad" in *The Upanishads,* translated by Eknath Easwaran (Tomales, Calif.: Nilgiri Press, 1987), pp. 60–61. See also *Shankara's The Crest-Jewel of Discrimination (Viveka-Chudamani),* translated by Swami Prabhavananda and Christopher Isherwood (Hollywood, Calif.: Vedanta Press, 1947, 1975), pp. 45–49.

3. *How to Know God: The Yoga Aphorisms of Patanjali,* translated by Swami Prabhavananda and Christopher Isherwood (Hollywood, Calif.: Vedanta Press, 1953, 1981), p. 173. I have taken the liberty of substituting the word "awareness" for the word "thought" in the original, for consistency with my metaphor.

4. All of the content and much of the language in this essay was provided by Jane Alter.

CHAPTER 4

1. The mystical branch of Judaism is called Kabbalah. In Kabbalah, the soul has five levels: *Nefesh, Ruach, Neshama, Chaya,* and, the highest, *Ye'chidah.*

2. E. B. Pusey, *Daily Strength for Daily Needs: An Inspiring Collection of Spiritual Passages in Prose and Verse, One for Every Day of the Year,* selected by Mary W. Tileston (New York: Smithmark Publishers, 1995), p. 85.

3. See his famous "Essay on Civil Disobedience"; also "Life Without Principle," and certain parts of *Walden.*

CHAPTER 5

1. The theories of karma and reincarnation hold that our "past" goes *way* back—to past lifetimes. According to these theories, we have all had many lifetimes on this earth, in each of which we all had innumerable different experiences. Each experience left an *impression* on us, a subtle residual memory-trace, and the more significant and/or traumatic the experience, the deeper the impression. All of these impressions are stored within our subconscious in what's called the *subtle body,* like the soul, and these impressions travel with the subtle body as it incarnates and reincarnates into different physical bodies. In other words, we carry with us and within us a complete memory-record of everything that ever happened to us. These memory-traces are called, in Sanskrit, *samskaras* (from which is derived our English word "scar").

From these *samskaras*—subconscious memory impressions of past experiences—derive our innate tendencies to feel certain feelings, our predispositions to think and act in certain ways, and all our negativity and pain. The feelings that we cannot make sense of from the point of view of this one lifetime—especially the big, negative, chronic, entrenched feelings in us—make perfect *samskaric* sense from the point of view of many lifetimes.

Fortunately, there also exists in us a dormant energy—called, in Sanskrit, *kundalini*—which, if awakened, can, over time, through God's grace and our own sustained efforts, completely eradicate all our *samskaras,* gradually freeing us from all the mental and emotional suffering caused by them—in effect, removing all our pain.

See also the essay "Karma and Reincarnation and All That Eastern Stuff" in chapter 8, pp. 240–242. For more information about *samskaras* and *kundalini,* see Sir John Woodroffe, *The Serpent Power* (New York: Dover Publications, 1974); and Swami Kripananda, *The Sacred Power: A Seeker's Guide to Kundalini,* (South Fallsburg, N.Y.: SYDA Foundation, 1995).

2. The "heart" referred to in this essay is the emotional heart, which contains all human feelings—to be distinguished from the spiritual heart referred to in earlier chapters, where there is only love and peace and joy. I have borrowed the concept and the phrase "The human heart is a package deal" from my friend Robbie Gass. Used with permission. Thanks, Robbie—for everything.

CHAPTER 6

1. I am indebted to Alice Miller for this idea. See her *Banished Knowledge: Facing Childhood Injuries* (New York: Doubleday, 1990), *passim,* and especially her *For Your Own Good: Hidden Cruelty in Child-Rearing and the Roots of Violence* (New York: Farrar, Straus & Giroux, 1990), pp. 97–98, 243.

2. "An Egypt That Doesn't Exist," *Open Secret: Versions of Rumi,* translated by John Moyne and Coleman Barks (Putney, Vt.: Threshold Books), p. 43.

3. Although this essay discusses male sexual addiction, it also has relevance to some aspects of female sexual addiction.

CHAPTER 7

1. For verbal convenience, I use the term "marriage" in this chapter to mean "marriage and all committed relationships," and I imply no bias against nonmarried committed relationships by this usage. Also, most of the couples presented in this chapter are heterosexual, reflecting the fact that most of the couples I've seen in my therapy practice have been heterosexual. I do not know homosexual relationships as well as I know heterosexual ones, but I have observed that many of the same issues, challenges, and opportunites for growth happen in both; and I believe that anyone of any sexual orientation in any kind of committed partner relationship would find familiar and hopefully useful material in this chapter.

2. See the writings of Harville Hendrix, especially *Getting the Love You Want* (New York: HarperCollins, 1988).

3. The English word "paradise" derives from a Persian word meaning, like *hortus conclusus,* "enclosed garden." The etymological implication is that if we can create the *hortus conclusus,* the one safe place, in our marriages, our marriages can be paradise.

4. I have borrowed the "healing balm" phrase from Harville Hendrix's audiotape *Safety* (Town Crier Recordings, New York, N.Y., 1992).

5. Like many other experiences on the psychological and spiritual journey, the experience of marriage, or any close relationship, can often be *tapasya.* "Tapasya" is a Sanskrit word meaning "friction which produces beneficial heat that burns off impurities." Any difficulty or austerity in life can be interpreted favorably as tapasya, and used as an occasion to turn within and discover an inner strength and an inner peace that transcends difficulties.

6. Yiddish, meaning "anything very long and complicated."

7. In my clinical experience with couples, the new consciousness most often strikes women first, who then become conduits of this consciousness to the men.

8. As Cicero said, "The first bond of society is marriage; the next our children; then the whole family, and all things in common."

9. See all of Hendrix's books, especially *Getting the Love You Want: A Guide for Couples* (New York: HarperCollins, 1988). Hendrix's "behavior change request" and his "container exercise" are two other excellent "forms" for the repair of marital talking.

10. I am indebted to Swami Anantananda for the phrase "conversation of discovery." See his brilliant book on the psychological/spiritual journey, *What's On Your Mind?* (South Fallsburg, N.Y.: SYDA Foundation, 1996).

CHAPTER 8

1. *Collected Letters of St. Thérèse of Lisieux,* translated by F. J. Sheed (London: Sheed & Ward, 1949, 1972).

2. Interestingly, the words "audio" and "obey" are etymologically related. The etymological implication is that when we hear the truth being spoken to us, we are supposed to obey it.

3. Lord Krishna explains this point to Arjuna in the sixteenth chapter of the *Bhagavad Gita:* "Let the Scriptures be your guide in deciding what to do and what not to do. Understand what they teach, and act accordingly."

4. *Newton Graphic* (now *Newton Tab*), Newton, Massachusetts, April 25, 1996, p. 13. A shorter version of this story also appeared as part of the article "The Journey of Inner Change" in *Darshan* magazine, SYDA Foundation, South Fallsburg, New York, July, 1999, pp. 17–24.

5. She would not, however, have seen us being sexual with each other. It is our belief that, in a culture like ours that is so unclear about sex and sexual boundaries, children should not see or hear their parents' sexuality.

6. An earlier version of this essay appeared under the title "What Is Fathering Anyway?" in *Mothering* magazine, summer, 1980, pp. 30–33.

7. See, for example, string theory. In a review of Brian Greene's *The Elegant Universe: Superstrings, Hidden Dimensions, and the Quest for the Ultimate Theory* (New York: W. W. Norton, 1999), Alan Lightman writes, "According to the theory, all of these ultrasmall strings are identical. But each of them can vibrate in different ways, similar to the vibrations of a guitar string, and the different notes thus produced create all the different forces and particles in nature" ("One Stuff," *Harvard Magazine,* July–August, 1999, pp. 25–30).

8. The Hindu sages say that the original word that God spoke to create the universe was Om (Aum), and that that sound now reverberates in every particle of matter in the universe. According to Hindu cosmology, in the present age— Kali Yuga, the Age of Darkness and Unrighteousness—the easiest and surest way to experience God is to sing sacred song ("chant the Name"). For more on the singing and chanting of sacred song, and for resources, see Robert Gass's excellent book *Chanting* (New York: Broadway Books, 1999), and the audiotape *Let Your Heart Sing: A Talk and Chant* by Swami Chidvilasananda (South Fallsburg, N.Y.: SYDA Foundation, 1998).

9. On the psychological, emotional level, the core wound in a human being is hurt. On the spiritual level, the core wound is ignorance of one's identity with the Self.

10. *Lalleshwari: Spiritual Poems by a Great Siddha Yogini,* rendered by Swami Muktananda (South Fallsburg, N.Y.: SYDA Foundation, 1981), p. 29. Used with permission. "*Sadhana*" is a Sanskrit word meaning "the way, the spiritual journey," or, literally, "that which leads straight to the goal."

11. Remembering, of course, that the Self-realized master Jesus specifically warns us against charlatans: "Beware of false prophets, which come to you in sheep's clothing, but inwardly they are ravening wolves" (Matthew 7:15). See also Matthew 24:11, Mark 13:22–23, and Luke 6:26.

12. "Higher Laws," in Carl Bode, ed., *The Portable Thoreau* (New York: Viking Penguin, 1982), p. 466.

PERMISSIONS

Grateful acknowledgment is made to the following publishers, individuals, and copyright holders for their kind and generous permission to reprint excerpts from:

Shelter from the Storm, copyright © 1974, 1975 by Ram's Horn Music. All rights reserved. International copyright secured. Reprinted by permission.

Transformation, SYDA Foundation, South Fallsburg, New York, copyright © 1986 by the SYDA Foundation. Used by permission.

The Power of Myth by Joseph Campbell and Bill Moyers. Copyright © 1988 by Apostrophe S Productions, Inc., and Bill Moyers and Alfred Van der Marck Editions, Inc. for itself and the estate of Joseph Campbell. Used by permission of Doubleday, a division of Random House, Inc.

Embracing the Exile: Healing Journeys of Gay Christians, The Seabury Press, copyright © 1982 by John Fortunato. Reprinted by permission of HarperCollins Publishers, Inc.

"It's Alright, Ma (I'm Only Bleeding)," copyright © 1965 by Warner Bros., Inc. Copyright renewed 1993 by Special Rider Music. All rights reserved. International copyright secured. Reprinted by permission.

"Be Lost in the Call," from *Love Is a Stranger: Selected Lyric Poetry of Jelaluddin Rumi,* translated by Kabir Edmund Helminski, copyright © 1993 by Kabir Edmund Helminski. Originally published by Threshold Books, 139 Main St., Brattleboro, Vermont 05301. Used by permission.

Night and Sleep: Versions of Rumi, translated by Coleman Barks and Robert Bly. Used by permission.

Safety, audiotape, duplicated by Town Crier Recordings, 59 West 19th St., New York, New York. Used by courtesy of Harville Hendrix, Ph.D.

"Galileo," words and music by Emily Saliers, copyright © 1992 by EMI Virgin Songs, Inc. and Godhap Music. All rights controlled and administered by EMI Virgin Songs, Inc. All rights reserved. International copyright secured. Used by permission.

For Your Own Good: Hidden Cruelty in Child-Rearing and the Roots of Violence, copyright © 1983 by Alice Miller. Reprinted by permission of Farrar, Straus, & Giroux, New York, and Faber and Faber, Ltd., London.

The Fragile Bond: In Search of an Equal, Intimate, and Enduring Marriage, copyright © 1988 by Augustus Y. Napier. Reprinted by permission of